GW00761273

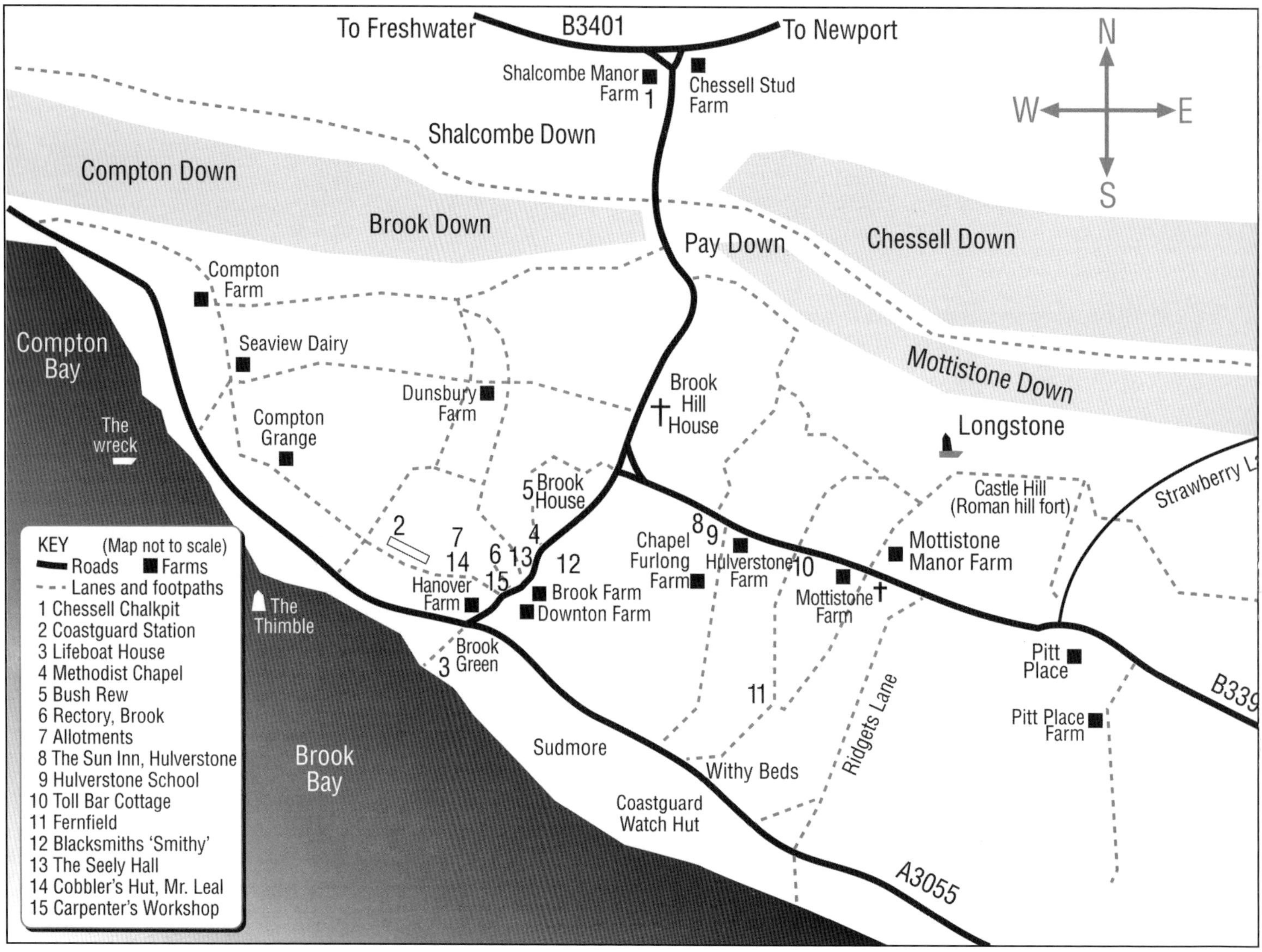

Map showing the farms and significant places mentioned in this book


First published in October 2010 by
*Brook - A Village History*

Reprinted March 2013




brookvillagehistory@yahoo.co.uk



ISBN 978-0-9567050-0-6




Printed by Crossprint Limited
Newport Business Park
21 Barry Way Newport
Isle of Wight PO30 5GY
Design: Daphne Denaro Brooke-Smith

heritage lottery fund
LOTTERY FUNDED

# Brook

## A village history

with Mottistone, Hulverstone and Chessell
Isle of Wight

Daphne Denaro Brooke-Smith and Susan Mears

# Contents

# Foreword

For me this book is a treasure trove. Much of the history captured here is ephemeral and personal and conveys the deep affection for the area felt by the people who lived and worked here for generations. It is special to me because my mother was born in Brook House in 1902 and my parents were married in Brook Church on a wet summer's day in 1924. My happiest childhood memories were holidays first at Mottistone and from 1952 in Phil Jacobs' cottage at the end of Brook Green. In 2000 we bought our own cottage in Coastguard Lane.

I wrote *Galloper Jack* in 2002 to explore the life and times of my grandfather, the politician and war hero Jack Seely, none of whose achievements gave him more satisfaction than being a rowing member of the Brook Lifeboat crew. When I had finished writing it I walked up the village from the shore with the ghosts of the past swirling in my mind. When I reached the doors of Brook Church and looked back down to the sea I wept with both sadness and joy.

This book will do that for you. That is what memories are for.

Brough Scott, MBE
October 2010

Brough and cousin, Mark Fletcher, sail a scow on Shalfleet Creek in 1949.

# Introduction

Aerial view of Brook village in the 1970s

This book offers an insight into the recent history of a small but unique area on the south-west corner of the Isle of Wight. It includes memories and photographs that record the way people lived and worked in Brook, Mottistone, Hulverstone and Chessell from the mid-19th century to the 1970s. It was a period of unprecedented change – from horse-power to jet planes, from self-sufficiency to supermarkets, from the Penny-Post and carrier's van to global communication. The economic and social relationships of the communities changed just as dramatically and are today quite different from when the lord of the manor and the rector, usually benevolently, decided everything; when 'everyone knew their place' and almost every community event was connected to the church.

In the period this book covers, and especially before the motor car was commonplace, villages and farms were busier places than they are today. People walked everywhere, led their animals, took tools from field to field and greeted everyone on the way with 'Whatcher you!' Communities were small, for example in 1901 54 households in Brook and Hulverstone held 221 people, with a further 90 or so living in Mottistone. It is therefore remarkable that this area had a school, a post office, a shop, a reading room, eleven working farms, a smithy, two churches, a chapel and a lifeboat service. The school even had its own orchestra. Many of these institutions were supported by the Seely family.

While there was never much money there was a strong sense of community and an even stronger sense of humour - as the local stories and nicknames testify. Everyone had one. In living memory there was 'Safe' Edmunds down Hoxall Lane, 'Broody' Barnes up at Longstone, 'Giant' and 'Stumpy' Barnes at Briar Cottage, and the 'Cuckoo,' a man who arrived from the mainland every Spring, played a tin whistle and slept rough.

Many of the families mentioned in this book still had descendants in the village in recent years: Hookey, Cassell, Newbery, Barnes, Whitewood, Morris, Bull, Jackman, Cooke and Seely are names that occur again and again. Some old names are found no more, but over the years other families have arrived and become part of the village. This book does not aim to be a comprehensive or academic study but reflects the wealth of material gathered up to this point. The importance of the land, some of the most fertile on the Island, is reflected in the chapter *Farms and farming*; the influence of the sea on this striking yet treacherous coast is shown in *Smuggling and the Coastguard Service, Fishing* and *Ship Ashore! Self-sufficiency and lucrative pastimes* and *Village trades and occupations* record the many skills villagers had, some of which have now died out.

This project began in 1996 with a note pinned to the Seely Hall noticeboard in Brook. Sue Mears (Stone) had inherited a collection of unique old photographs from her uncle, Bert Morris, and was looking for others to work with her on preserving them for posterity. Julia Denaro passed Sue's message on to her daughter Daphne, who had already begun looking at census returns and had mapped the graveyard. Since then this book together with the exhibition it has grown out of, have developed substantially. Compiling the book has involved close collaboration with people whose families lived all their lives in the area. Most of the photos are family heirlooms, lent by local people. They have also lent some wonderful reminders of everyday life in farm, house or forge, as well as at sea. Best of all, they have told their own stories in their own words.

We owe many thanks to them, to the Heritage Lottery Fund and to everyone who believed in and supported us through the project. We hope this record helps ensure that the villagers, their way of life and the strong pride they have in the area they grew up in, is preserved and not forgotten.

**Notes**

- We have not had space for the full versions of people's memories, the history of houses or the exceptional natural history of the area. In a companion publication we intend to publish the complete memories of those who have contributed to the project. The forthcoming *Brook - A village history* website will contain much that we cannot include here. If you can contribute to the project please contact the authors via **brookvillagehistory@yahoo.co.uk**.
- Historical records mainly focus on public moments and, as a result, it is rare to find records of women's lives in the villages. This lack will be partly remedied when we publish the full version of local people's memories.
- Brook or Brooke? Over the years we find various spellings for Brook: Broc, manerio del Broc, Broke, La Broke, Brouke and Brooke all appear. Nowadays, the village is Brook, but for much of the period covered by this book it was Brooke. The road signs in Shorwell and Chessell still have Brook with an 'e'. We have therefore used the spelling 'Brooke' for events and institutions such as the Lifeboat and the Regatta that were contemporaneous with the earlier spelling.

A photograph from the collection of Rita Whitewood (1921-2005).Today we are as familiar with the crumbling cliffs of Brook Bay as the women who perched on them all those years ago. Rita lived in Brook all her life and encouraged us with her memories and her goading, *You're never going to finish that book..!*

# Early history

Brook Bay in the 1970s. Right: an Iguanadon dinosaur the size of a bus. It was vegetarian and fed on pine forests in the area. Below: a fossilised Iguanadon ball joint found in the sea off Brook.

*What is now the coastline of Brook was once a river valley within a large land mass.*

Some of the earliest living creatures in this area were the dinosaurs, one of which left a footprint in the fossilised pine raft at Hanover Point in the late Cretaceous period, many millions of years ago when the chalk deposits of today's cliffs and downs were formed.

**The earliest human inhabitants**

What is now the coastline of Brook was once a river valley within a large land mass. The flint tools used by our Mesolithic forbears (7-8,000 B.C.) are often found around the coastline and in the Brook area. They reveal a fertile land and an industrious population. People were highly mobile and moved around large areas, stretching out where now there is nothing but sea. As sea levels rose during the Mesolithic period the Island was formed and cut off from what is now known as the 'mainland'. From then on an important and enduring factor in Brook's history developed – its close relationship with the sea. Settlements, as we know them, only began in the Bronze Age around 2,500 B.C. Over the following centuries there appears to have been a process of harmonious integration of successive 'incomers'. The archaeological remains found locally have been predominantly tools, coins and jewellery rather than defensive weapons.

The Longstone, Mottistone in the 1960s when the area was forested.

It is only during the Neolithic period, about 5,600 years ago, that we find the first evidence of land clearance and farming. Small areas were cleared and crops grown, although Brook inhabitants probably still relied on hunting, fishing and gathering of wild food such as fruits and shellfish for much of their diet. The Longstone dates from this time and is probably the oldest man-made monument on the Island. Standing on a ledge at the foot of the downs above Mottistone, the stones are thought to have guarded the entrance to a long barrow, a communal tomb.

Later, in Anglo-Saxon times the Longstone was used as a 'Moot place'where the lords of the manor held court hearings.

**The Bronze Age**

When we reach the Bronze Age, between 2,500 and 700 B.C., we begin to get a clearer picture of what life was like in Brook. Downland and lowland were cleared extensively and the now familiar landscape began to emerge. It is

Bronze Age flint tool for scraping animal hides clean.

thought that our modern villages and some of the farms are on the very spots our Bronze Age ancestors chose. Recently, a well-preserved hurdle fell out of the cliff at Chilton Chine - its uprights interwoven, still in its own block of soil, and carbon-dated to exactly 2,000 B.C., the beginning of the Bronze Age. The hurdle may have been part of a structure for living in or fencing for a land division boundary. Small farmsteads probably had sleeping huts, cooking compounds, workshops for weaving and other activities, as well as barns and byres. A typical farmhouse was a timber post roundhouse made of huge uprights in-filled with wattle and daub and roofed with thatch. Each farmstead housed between 15 and 29 people. They farmed crops such as barley and kept animals. The most important community members were buried in round barrows high on the downs. Unfortunately, later generations have robbed these tombs so we have very little detail about who was buried there. Records as early as 1237 talk about people opening up Isle of Wight barrows to search for treasure; later generations had more prosaic but even more destructive motives. A Victorian antiquarian thunders:

*Men were lately digging at the side for gravel and flints, and found human skeletons side by side, almost in a circle, with their faces towards the barrow... it cannot be too much reprobated that ignorant peasants...who are unable to afford any reliable information as to what they discover...should thus invade the sanctuary of the dead under the authority of a road contractor.*

**Iron Age and Roman times**

By the Iron Age, tribes from the Island had become involved in overseas trade with Britain and areas all over the Roman Empire. Local Island pottery dating from this time is called Vectis Ware, and has been found around the Brook area, confirming that Iron Age people continued to live and farm in the same areas as their Bronze Age ancestors. In 1948 a well in the form of a column of stonework appeared in the cliff face. The pieces of pottery found at the bottom established that it had been in use from the first century A.D. There are a number of Iron Age hill forts on the Island and the earthwork 'Castle Hill' on Mottistone Down is thought to have been one of these. The Roman invasion of Britain had less impact on the Island and on Brook than it did on mainland Britain. It is thought that treaties between the Iron Age tribes inhabiting this area and the Romans ensured that an established rural farming life could continue through the Roman period. One enduring legacy of the Romans was their contribution to the diet – they introduced rabbits and apples.

Roman Denarius coin found in the locality

**The Anglo-Saxon period**

After Britain was abandoned by the Roman Empire in AD 410, the Island was one of the first places to be visited by the Anglo-Saxons who eventually settled and farmed here alongside

The Bronze Age burial landscape known as Five Barrows on Brook Down contains both bell and disc barrows.

the existing population. An early Anglo-Saxon cemetery at Chessell shows us that the people who lived here were buried with grave goods such as swords, brooches, buckets and household pottery. Finds included a particularly fine 6th century square-headed brooch and a sword mounting. The quality of these finds suggest that the elite class, at least, was prosperous and sophisticated. Later in the Saxon period, the Island was divided into long thin parishes so that each parish had access to both coasts, the Solent and the high seas. The boundaries to these parishes can be identified by Late Saxon charters. Brook was originally in Shalfleet Parish. Hulverstone, and part of Brook Green, remained so until 1889.

New Forest slipware pot 300-307 found at Brook

**The Normans and the Domesday Book.**

The great Domesday Book was compiled by the Normans as a record of who owned what, so that King William could raise taxes. It took 20 years, until 1086 AD, to complete and gives us the first documentary evidence of life in Brook. The record reads:

> *King William holds BROOK in demesne, Earl Tosti held it. Then at 3 hides. There is land for 6 ploughs. In demesne are 2 ploughs, and 3 villans and 7 bordars with 2½ ploughs.*
>
> *There are 9 slaves and a mill rendering 15d, and 6 acres of meadow. TRE it was worth 7l; and afterwards 6l; now 7l; and yet it renders 7l more.*

Compton is listed as a separate settlement having: *1 hide (3 in Tosti's time) land for 4 ploughs – 1 in demesne, 7 villans and 3 bordars with 2 ploughs and just 1 serf.* It is unclear whether Dunsbury, if it existed at all then, was counted with Brook or Compton. There is no mention of Hulverstone, but again this does not mean it was uninhabited. The Domesday Book counted freeborn men who were the head of a household; serfs were also included in order to raise the tax liability of some households. Multiplying that figure by five gives us a population for Brook of around 95 people, with a further 30 at Compton. Hides and ploughs are measures of land – a hide was roughly 120 acres, so Brook boundaries covered around 360 acres. A 'plough' was the same size but specifically arable land. While villans, bordars and serfs all 'belonged' to the lord of the manor, villans were the wealthiest and typically owned between 20 and 40 acres of land, working for the manor two or three days a week and for themselves the rest of the time. Bordars might only own 10 or 20 acres. Some authorities suggest bordars lived on the outskirts of settlements and had assart rights in the woods (the ability to clear woodland and create arable or pasture land). Serfs were usually landless. Why nearly half the population of Brook were serfs is unknown – on a national average, only about 10% of men were serfs. Is it possible that there was a large manor house here and that many of the serfs were household servants?

The mill at Brook had a low rateable value and was therefore presumably of minor importance. Its location is unknown – but there are banks and earthworks and an old stream bed around the barn on Brook Shute (which is apparently mentioned in the Domesday Book). Could it be that the first building here was a mill and that the stream later dried up?

**The Medieval period**

The Mackerel family became lords of Brook some time towards the end of the 11th century. Again, varied accounts make this period difficult to unravel. We know that one William Mackerel granted the tithes of the mill and common pasture to the Abbey of Lye in Normandy before 1189. We also know that in around 1200, another William, his great nephew, granted the

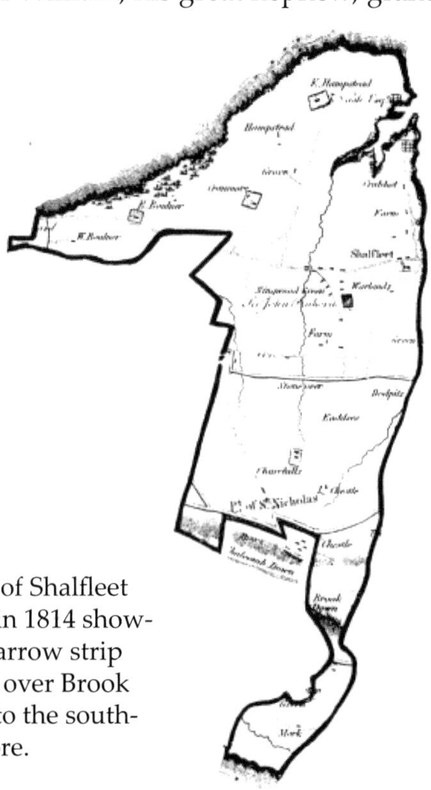

A map of Shalfleet parish in 1814 showing a narrow strip of land over Brook Down to the southern shore.

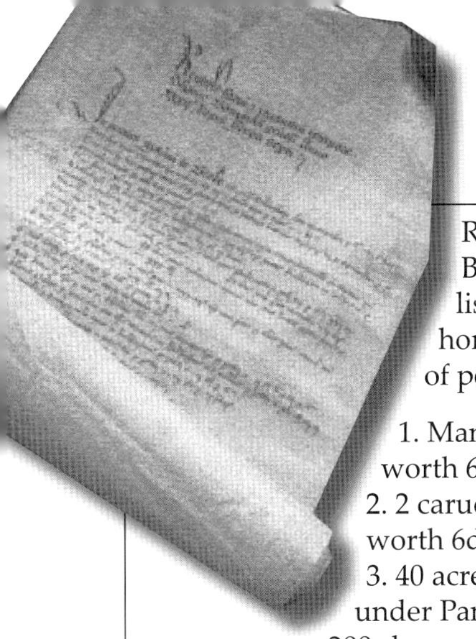

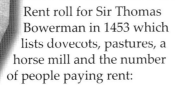

Rent roll for Sir Thomas Bowerman in 1453 which lists dovecots, pastures, a horse mill and the number of people paying rent:

1. Manor of Broke, 1 dovecot, worth 6s 8d
2. 2 carucates of land, 200 acres worth 6d an acre
3. 40 acres of pasture lying under Pandowne and pasture for 200 sheep and 200 ewes worth 2d per acre
4. 1 messuage in Hailferston, with 12 acres of land called Knollehay in Holferston and Motteston, held of John Chike and worth 6s per annum
5. 4 fishponds
6. 1 horse mill with 1 butt of pasture, John Lysle

advowson (the right to appoint a priest) of the chapel at Brook to God's House, Yarmouth or Eremue Hospital. Importantly, this also confers the right to the tithes. Sometime towards the end of the 13th century Brook passed by marriage into the de Glamorgan family. Also at this time we know that the Passelewe family held half a knight's fee at Hulverstone from the lords of Brook (a knight's fee was about 12 hides or 1500 acres). Within two generations of acquiring Brook, a quarrel broke out between Isabel de Glamorgan, who had been left a lifetime interest in the property but tried to sell it, and Thomas Haket, the guardian of her brother, Nicholas Glamorgan, who was the male heir but 'an idiot.' Nicholas died without heirs and Brook was divided between his five sisters. Isabel, the eldest, appears to have married twice, once to Godfrey Hunstan (or Hanson) and once to Geoffrey de Roucle, or Rookley. In 1370 we find Geoffrey calling himself 'Geoffrey Roucle de la Brook.' However, the family were not to enjoy Brook for much longer; in 1445 Geoffrey and Isabel's son John gave Brook to John Lisle, John Stoure and Thomas Bowerman, and in 1450 Lisle and Stoure transferred their shares to Bowerman, who had married Joan, one of the daughters of John Rookley. It wasn't until 1566 however, that the Bowermans owned all of Brook – some portion of it had been inherited by Thomas Haket, guardian of Nicholas – and passed through several generations until one George Gilbert sold it to Thomas Bowerman. Most recorded history is of the great families – we have scant evidence of what was happening to the ordinary inhabitants of Brook. One can be

This large early dovecot survives at Shalcombe Manor, Chessell and will have supplied its owners with valuable food. The close-up is of one pigeonhole.

certain that they continued to fish and to farm. We know that there were warrens at Brook and Hulverstone and rabbits were a major source of food.

**The Bowermans**

The Bowermans were lords of Brook from 1450 to 1792, with the Rev. Thomas Bowerman, who had several daughters but no sons, remaining as Rector of Brook until 1833. Although they were here for over 350 years, relatively little is known about the Bowermans. We know from a rent roll dated 1463 that the Bowrmans (sic) owned property in Dorset and Hampshire and throughout the Island. Brook House had a dovecot, a fishpond, stables, an orchard and a 'messauge' or kitchen garden as well as a 'pleasance' – a formal garden for pleasure and recreation (often the province of the women of the house who would take their spinning and needlework outside in fine weather). In 1488 we hear that the Governor of the Island mustered a force of 40 gentlemen and 400 men including those from Brook and Mottistone. Armed with pikes, longbows and arrows, they went to France to support the Duke of Brittany against the King of France. Every man was killed in the battle except for one young boy, Robert Cheke, who made his way alone on foot back to his home in Mottistone. We can assume that Brook was a house of some importance because in 1499 it was the scene of great festivities on the occasion of Henry VII's visit to the Island. The King was entertained by Thomas Bowerman and Joan his wife and we are told that: *a bountiful repast was placed on the tables, to which ample justice was done by all present. About 70 sat down to supper, including the gardeners and other servants and friends.* On leaving, the King gave Dame Joan Bowerman his drinking horn as a keepsake and granted her a fat buck annually from his forest at Carisbrooke. There is little recorded history between then and the Civil War, although we know that John Cheke (1514-1557), academic and personal tutor to Edward VI, was from the Cheke family of Mottistone. Less admirably, in Elizabeth 1st's reign a Spanish ship was wrecked off Brook Bay and the unfortunate sailors were, according to legend, lured ashore, drugged, murdered and buried in a copse next to the churchyard. In the Civil War Sir Thomas Bowerman supported Cromwell and was MP for a short time. During the Commonwealth William Bowerman 'an extreme radical' was variously Captain of the Brook Militia, Deputy Governor of the Island, a magistrate and MP for Newport. We are told he also appointed Cromwell's personal preacher to the local living. The hearth tax returns for 1664 show that Brook Manor had fourteen hearths – it was obviously a substantial house. There were a further 23 households recorded in the parish. These records show a relatively prosperous Mottistone in 1664 (see below). Mrs Dillington obviously lived at the Manor with its eleven hearths. Nine other houses had between three and four hearths. N.B. 'Hearth' could include fireplaces in living rooms, brew houses, etc. The number of wells shown in old maps is also an indication of a relatively large population in Mottistone in the 16th Century.

**Hearth Tax records for Mottistone in 1664**

| | | | |
|---|---|---|---|
| Mrs Dillington | 11 | David Urry | 2 |
| Mr King | 5 | Thomas Cooper | 3 |
| Widd Blore | 2 | John Orchard | 1 |
| Thomas Gustard | 2 | Francis Browne | 2 |
| Andrew Brewer | 1 | Thomas Joliffe | |
| Widd Day | 3 | for Gilberts | 1 |
| William Wavell | 4 | Widd Hollis | 2 |
| Mark Therle | 4 | John Bull | 3 |
| William Jackman | 1 | | |

In 1792 William Bowerman sold Brook Manor to Henry Howe. Troops were stationed near here during the Napoleonic Wars – Hanover Point and Hanover House are believed to be named after a German regiment, stationed here to resist an invasion that never came. It is startling to discover that in 1797 there were 4,500 soldiers

Wooden canister of grape shot found under the sea at Brook.

on the Island and a further 3,000 Islanders under arms. In the 1860s another threatened French invasion led to the building of the first Military Road. Around 1857 (the date is unclear), John and William Howe sold the estate to Charles Seely, MP for Lincoln, a wealthy mill and coalfield owner from Nottinghamshire. The Seely family and the impact they had on the locality and villagers' lives features strongly in this book. One convoluted aspect of Brook history is the Tithe Dispute. For over two hundred years, from the 13th to the 16th century, the rectors of Freshwater claimed that the tithes of Brook belonged to them and the lords of Brook resisted the claim, both sides pursuing their claims with vigour. In the 1660s Thomas Bowerman enclosed a churchyard and instigated a register of Births, Marriages and Deaths in order to consolidate his claim. It is during an early round in the tithe dispute that we find the first authentic voice of an ordinary person talking about their life in this area of the Island. Around 1565 Agnes Graunt, a fifty year old farm servant from Compton, gave witness in a court hearing. Some fifteen years earlier Agnes was working at Freshwater Parsonage (then rented by Captain Girling and his wife, who were clearly eager to make sure they received all they felt was their due). Mrs Girling rejected some tithe cheeses saying they were: *not fitt or lawful tyth cheses,* because they were: *newly had owt of the presse and sent…vpon the borde without salte or clowte and therefore.* Here is the voice of Agnes speaking to us down the centuries, telling us what it was like to be an Elizabethan dairymaid: *The milkying of ewes is commodious and profitable to the owners, although troublesome and painfull to the servants. And ewes mylk renned yeldeth much more crud than cow mylke, and mingled with cow milke increaseth the dayrie.* This book is based on the recollections of ordinary people like Agnes. This is their book and their story.

# Smuggling and the Coastguard

Brook coastguards in front of the coastguard station, c. 1868.

*Coastguards were stationed at Brook from 1817, mainly to combat brandy smuggling from the Channel Islands, Cherbourg and Barfleur.*

A visitor to Niton in 1860 said, ' The whole population here are smugglers.' The same was true of Brook and Mottistone, where smuggling was a core part of the village economy. Writing in the WI Scrapbook in 1958, Mrs Buckett remembers hearing how: *When the fishing season finished, the adventurous characters took to making trips to France on dark nights for their livelihood. This was usually to the Cherbourg peninsula where three gallon tubs were purchased for 10 shillings each and were tied in pairs ready for carrying when landed here. When purchased in France, the brandy was colourless like gin and much over-proof. Before selling it in this country it was coloured with burnt sugar and the alcohol level lowered by the addition of water.*
In 1930 Jack Seely remembers David Hookey, the blacksmith, saying 'My grandfather said things were not so unhappy as you

*We were on the front line for imports.*

might think in those days; the smuggling was a real help to all classes.' He was talking, probably, of the period 1830-1850, when a crewman earned £3 to £5 a trip and a tub carrier earned from two shillings and sixpence to five shillings for a night's work. This was at a time when agricultural wages were about ten shillings a week. There was no social stigma attached to smuggling, Lieutenant Dornford and his crew

*The smuggling was a real help to all classes. A tub of brandy was always left at the farm and the Rectory.*

of seven coastguards were charged in 1836 with collusion. Part of the evidence being their friendship with Mr Rogers of Compton Farm, ' a person in the habit of affording every accommodation to smugglers,' according to the Supervisor of Excise. 'Do you not know,' said Lieut. Dornford, 'that Mr Rogers' relatives and connections are among the most wealthy and respectable on the Island? Was he not a yeoman of the highest respectability?' The Reverend Collingwood Fenwick, the land-owning rector of Brook from 1833 to 1856 said: *The people engaged in smuggling or benefiting by it, do not feel it a moral offence and make no secret of their success when the danger is over.* But they did not always succeed. In about 1830 the Brook coastguard caught James Buckett (much later the first coxswain of the Brighstone Lifeboat), grappling for his tubs at Chilton Chine. In 1871 Lieutenant

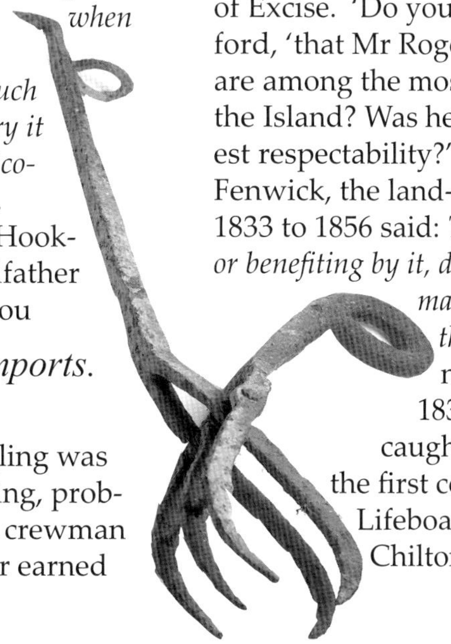

Rattray and his men from the coastguard cottages surprised Mr William Cooke (1811-1902) of Brook Green as the carriers were picking up his tubs. The sentence for James Buckett was to serve in the Royal Navy for five years, and that for William Cooke was a year in Winchester Prison.
The local fishermen, who knew every inch of the coast as well by night as by day, were in demand by smuggling vessels from the Solent who would take a local hand on each 'run'. As the 'crop' was landed, a gang of carriers (local villagers) picked up the tubs and carried them inland. A tub or 'half-anchor' (pictured) weighed 56lb when full, so the carrier might bear 1 cwt for several miles. It contained four gallons of brandy which in the 1830s cost only four or five shillings a gallon in

France but thirty-six shillings a gallon in England if the duty was paid. The tubs were hung round the boat, weighted with stones, and dropped in shallow water off the shore, leaving the boat to continue to its usual mooring with no evidence of its activity. Later the grapnel and peep tub were used to find the 'crop' and pull it in (although the coastguard might also look for it in the same way). A favoured way to get contraband up the cliffs was to haul the tubs up on ropes, and a local story tells how a group of smugglers were caught red-handed doing exactly this. The local riding officer spent much of his time patrolling the coast on a white horse, and the yarn tells of a Brook man who enjoyed similar excursions on his black mount. Anxious to avoid being confused with the hated customs officer (and thus risking a bump on the head from his smuggling pals), the Brook man had developed an elaborate code. On reaching a hill, he would gallop up, and walk down. So when the smugglers were

*The people engaged in smuggling, or benefiting by it, do not feel it a moral offence and make no secret of their success when the danger is over.*

**SMUGGLERS' HIDEY FOUND AT BROOK**

Joe Morris outside 2, Old Myrtle Cottage with smugglers' jars and barrel found hidden in a bend in the chimney.

An interesting discovery this week has produced a new link with smuggling days along the channel coast of the Island. Workmen engaged on alterations to 2, Old Myrtle Cottage, Brook, found a six gallon brandy cask and three glass bottles or jars of four, five and six gallons capacity in a chimney 'hidey.' The cask is in perfect condition and the jars are uncracked, but the woven withies around the two large ones have rotted. The glass is dark green.
The containers were found behind a bend in a chimney stack between the main building and a lean-to, which is being demolished. No entrance to the hiding place was apparent.
Mr J C Morris, owner of the property, who lives next door in Rectory Cottage, estimates that the bottles and cask have been stored away for at least a century. He told a County Press representative that he had known the cottage for 70 years and the existence of the hidey was never suspected.

*The carrier might bear 1cwt for several miles*

Courtesy of the Isle of Wight County Press, 1958.

*The journey was dangerous in a small, open boat and could only be undertaken in what was called 'the darks', that is to say three days each side of the new moon.*
*Forever England,* J.E.B Seely,

hauling tubs up the cliff face, they saw no danger at the approach of a man on a black horse that galloped uphill and walked down. Only when the riding officer was close enough to be recognized did the lookout realise his mistake — and by then it was too late. Most of the gang were at the top of the cliff, and got clean away; but the man loading tubs at the bottom spent a year in prison for this unfortunate error. The gentry allowed their woods and barns to be used and stables and cowsheds contained much valuable cargo for short or long periods. Brooke House was no exception and in his book *Forever England* (1932), Major General Jack Seely records how: *Even in my grandfather's time a tub of brandy was always left at both the farm and the Rectory. Our old butler, by name Linggar, told me that in 1884, 'Your grandfather (Charles Seely) came into the stables (Brooke House) the morning after the convict ship had come ashore on Brighstone Ledge. He found a tub in the corner of one of the loose boxes, made a terrible to-do, and handed it over to the coastguard. I heard him say myself that it was wrong to defraud the revenue and that he would have nothing to do with it. It was a great pity, for it was the best brandy they had ever landed; but then, you see, Master Jack, he was an M.P. and he had to say it. We all understood that well enough.'*

A peep tub used for locating contraband stored under the sea.

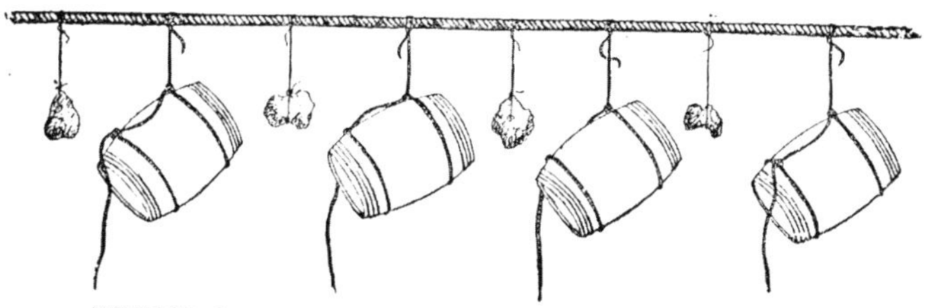

METHOD OF SECURING TUBS AND STONES FOR SINKING.

Brook inventiveness is illustrated in this story recounted by Fred Mew in *Back of the Wight*:

> I had a talk with a noted Brook man, Phil Jacobs, who showed me with pride, and justifiable pride, too, a certificate from the Royal National Lifeboat Institution, awarded for over 40 years' continuous service with the Brook Lifeboat... Phil laughed heartily as he told me the tale of a cargo of tubs sunk just east of where he lives (Sudmore). It came on to blow and the tubs began to break loose and wash ashore during the day, and, to make matters worse, the coastguard had wind of the fact that there had been a cargo in the vicinity. What was to be done? They could not be lost without an effort. Someone had a brainwave; there were large heaps of seaweed lying along the shore, and it would be a good plan to get a few loads for the garden. A pair-horse wagon was got from the farm and was soon returning with a heaped-up load of weed. So far, so good, but the coastguard officer is seen coming along to them; has he smelt a rat? No, he merely looks and passes on, intent on his job of trying to find tubs, and away that load went to safety.

Fred Mew recounts an unusual hiding place for contraband in Mottistone: It was about the year 1872, when John Cook, a carter could be seen ploughing a deep wide furrow in a field near a withy bed. Farmer Brown, who was passing at the time remarked on its dimensions to the old man, 'That's throwing it well open, carter!', to which John replied, 'I must do summat to please the old man.' The furrow was left open at night but by the time morning came it had been ploughed in again and that part of the field lay fallow for many months. When the new bailiff questioned why that part of the field was not being used, he was put off by an evasive reply and never discovered that a crop of contraband tubs lay concealed in the furrow for seven months. The larger tombs in Mottistone churchyard were also reputedly used for this purpose.

*The coastguard building commands a panoramic view out over Brook Bay. On a summer's day the view is second to none, with some of the finest sunsets seen. On a cold, wet, stormy winter's day - it is something else besides.*

The Preventative Water Guard, as the Coastguard Service was called before 1822, was established in Brook as early as 1817. Maps of the time show a couple of customs and coastguard buildings on the cliffs to the west of Brook Chine. The station was called *Freshwater* in those days with the name changing to *Brook* in 1838. By 1841 the census shows four coastguards living in Brook and in October 1861 the Lords of the Admiralty purchased land from Charles Seely for £300 to build a more substantial coastguard station. Between Hanover Point and Chilton Chine a permanent two-man coastguard watch was maintained and the number of coastguards rose to six in 1861 and settled at five from 1881 to 1901. The census shows families with as many as eight members living in the individual cottages. Before Brook had its lifeboat station, the coastguards took part, with the villagers, in rescuing men from shipwreck. In 1838 Lieutenant Symons and the Brook coastguard rescued the crew of the brig *Claire* wrecked at Brook. By that time all coastguards belonged to the Navy. During the smuggling years, their work could be dangerous. Two Brook coastguards beaten up at Freshwater Gate in 1835 were in bed for five weeks afterwards. But there was prize money for a capture a nd in any case it was usual for the smugglers to leave a little of their 'crop' with the coastguards. The Brook census returns show that many of the coastguards came from Cornwall, also a busy smuggling area – it takes one to know one... Joe Hulse who was born at Brook Coastguard Station has looked into the origins of the building and the service: *Until the late 1800s the vast majority of ships still used sail as their main power. The 'back of the Wight' proved to be the final resting place for a large number of ships together with their crews and passengers. Brook Bay was no exception and the strong prevailing south-westerlies meant that the bay acted as a trap for ships under sail (and later those with engines but no radar, in times of fog). Once there, they had no sea room and were trapped against a lee shore. In the 1850s local clergymen realised that something needed to be done to save lives. Even after 1860, when both Brook and Brighstone lifeboats came into service, the*

## A dangerous and unpopular job

*problem was who would keep a lookout? Until this time the coastguard had been an armed, quasi-military force, whose principal job had been to assist and back up customs and excise in the campaign against smuggling. It was soon realised that while patrolling the coast on the lookout for smugglers, they could also provide the lifeboat crews with a lookout for ships in distress. The Station comprised of six terraced cottages for the coastguard team, together with a 'watch*

Chief coastguard Edward Stone in the 1870s.

*room' at the western end of the building and an equipment store room underneath. A separate washhouse, containing two wood fired coppers, completed the station. The watch room view to the east was partially obscured by Brook point (erosion of the cliff since then has modified the view somewhat) and a wooden lookout hut was built on the cliff near Sudmore point to extend the lookout range of the station. A telephone linked the two sites in later years, and the Sudmore lookout became the principal watch site.*

In his book *Coastguard!*, William Webb describes how: *The men were forbidden to leave their posts on the shore even when wet through. There was a high level of sickness as a result but when a man reported sick he was stopped one-third of his pay*. Coastguards frequently worked a 16 hour day, or rather, night. Every night they were assembled in the watchroom and armed with a musket and bayonet. No man was given his instructions and position before he reported for duty and he was forbidden to communicate with his family after he had received them. One of the most unpopular duties, because it took place in the daytime rest hours, was 'creeping.' This involved rowing out and dragging an iron grapnel

*On night watches coastguards were given a 'one-legged donkey', a stool with a single leg on which to rest. If the guard dozed off the stool would collapse...*
William Webb, *Coastguard!*

or 'creep' along the bottom to hook up sunken goods. While the coastguards were not entirely welcome, they and their families became part of the life of the village and from the 1860s a new baby arrived at the coastguard cottages in most years. The coastguards' skills also contributed to the community as the following newspaper article of 1898 shows:

May 21st 1898

**Crushed by infuriated bull**

On Tuesday morning Charles Cleal employed at Brook Farm whilst attending to the cattle was crushed against the stable wall by a bull which became infuriated when being moved from one stable to another, and the unfortunate man sustained the fracture of two ribs. First aid was skillfully rendered by chief coastguard T Hennings, superintendent and secretary of the Brook division of the Isle of Wight Ambulance Association, until medical assistance arrived.

Relationships between the local fishermen and the coastguards were sometimes strained. The following interchange and court case between John Hayter (a fisherman who had just been appointed coxswain of the Brooke Lifeboat) and the Brook Chief Coastguard, shows the tensions:

**John Hayter v Board of Customs, 1861**

On the 15th May 1861 the Treasurer of IOW Lifeboats, wrote to the Customs Office in Cowes on behalf of John Hayter whose fishing boat had been seized by the coastguards:

*Mr John Hayter the coxswain of the Brooke lifeboat having called on me this morning stated that his fishing boat had been seized by your orders on Monday 10th inst...and he is thereby prevented from following his occupation and gaining his daily bread as a fisherman. The only reason for the seizure being that his name was painted on the inside instead of the outside of his boat and Hayter not being aware that he has in any way acted contrary to the laws of his country, feels deeply that his liberty as an Englishman, when following an honest calling has been interfered with in a most arbitrary manner . . .*

Seven days later Lieutenant Cutajar (Chief Coastguard), Brook replied: *I have the honour to report that on the 9th inst. I observed a boat on which the name was so effaced as to be quite unintelligible. I informed him (Hayter) that the law required that every boat should be legibly marked with the name and port or abode of the owner... The weather being fine I allowed him 24 hours to complete the work and informed him that unless it was executed I must seize the boat. I found that my request had not been complied with, I allowed him a little longer. Finding that all my efforts to obtain compliance with the law were fruitless, I was reluctantly compelled to desire my man to seize the boat.*

Five days later the Board of Customs decreed: *Upon the provision of the law being duly complied with the boat may be restored but the owner is to be cautioned as to his future conduct.* Two months later nothing had happened and the Customs office in Cowes wrote to the Customs Board in London: *it appears that Hayter refuses to take his boat on the ground that she has deteriorated in value or become useless since her seizure.*

The Board of Customs in London replied: *The only course now open is to treat the boat as condemned. . the owner appearing determined not to receive the boat back . . . care should be taken to give him the notice required by the Act.*

In August things were still at an impasse. By this time the Chief Coastguard in Brook appears exasperated: *I beg to report that Hayter's boat is in as good a state as she was on the day she was seized. The fact of Hayter's refusing to take the boat (is) that she was getting useless to him and at the time of the seizure he was already provided with another and a new fishing net, which they worked ever since. Hayter is a very obstinate man and his only reason for refusing to take the boat back (is) that he never intended to work her again.*

To resolve the situation once and for all, the Chief Coastguard in Brook visited Hayter (who lived all of 300 yards away from the coastguard station...) on 16th August 1861: *I have been to John Hayter with the letter which I read to him but I could not leave with him as he would not take it. I should be glad to hear from you what I am to do with it. I hope the Board will see what an obstinate fellow we have to deal with ... it's quite miserable to have to deal with such a fellow, when I read him the letter he would not stop to hear however I followed and read it to him ... I think the best way is to send it to him by post. I sincerely hope that the Board will soon settle this affair.*

By the 31st October instructions were given from London to sell the boat to the best bidder.

A Brook coastguard takes rifle practice at Hulverstone School in the 1890s.

Lantern with one side blacked out.

Joe Hulse describes the coastguard station as it was when he was growing up in the 1950s: *Cottages numbered 1, 2 and 3 are the smallest and were for the junior members of the team. There was an entrance door at the rear of each building, a hall with the pantry and stairwell forming part of it. The kitchen with its coal-fired cooking range and the front room completed the downstairs with three bedrooms upstairs. Each cottage had a coal shed at the top of the garden, behind which, was hidden the toilet. Numbers 4 and 5 are larger and were used by the senior team members with number 6 for the Head Coastguard. Extra garden plots between the western walled garden and the boundary with 'Flaxtead' were allocated to each cottage for growing vegetables. There was no electricity, mains water or drainage for many years. Water was obtained from a hand pump located on the western garden wall, between the watch room and number one. The station also had a well and all the cottages had rain water tanks fitted to their fronts, including the wash house. Finally a flag pole was erected onto the front garden between numbers 3 and 4. My life started in number 3 where Mum and Dad, Edie (Morris) and Joe Hulse lived in 1945. The coastguards were Mr Johnson, Mr Timothy and Mr Hanlon. In the mid-1950s numbers 1 to 4 were sold off. Gran and Grandad were unable to afford the £100 for their house as farm wages in those days did not allow people to have savings. Number 2 was never changed all the time Gran lived there. Right up until 1965 cooking was done on a range supplemented by primus stoves and lighting was via candles, torches and oil lamps. All water came from an outside tap and washing was done in a bowl in the kitchen and emptied into the drain outside the back door. The house had no bathroom. The benefits of living there were a warm kitchen in the cold winter and a regular supply of fresh vegetables from the garden. Of the later coastguards I remember there was Mr Hoyles, Mr Mashiter, Mr Cooper, Mr Stokes, Mr Bastable and Mr Bevan. Mr Bastable was the last Head Coastguard with Mr Bevan as his deputy. The Station finally closed around 1969.*

## The Later Years

At the start of World War II most regular coastguards went back to sea and local volunteer auxiliaries took over under the control of two or three older regulars. The old stations remained at Freshwater, Brook , Brighstone, Atherfield and Blackgang – the 19th century pattern of stations every three miles had been able to keep in touch by semaphore. The local men kept watch whenever the weather threatened. They did good work, for example in 1955 getting the stranded yacht *Pintail* to safety and looking after the three crew at Hanover House and Chine Cottage. In 1964 they got prompt aid to the cargo ship *Brother George* aground in Brook Bay. Robert (Bob) Cassell, lived all his life in Hulverstone and Brook and describes work as an auxiliary coastguard over 25 years in the 1950s and 60s: *At first I was Watch Keeper. There is a hut just up the road on the cliff where we did a constant lookout watch - day and night. There would have been three of us in the day and two at night. If I started at 8 o'clock at night I came off at 2 o'clock in the morning. We used to be watching for any boats in distress or shipwrecks. If the wind came up and the weather was rough, you had to ring through to Freshwater and put them on watch too, and Ventnor. I never seemed to have any time for myself and came off Watch Duty and went on the Coast Rescue Service up until 1977. In this I was not on duty all night but could be called out by the watcher. I had the long service medal for that. If a boat was in distress and was near enough we used to fire a rocket over to it.*

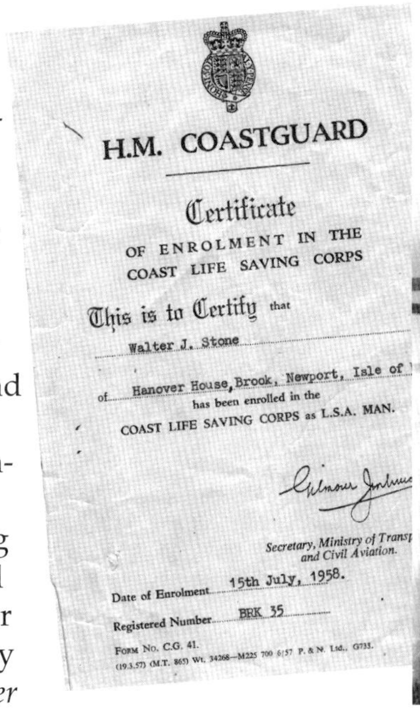

H.M. COASTGUARD

Certificate

OF ENROLMENT IN THE COAST LIFE SAVING CORPS

This is to Certify that

Walter J. Stone

of Hanover House, Brook, Newport, Isle of

has been enrolled in the COAST LIFE SAVING CORPS as L.S.A. MAN.

Secretary, Ministry of Transp and Civil Aviation.

Date of Enrolment 15th July, 1958.

Registered Number BRK 35

Form No. C.G. 41.

Cyril Toogood outside the Watch house at Sudmore, Brook in the 1950s.

By the 1960s radar and helicopters took over and only two regular coastguards remained at Brook. The station closed in 1971. The Brook men were then controlled from Atherfield; but that station closed in 1988 and with a retirement party at the Sun Inn for Mr Ken Newnham at Shorwell (the last local coastguard in charge) the story of the coastguard at Brook came to an end.

Brook Coastal Rescue Service in 1960.

Back row left to right: Bill Cook, Walter Stone, PC Hunt (Calbourne), Bert Morris, Tony West, Ralph Cook. Front row (left to right): Ted Bastable, Haifa Strickley, Robert Cassell, District Officer Shields, R. Rodgers, Alan Elliman, Frank Bevan. Above: Brook coastguard cap and button.

# Fishing

Brook shore when a number of wooden rowing boats were regularly fishing.

*Some days, but not very many, all is easy. The dawn is clear, the sea is calm.*

The villages on this coast originally developed as small fishing and agricultural communities with a few farms and fishermen's cottages. The 1841 census shows seven fishermen living in the village. This reduced to only two in the censuses of 1861 and 1871 but by 1881 had increased to eight. In the 1920s we know that twenty fishing boats worked out of Brook Bay and in living memory Alf Woodford chugged the round of his lobster pots in his white painted boat and sorted his catch in the tarred shed on Brook Green nicely named 'Seashell'. Therles, the cottage Alf lived in has changed little and the cluster of houses on the Green still gives an impression of what the huddled line of fishermen's cottages must have looked like. The undercliff at Sudmore, to the east of Brook Green, had particularly good fishing grounds. Withies for making crab and lobster pots were also planted there. The chief catches outside the mackerel season were prawns and lobsters. In the old days Brook fishermen would be out early in the morning to catch the prawns, cook them and take them to Newport to be put on the train for Billingsgate fish market in London. Pat Tyrrell remembers: *Brook Bay prawns were what Alf caught in his later years, they were big prawns and he always had a sale for them.*

*Caught in Brook in the morning, eaten in London that night. ..*

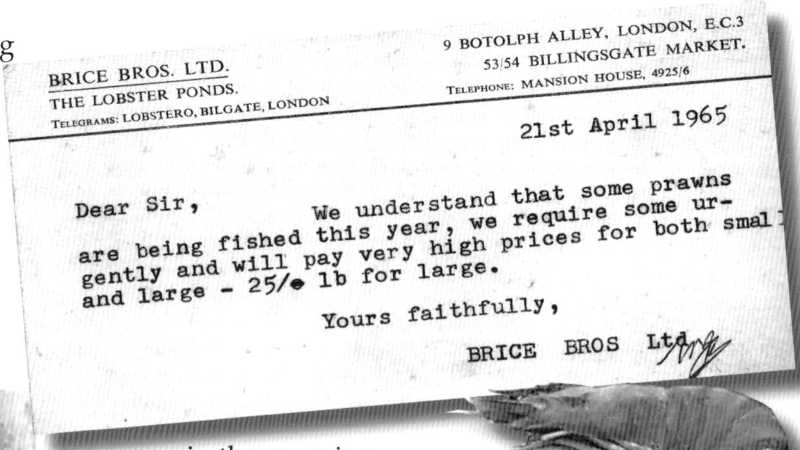

BRICE BROS. LTD.
THE LOBSTER PONDS.
TELEGRAMS: LOBSTERO, BILGATE, LONDON

9 BOTOLPH ALLEY, LONDON, E.C.3
53/54 BILLINGSGATE MARKET.
TELEPHONE: MANSION HOUSE, 4925/6

21st April 1965

Dear Sir, We understand that some prawns are being fished this year, we require some urgently and will pay very high prices for both smal[l] and large - 25/- lb for large.

Yours faithfully,

BRICE BROS Ltd

Alf Woodford, Steve Thompson and Alec Ballard at Brook with a big catch of prawns.

Pat Tyrrell remembers Alf Woodford and his withies:

Alf had a withy bed up at Sudmore on the left as you go towards Chilton; he used to cut all these withies and when he wanted to take them down to his house he'd carry them down on his back; all you'd see was a pair of legs and a great big pile of withies walking down the Military Road! It was like a big round bird's nest but Alf was under there somewhere! He was only a little man, but very strong. He knew how to cut the withies so he had a continuous flow from one year to the next. I never went in there much because Alf always used to say there was some very big snakes there… In the Summer it was wet and cool and adders used to like being there, so Alf said, and there were some that were four or five foot long. Maybe he said this to discourage people from going in there... The withies were stacked outside the shed in the open to weather. Withies are very pliable, like a bit of string and you could nearly tie a knot with them. Of course when Alf made his lobster pots in the winter he'd sell more than he kept for himself. I suppose he'd replace any that had got worn, but mostly he made them to sell; that was part of his living. It was a very skilled job, even in the sixties, with not so many folks doing it. He had perhaps twenty or thirty lobster pots outside his hut all black with tar and piled carefully on top of one another, about eight foot high. They were ordered by fishermen from all around. I don't know how much you could get for a lobster pot in those days but I expect he made enough to buy his groceries every week.

**Withies and lobster pot-making**

The making of lobster pots was a flourishing industry with pots being sent as far afield as Ireland. Marshy land at Sudmore, to the east of the village, was ideal for growing willows – or withies. The pliable shoots were cut in January each year and stacked in large sheds. Later they were trimmed to size, the ends sharpened, then they were woven into cunningly-shaped baskets from which no lobster could exit. The same wetlands that provided withies for lobster pots provided candle rushes for giving light. The practice was to nearly strip the rushes (not the leaves), leaving one thin strip for rigidity. The pith (kept intact with its strip) was dipped in mutton fat which could then be lit.

Ella Hookey ('Mrs Tom') wrote in the *WI Scrapbook* in 1958:

Fishing was another industry in which about eight men were occupied in Brook. My father (Frank Cooke) fished in summer and in winter occupied himself in making lobster and prawn pots, generally admitted to be the finest obtainable. He had orders for these from different parts of the country some even going to Ireland. When I was about twelve years old an exhibition of handicraft was held in Newport - and my father had an award of merit for his pots. He rented withy beds and cut them in January each year, stacking them in large sheds. These were trimmed and sharpened and then soaked before they were used. Then they were woven into the baskets and this was a great art which has been handed down to the present day for we still have Mr Woodford on the Green who makes these baskets.

Lobster pot made by David Hookey of Downton Farm. David was taught to make pots by his uncle, Alf Woodford of Brook Green.

The cottages on Brook Chine were known as 'France.' Those who lived there were independent of any landlord (as good as abroad) and able to live off fishing and whatever was washed up onto the shore.

A 'keep' used for freshly caught prawns. Made out of withies and preserved with tar. If a fisherman hadn't caught enough prawns to sell, the catch was kept alive submerged in the keep until required.

Frank Cooke (left and below) takes a rest on the cliff top at Brook in the 1920s. By the time he died he was very well-off and owned properties in Freshwater Bay.

## A PRE-EMINENT ISLAND INDUSTRY

Mr Cooke and his father and grandfather before him have carried on this industry for about 150 years, and it is still being maintained by his son Mr Herbert Cooke. The Cookes of Brook have won a wide reputation for their fish-pots, having for many years supplied the south coast of England and even Ireland. The red withies used for making the pots are grown on a four acre plot of ground near the Military Road, which the family have rented from the Seely Estate for many years. Mr Cooke is seen in the accompanying photograph just commencing a pot. In his younger days he made as many as six a day, but now is satisfied to make one. He is wonderfully active for his years and enjoys splendid health. He comes of a long-lived stock of fisher folk. His father (William Cooke of Mottistone lived to 91) and he has two sisters residing in Brook, Mrs Hayter who is 87, and Mrs Johnson, 85. Mr Cooke has also a worthy record as a lifeboatman, having been a member of the Brook crew for 30 years.

Courtesy of the *Isle of Wight County Press*

Mr Frank Cooke, aged 83 of Brook, making fish-pots outside his house near the shore.

In *Forever England* (1932) General Jack Seely describes the daily risks that Brook fisherman had to take in deep swells and breakers that no boat but the lifeboat could survive:

I will try to describe a fisherman of today who lives in a cottage quite close to the sea. His wife is dead, and he has one child. His mother is ailing and he is the sole means of support.

Although he is fifty years of age, he still has fair curly hair, steel blue eyes and a strong frame. The material of his trade, all of which he has bought or made himself, is a fifteen foot six open boat, lobster pots and prawn pots…each day he must try to get afloat in order to make enough to give comfort to his mother and child.

Some days, but not very many, all is easy. The dawn is clear, the sea is calm. All alone in the morning twilight he puts the little wooden ladders, well-greased, down the beach towards the sea, pushes his boat down along them until she is nearly waterborne; then puts in the gear; with one hard push gets her afloat, jumps in, seizes the sculls and with a few deft strokes gets her clear of the rocks. Then he steps, first his mast, then his rudder; hoists his spritsail, and with the light morning breeze sails to his fishing ground, beyond the outlying edges, three miles out to sea. There, in seven fathoms of water, with only a slight swell to hamper him, he hauls his pots, puts the catch in the boat, rebaits the pots, having carefully seen that the weighting stones are all in place, and lowers them again.

I have tried to describe a good day, but what about a bad day? The sky is red in the east and, a more sinister thing which we all dread, there is a reflected pink glow in the west. Presently a strange thing happens – I sometimes think the most awe-inspiring of all my own adventures in peace and war. A great heave of sea comes along, lifting us high in the air, as if some giant standing on the bottom, fifty feet below, were lifting the boat with his hand…and then comes the terrifying sound just beyond us, between us and our home – the great roar of the roller breaking on the outer ledge. We look at each other and my friend says: 'That's a big ground-sea. We had better be getting home'.

*A great heave of sea comes along, lifting us high in the air, as if some giant standing on the bottom, fifty feet below, were lifting the boat with his hand…*

Arthur Buckett and Charlie Newbery back from fishing on Brook Beach. They have a sail in the boat as well as oars and a basket for their catch which is similar to those made by Alf Woodford and Frank Cooke.

Roland Hayter, lifeboat coxswain, and Alf Woodford fishing from Sudmore, Brook Bay, in the 1920s.

Pat Tyrell remembers spending time as a boy with Brook fisherman, Alf Woodford:

Alf was a very nice, very kind man and a bit of a character; probably one of the last characters in the village and the last longshoreman in Brook. When I left school in 1958 Alf would have been about sixty I suppose, and had a hut down on the undercliff below South Hills, a field belonging to Mr Hookey of Downton Farm. Alf worked down there all his life. A single man, he only had himself to look after so it was quite easy for him to make a living. He used to put out lobster and crab pots and had a boat; it was about fifteen foot long and made of wood, clinker built.

Alf lived on Brook Green, in Therles, a house that didn't have much of an outlook, right behind Chine Cottage where Alec and Bill Ballard lived. Alf's journey to work took him up the garden, over the fence into South Hills, up to the corner of South Hills and down onto the undercliff; it took him less that ten minutes to get there.

I could smell Alf's pipe in the morning, if he was about.

He always had a pipe in his mouth; a lot of folks did in those days; he smoked a very distinctive tobacco which he bought at Brook shop. Alf used to go out mostly after lobsters and crabs, although I can remember him catching a lot of mackerel and bass, and he was very keen on pouting. He used to sell whatever he caught. I always wondered how he got in contact with anybody to buy them as he never had a phone. There was a phone box in Brook but I can't remember Alf using it, I don't know if he even knew how to use it. I suppose it was just hearsay and somebody found out he'd had a good catch and came down to buy his fish.

The hut that Alf had down on the undercliff was a very nice boathouse about twenty foot square, made from tin with a wooden floor and painted black every couple of years. It was just up on the undercliff from Brook shore on the Chilton side of Brook beach. Alf kept all his bits and pieces in there - bits for mending fishing nets and lobster pots; old bits of rag, bits of tarred rope... a tidy hut with things stored in little heaps.

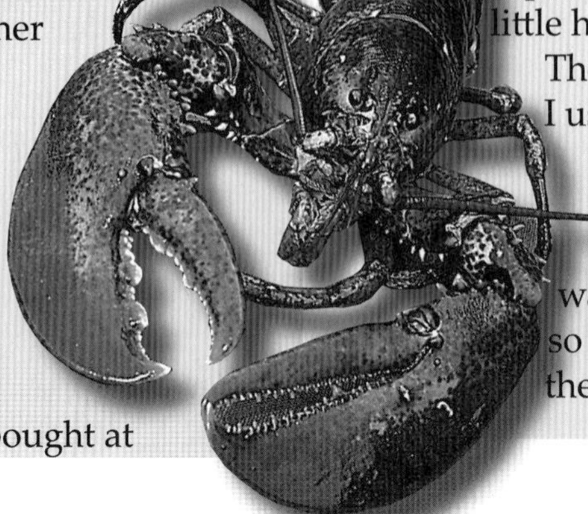

The boat was just a one-man boat. I used to go to get the cows from South Hills about six o'clock, perhaps a little earlier, and by the time I got up there he was gone; you couldn't see him, so he went out quite a long way. In the winter months Alf used to make

Alf Woodford's prawn pot used for cooking in the fireplace at 'Seashell' before selling the prawns to locals and holiday-makers .

lobster or crab pots in a little hut he had on Brook Green (Seashell). I really enjoyed spending time, usually together with Dave (Hookey), on winter evenings in this hut. An oil lamp, like a tilley lamp, gave quite a good light; there were a couple of chairs and a fire… I can't really remember if it was an open fire or if it had a door on it, but there was a fire and it was always very warm. We'd get there about seven, Alf was already there and he'd welcome us into the hut. We'd sit down and Alf was making these prawn and lobster pots. He always had a bottle with a bit of brandy in it and used to say he'd got it as a 'present'… He used to go out in his boat fishing a long way out, and I think French fishermen, who had bigger boats than Alf with an inboard motor to go a lot further and a lot faster, would meet him out there. I don't know what they'd exchange or if Alf exchanged anything at all, but sometimes I think they'd give him a bottle of brandy, or maybe two bottles. Only just a present, not smuggling or anything like that. I remember the bottles were a bluey colour and had a cork. Alf kept two or three little tin cups in this hut and he'd pour out a drop of this brandy for each of us, only two or three mouthfuls. I didn't know much about brandy then, but when I look back on it that was the best brandy I've ever tasted - lovely stuff and when it went down your throat it tasted beautiful!

Anyway we used to sit in this hut night-time with the fire going; Alf used to make his pots and chuck bits on the fire so it would burn up and get warmer and warmer - you could nearly drop off to sleep! Sometimes we'd stay in there talking for perhaps two or three hours; it was seven when you went in there and nearer ten by the time you'd finished. Time would just fly talking to Alf. He was a man with a lot of stories about Brook and the surrounding district. It's a pity a lot of these stories went with him when he passed away.

Up on Downton Farm where I worked we had a dairy. If Alf had a big catch of mackerel, for instance, he'd bring them up to the farm; this would be about June time. We had a bath in the dairy on the floor; it was a very cold room to keep the milk and cream cool; we had what they called a dolly bath I think; a very shiny galvanised bath, always kept clean. If Alf had a lot of mackerel, he'd bring them up in a sack on his back; we'd half fill the bath with water and might have say thirty nice big mackerel in there and we'd sell them from the dairy. I don't remember them being gutted, perhaps he gutted them … they were there in view in the dairy, and the people who bought the milk would perhaps have a couple, they were only about sixpence each in old money; not much of a price in those days. In those days it seemed to me all the fish, especially bass and mackerel, seemed bigger and more plentiful.

Alf used to tell me that mackerel were a bit of a nuisance; you'd get in a shoal of mackerel and

Alf Woodford outside Red Cottage, Brook Green, with a record catch of sea bass.

couldn't get down below them with your line - with two or three hooks on your line, in about half a minute you'd pull in three mackerel and then you'd start again, you don't get that today. I can remember at the end of May or into June on a warm day, the sea would be boiling for about two hundred yards square with shoals of mackerel, after the whitebait that they'd feed on. I've known mackerel to push the whitebait right up onto the shore - you could wade out up to your knees, pick up mackerel and throw them onto the shore. You don't see that now, but I can remember doing it - what I'm trying to say is that there was a plentiful supply of fish in them days for Alf to catch. He also used to catch a lot of pouting and always had orders for them at the right time of the year. Today I don't think you see them much for sale – I can remember eating one and they seemed a terrible bony fish and not very nice at all. He used to say he had what you call a 'poutmark'. Pouting would live in a hole on the seabed, so that on the seabed you'd have this hole that went down fifteen or twenty foot perhaps, which Alf called a poutmark. He said he knew where these poutmarks were because he used to line up somewhere on the Downs when he was out there - perhaps one of the five barrows, another hump, or a tree - which he'd line up with perhaps a chimney pot in Brook – get the two in line and he'd manoeuvre his boat so that he knew when he was over the poutmarks and start to fish. I suppose it took a bit of manoeuvring, maybe twenty foot one way or the other, but once he started catching the pout he knew he was over the mark. I've always thought nobody would do that now, but he did it all his life and that's how he caught his pout. Alf mainly caught lobsters and crabs when I was working at Brook; he wasn't a young man when I knew him, I think he used to catch a lot more fish in his younger days and be able to sell them but had slowed down a bit by the time I knew him. I remember that at Brook in the summer the sea used to come up and they used to call it a ground sea; the waves would come up and break thirty or forty yards off the shore, surging and boiling right up to the foot of the cliff. A ground sea would come on quite suddenly; Alf might have gone out in the morning in a very calm sea, but while he was out there a ground sea could come up and he'd have a job to get back in. The waves mightn't look very high from the shore but I expect when you were out there they were five or six foot high even in the summer. The wind would come up as well. Mrs Hookey would come out to me if I was going up to South Hills to get the cows in for the afternoon milking, 'Pat, when you get the cows can you have a look and see if Alf's boat's in? ' She was being kind you see, because she knew this ground sea had come up over a few hours and that Alf would have been out there; that was for safety's sake and because she cared about him. I'd walk up to the top of the cliff and look over ... Alf's boat was always in. He was very clever at reading the weather - I think if he went out in the morning he'd probably know what the weather was going to be like six or seven hours from then. Mrs Hookey said that to me more than once.

I went out with Alf a couple of times; what I didn't like was that these ground seas came up so quick; it used to frighten me. I only went out with him twice as I can remember and then not very far. I think Alf must've got caught out there at some time and found he could manage alright, so I'm sure if the waves had come up he'd have known what to do to get in alright.

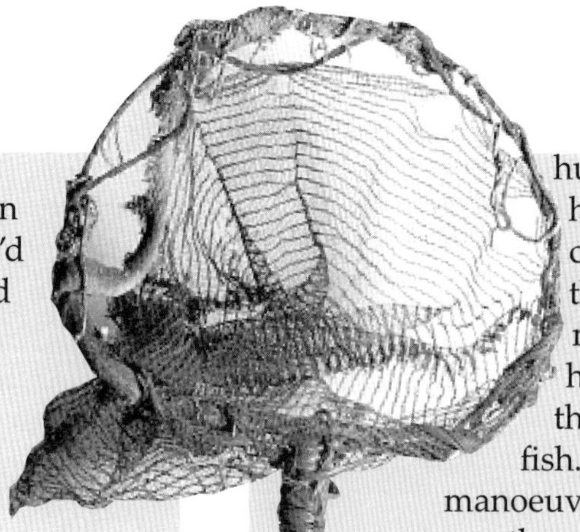

A fishing basket and prawn net found on a Brook farm and likely to have been made and used by Frank Cooke or Alf Woodford.

I think it was in his late seventies or his early eighties when he had to pack up fishing altogether - even then I think he still used to make a few pots. I liked most things about Brook and one of them was Alf Woodford; a bit of a character, a very quiet man, he never caused no trouble, never argued - didn't say a lot actually, but a very nice man. I'm always pleased to think about him, an old fashioned man who when he talked to you could make you feel a grown-up even though you were only fifteen.

Alf Woodford as locals remember him. You can imagine him talking as you look at him.

Like all good fishermen, the best places for catching fish in living memory was a secret known only to Alf and David Hookey. Anne Ham (Hookey) remembers how: *when it came to divulging any of his fishing grounds, Uncle Alf was close. My brother was of the same mind, BUT David did at the very last tell my husband, George, where to fish for BASS......Guaranteed !! Sadly though, George was sworn to secrecy...*

Janet Ash (Stone) remembers:

*My partner Len, a keen angler, was told many times by Uncle Bert about an occasion when he was fishing with Alf Woodford. They would row the boat out a fair distance, dropping the net, then row back in a big circle, dragging the net in. When Bert could touch the sea bed with his oar, Alf would jump out ready to pull the boat in. On one occasion Bert gave the ok and Alf jumped out. Unfortunately on this particular occasion he jumped into a gully and disappeared, only his cap was left floating on the water. He did surface but Bert found it highly amusing. Each time he told the story, and he told it a lot, he would find it more amusing. I can remember the fish being sold to neighbours on a Sunday morning from tin baths in the shed. They were big fish with very red gills and I remember how tasty they were. No doubt they were fried in butter!!*

As an experienced seaman, Alf Woodford had a healthy respect for the sea and did not like to take people out fishing with him: *If something happens I've only got myself to worry about.* When he died a well-thumbed mariner's version of Psalm 23 was found among his few possessions:

**Psalm 23, Mariner's Version**
**Captain John H. Roberts, 1874**

The Lord is my Pilot, I shall not drift.
He leadeth me across the dark waters and steereth me in the deep channels.
He keepeth my Log and guideth me by the star of holiness for His Name's sake.
Yea, though I sail amid the thunders and tempests of life, I shall dread no danger, for Thou art with me;
Thy love and Thy care, they shelter me.
Thou preparest a harbour before me in the homeland of eternity;
Thou anointeth the waves with oil, and my ship rideth calmly.
Surely sunlight and starlight shall favour me on the voyage I take, and I will rest in the port of my Lord forever.

Glass floats, like those above, were commonplace on Brook beach in the 1950s, but are very rarely found today. Made in Japan, they are hollow glass balls with air inside to give them buoyancy. Each float had its own net and a long line of them was attached to huge fishing nets to keep them afloat. Most of these floats are in shades of green because that is the colour of glass from recycled sake bottles.

*Fishing out of Brook on a calm day is a wonderful feeling. It is so tranquil and peaceful to head out to sea and enjoy the open waters.*

In the 1950s Bert Morris and Walter Stone of Hanover House enjoyed fishing from their rowing boat named *Fantoddle*. Many fish were caught and villagers would come and buy the fresh fish at the shop in Hanover Stores. On one occasion half a tonne of bass was caught and sent to Portsmouth for 4d per pound.

Chris Braund with lobsters caught at Brook in 1976.

**Chris Braund remembers fishing with David Hookey at Brook:**

David Hookey of Downton Farm was one of the last Isle of Wight farmers to work both on the land and the sea. David's speciality was prawn fishing; he grew his own withies, harvested them and then made his own pots during the winter months. The old fishermen kept their boats at Brook Point, not where the slip road is now; this is before the land slip. Dave kept his boat at home in the farmyard and would bring it down to the beach with his small tractor. He would then drive to Brook Point before he would launch his boat so he was fishing the same ground as the old men.

I am not sure but I believe that his old boat belonged to his father. It was clinker built (wood) in Ventnor and was about 16 feet long, Dave never sat down to row but stood facing the bow and pushed the oars. In the autumn months we would take his boat and fish with a large net at Compton beach the same as the Chale Bay fishermen used to catch mackerel years ago.

When Dave was not fishing he loved to be under the water. He was a very good diver and loved to explore the seabed looking for anything of interest. He helped me out several times when I had a lobster pot stuck under a rock and could not get it up.

**Simon Homes compares fishing off Brook in 2009, with earlier years:**

Fishing at Brook today is much as it always has been. Even with lighter boats and modern equipment, the rough sea and huge Atlantic swells still limit the days you are able to launch safely. Over the last four years spring and summer conditions have been dictated by a busy Atlantic which keeps throwing areas of low pressure in our direction. If a swell arrives you can normally guarantee the arrival of wind and rain in a couple of days.

A day's fishing for bass and mackerel can be very exciting. Brook, Freshwater, Compton, Sudmore, Dutchman's, Atherfield and Blackgang still attract huge shoals of mackerel and bass which usually arrive in May or when the blossom starts to fall. A good sign is when you see birds including gulls, gannets and guillemots following the shoals and feeding on the smaller fish (sand eels/whitebait). A friend of mine even saw puffins early one morning. Other fish that provide great sport include ray, wrass, pout, cod, tope, brill, turbot and plaice. The past few seasons have seen the arrival of warm water species such as squid and sunfish. You may even spot a porpoise or dolphin. Sunrise and sunset on a calm day are usually when fish come to the surface. This can look like a 'feeding frenzy' with the sea bubbling and fish jumping all around you. Twice, whilst fishing in the summer I have noticed such a feeding frenzy come to a sudden halt and the oily, eerie sea turn lifeless. Then a thresher shark has surfaced after feeding on the mackerel and bass!

Nowadays boats are often made of aluminium which makes launching easier and nets and pots are made of modern synthetic materials. Many boats use rod and line fishing, which is described as 'sport fishing' and often release the fish back into the sea to aid fish stocks. Electronic aids can now provide data on where fish could be found and, while it may sound easier, catching fish still requires a great deal of skill and knowledge.

Simon Homes with his boat and a catch outside Hole Cottage, Mottistone.

# *Ship ashore!*

# The work of Brooke Lifeboat

HMS Triton, a dredger wrecked off Brook Point, November 1904. We believe the man in the middle is the Rev. Leslie Morris, Hon. Sec. to Brooke Lifeboat.

*The Brooke Lifeboat alone is credited with saving 381 lives between 1860 and 1937*

The stretch of coast between the Needles and St Catherine's Point is the most treacherous on the Isle of Wight. The clay and smooth rock slabs known as Brook and Brighstone Ledges extend half a mile out to sea, stretch for six miles and have claimed many ships and lives in thick fogs, heavy ground swells and wild south-westerly storms. For hundreds of years, 'wreck,' like smuggling, was an important source of income for Islanders. Cargoes they came across in this way included valuable building materials, spices, salt, sugar and wine. If the longshoreman could not use the goods themselves they would sell them on, often using the smugglers' distribution routes and networks. The timbers from wrecks were used to build houses, sheds and boats; the panelling in Mottistone Church roof, for example, is taken from the *Cedarine*, wrecked in 1862.

Brooke Lifeboat Station was established in 1860. Before then rescues were carried out by the coastguards and prior to that by the local longshoremen. Between 1860 and 1937, when it was closed down, the Brooke service is credited with saving 381 lives. It was a succession of wrecks along this coast in 1859 that resulted in committees being formed by the rectors of Brooke and Brighstone and Charles Seely.They raised enough money for the Royal National Lifeboat Institution to build two boats, one for each village. From then on everyone in Hulverstone, Mottistone and Brook was in some way connected with Brooke Lifeboat. For a start, to launch the *Susan Ashley* (1907 - 1937) thirteen crew members, ten heavy horses and up to thirty helpers were needed. Six horses were needed to launch the boat and ten to recover it when it was heavy with sea water. The crew of thirteen included five oars on each side, a coxswain, a second coxswain and bowman. Support work on shore included keeping a chest of dry clothes always ready for those shipwrecked and we are told that in the 1850s, before John Dennett's and then Colonel Boxer's rocket was regularly used, the smithy at Downton Farm had been

*Villagers on the south coast of the Island were poor and 'wreck' was an important source of income*

experimenting to create a line to wrecked ships by firing a canon ball with a line secured through the middle. Although they perfected the drilling of a hole through the canon ball, the line always broke when fired. The lifeboat house still stands but the original launching path has long since been worn away by the sea. The doors of the lifeboat house are in the end away from the sea to allow them to be opened in stormy weather when the prevailing south westerlies funnel up from the sea. Robert Cassell recalled the drill in the 1930s:

*Just before a practice or any launch, the chief helper would come along and issue badges. If you never had a badge, you never got paid. The coxswain used to organise everything. Ordinary helpers used to get three shillings and sixpence summertime and five shillings wintertime for every launch. That extra bit of money was a godsend in the winter. Rowing was difficult and very hot work. You had great oilskins on and lifejackets and when you was pulling on the oars out through the breakers…well you would get ever so hot. The sweat would just roll off of you and come through the oilskins and you would stick to the seat and have to wrench yourself off.*

The lifeboat was away in less than an hour after the gun went off: *At Brook we had a light on the beach made from a forty gallon drum half full of carbide and because the fog was so thick the coxswain called out to us as they rowed away 'Keep that light burning won't you'. They wanted to be able to see to come back. It gave a magnificent light. One time we lit a fire and sat around and had a smoke and one thing and another while waiting.*

*Everyone in Hulverstone and Brook was in some way connected with the lifeboat because to run the lifeboat 13 crew members were needed and about 25 to 30 helpers.*

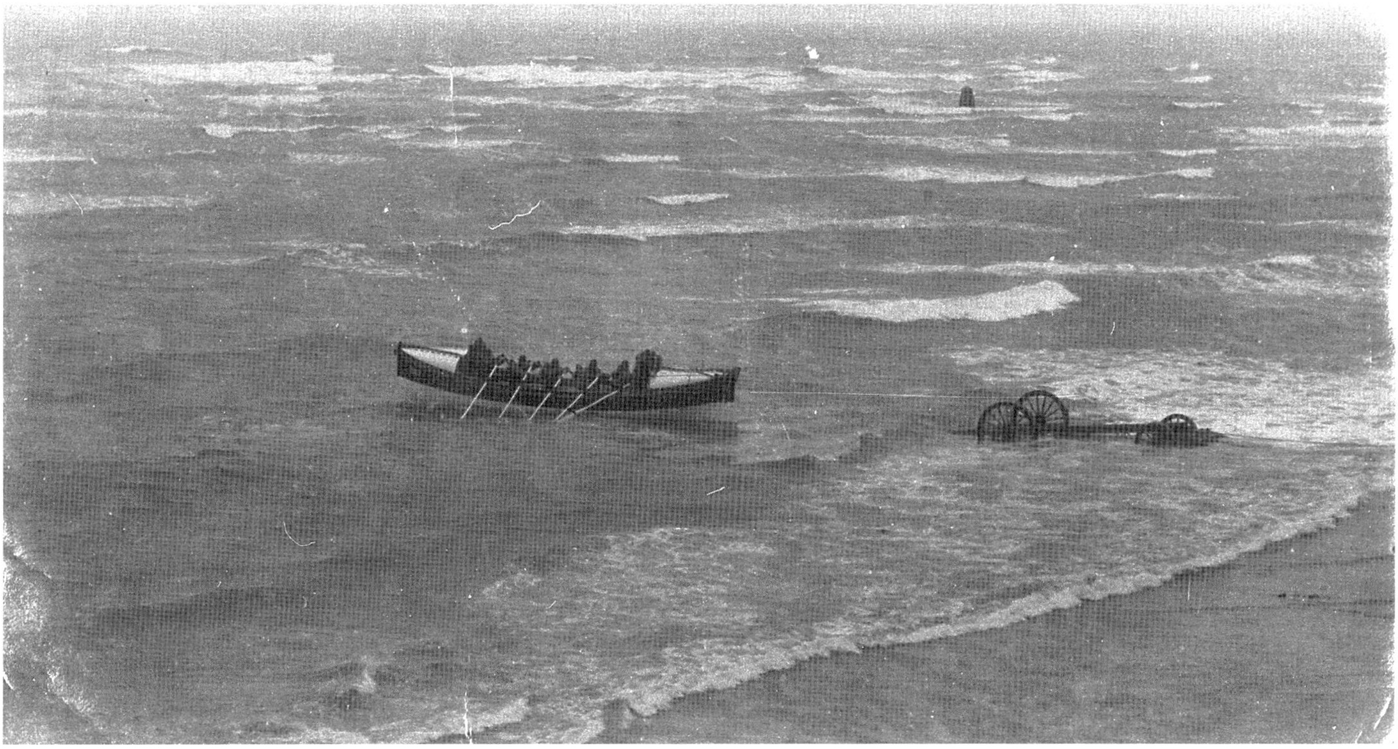

The following account is from Barbara Heal (Hookey) who at three or four years old remembers a launch in the early 1920s:

I was staying with my aunt and uncle near Brook. We were just sitting down to Sunday dinner when we suddenly heard an urgent hammering on the front door and a boy's voice calling, 'Ship ashore.' Before we could answer he was gone. With no time for our meal, Uncle and I and his horse headed a mile or so for Brook Green to help launch the lifeboat. Monarch of all I surveyed, gripping hard to his thick black mane I rode bareback on Captain, who for all his huge height and girth was gentle as a lamb. My small child's legs stuck out at right angles and buckled under me when I was lowered to the ground at the lifeboat house. Though all seemed bustle and confusion everyone knew his job, and soon Captain, with I think above five more equally huge carthorses, was hauling the heavy boat on its carriage along the road and down the path to the beach. There were more horses waiting, for all the farms near Brook made horses available at short notice for their invaluable share in saving life at sea – in this case a small coaster stranded on rocks just off the Hanover Point...

Helped by men from the village, the horses strained with the undertow dragging the pebbles against their legs. They appeared quite calm with the cold water splashing high on their legs. Perhaps the soft encouraging voices of the carters kept fear at bay. Suddenly the coxswain shouted 'Launch!', all oars dipped together and the lifeboat was off her carriage on the crest of a huge wave, heading westwards into the turbulent seas. A few minutes and the one sail was hoisted. The men still rowing strongly were now making better headway towards the stranded vessel, but we were not meant to see a rescue this day, for having lightened the vessel by throwing out some of the cargo she floated off -–the lifeboat was not needed. It returned to the shore where both watchers and horses dragged her back up the narrow path to the lifeboat house.

*In Living Memory,* IOW Federation of Women's Institutes.

The Susan Ashley 1907- 1937.

# Wrecks 1301-1964

A record of vessels ashore between Compton Chine and Chilton Chine, Isle of Wight.

| | | | | |
|---|---|---|---|---|
| 1. | 1301 | Unidentified | Sh. | Calais |
| 2. | 1320 | St Mary | Sh. | Santander |
| 3. | 1616 | Unidentified | | Wreck at Brooke |
| 4. | 1632 | Unidentified | | Wreck at Compton |
| 5. | 1635 | Phoenix | Sh. | British |
| 6. | 1659 | Moore | Sh. | Dutch |
| 7. | 1670 | Unidentified | Sh. | Wreck at Brooke |
| 8. | 1749 | Warren | Sl. | British |
| 9. | 1751 | Jonge Hanse & Gereton | Gl. | Dutch Friesland |
| 10. | 1753 | Unidentified | Bt. | British |
| 11. | 1754 | Diana | Sn. | New England |
| 12. | 1754 | Mary Anne | Dg. | French |
| 13. | 1755 | St Peter | Sl. | French Dieppe |
| 14. | 1755 | Samuel | Sn. | British |
| 15. | 1757 | Jonge Bonne | Gl. | Dutch |
| 16. | 1758 | Cyprus | Sn. | British got off |
| 17. | 1760 | Koornbears | Gl. | Dutch |
| 18. | 1760 | Vries Van Leuwaarden | Gl. | Dutch |
| 19. | 1760 | Unidentified | Ct. | French Privateer |
| 20. | 1766 | Identified | Sn. | British |
| 21. | 1769 | Bergetha and Marie | Sh. | Norway |
| 22. | 1770 | Noordster | Sh. | Dutch |
| 23. | 1770 | King George | Sn. | British |
| 24. | 1770 | North Star | Sl. | British |
| 25. | 1775 | Robert and Sally | Sl. | British |
| 26. | 1778 | Unidentified | Ct. | British |
| 27. | 1778 | Der Fuhrman | Sh. | Swedish |
| 28. | 1778 | William and James | Sl. | British |
| 29. | 1779 | Fothergill | Sl. | British |
| 30. | 1783 | Flying Fish | Ct. | King's Cutter |
| 31. | 1784 | Vrow Geloof | Sh. | Dantsic got off |
| 32. | 1784 | San Miguel | Br. | Spanish |
| 33. | 1784 | John and Jane | Ct. | British |
| 34. | 1785 | Juffrow Anna Louisa | Br. | Dantsic |
| 35. | 1785 | Dorothy and Charlotte | Sh. | British got off |
| 36. | 1785 | Juene Dragon | Br. | French |
| 37. | 1786 | Juno | Sh. | Dutch |
| 38. | 1789 | Liberty | Br. | British got off |
| 39. | 1791 | | Br. | British |
| 40. | 1791 | | Sh. | British Got Off |
| 41. | 1794 | General Clark | Br. | British |
| 42. | 1795 | Nra Sra Dpiler | | Spaniard |
| 43. | 1795 | | Hoy | Swedish |
| 44. | 1797 | Buene Elenna | Sh. | Venice |
| 45. | 1803 | Louisa | Sc. | Hamburg |
| 46. | 1804 | Andalusia | Br. | Portugal |
| 47. | 1805 | Triumph | Hoy | French Bordeaux |
| 48. | 1806 | | Gl. | Prussian |
| 49. | 1806 | Hope | Br. | British |
| 50. | 1813 | Good Advice | Sl. | British |
| 51. | 1814 | De Good Verwagting | Gl. | Dutch |
| 52. | 1819 | Elise | Br. | French |
| 53. | 1821 | Herman | | Hamburg |
| 54. | 1821 | Ales | Br. | Russian |
| 55. | 1825 | Friendship | Sc. | British Got Off |
| 56. | 1826 | Providence | | British Got Off |
| 57. | 1829 | Carnbrea Castle | Sh. | British |
| 58. | 1830 | Unidentified | Ct. | British Smuggler |
| 59. | 1830 | HMS Wolf | Sl. | HMS Got Off |
| 60. | 1830 | Crown | Sh. | British Got Off |
| 61. | 1836 | Atlanta | SS. | British Got Off |
| 62. | 1836 | L'Auguste | Sh. | French St.Malo |
| 63. | 1838 | Claire | Br. | British |
| 64. | 1845 | Siam | Bk. | British Got Off |
| 65. | 1847 | HMS Sphynx | Bk./Sl. | HMS Got Off |
| 66. | 1852 | Japara | Bk. | Dutch |
| 67. | 1856 | George Lord | Sc. | British |
| 68. | 1858 | Abby Langdon | Sh. | American |
| 69. | 1857 | Temerario | Bk. | Portuguese |
| 70. | 1857 | Nra Sra Del Carmen | Ct. | Spanish |
| 71. | 1859 | Sentinel | Sc. | British |
| 72. | 1861 | John Wesley | Sc. | British |
| 73. | 1867 | Fannie Larribee | Sh. | American Got Off |
| 74. | 1871 | Hephzibah | Sc. | British |
| 75. | 1871 | Cassandra | Bk. | British Got Off |
| 76. | 1872 | Roland | Bk. | Norwegian Got Off |
| 77. | 1872 | Malcolm Brown | Bt. | British |
| 78. | 1872 | L'Etoile | Br. | French St Malo |
| 79. | 1873 | Woodham | SS | Norwegian |
| 80. | 1874 | Hermoso Habenero | Br. | Spanish |
| 81. | 1875 | Blanche Marguerite | Bk. | French |
| 82. | 1876 | Mignonette | Bk. | British |
| 83. | 1878 | Ithiel | Sn. | British |
| 84. | 1878 | Charles Emillie | Lg. | French |
| 85. | 1878 | Dalton | SS | British |
| 86. | 1881 | Joseph and Mary | Sc. | British |
| 87. | 1883 | Castle Craig | SS | British Liverpool |
| 88. | 1886 | William Thornborrow | Sc. | British |
| 89. | 1891 | Henri et Leontine | Bt. | French |
| 90. | 1894 | Ossian | SS | British Got Off |
| 91. | 1895 | Noordster | Bkt. | Dutch |
| 92. | 1896 | Joanis Millas | SS | Greek |
| 93. | 1899 | Moland | Bt. | Norwegian |
| 94. | 1902 | Gedania | SS | German Got Off |
| 95. | 1902 | Kinfauns Castle | SS | British Got Off |
| 96. | 1904 | Gladys | Kt. | British Got Off |
| 97. | 1904 | Triton | SS | Spanish Got Off |
| 98. | 1906 | Briton | Br. | British Got Off |
| 99. | 1910 | Rene | Kt. | French |
| 100. | 1916 | Souvenir | Bk. | Norwegian |
| 101. | 1917 | Mientje | Sc. | British Got Off |
| 102. | 1917 | Indutiomare | SS | Belgian |
| 103. | 1917 | Westville | SS | British |
| 104. | 1918 | Molina | SS | Norwegian |
| 105. | 1930 | B.A.S.P. | Lb. | British Got Off |
| 106. | 1940 | Warwick Deeping | St. | HMS |
| 107. | 1947 | Carbon | SS | British Tug |
| 108. | 1959 | Phantom Wreck | Sh. | |
| 109. | 1964 | Brother George | SS | Liberian Got Off |
| 110. | 1964 | Witte Zee | Ms. | Dutch Tug |

Bk. = Barque

Br. = Brig

Bkt. = Barquentine

Ct. = Cutter

l. = Galiot

Kt. = Ketch

Lg. = Lugger

Sc. = Schooner

Sh. = Ship

Sl. = Sloop

Sn. = Snow

SS = Steam Ship

Courtesy of Nova Scotia Museum

# Early rescues

**1301**
The King, Edward I, and the local landlords split the proceeds from a ship *Calais* 'broken on the rocks' at Compton.

**1659**
The Dutch ship *Moore* went ashore at Brook Bay with a valuable cargo which included some silver plate. Rumour has it that the crew, when they saw no chance of getting her off, were induced by one of the inhabitants of Brook to take refuge in his house. Here, it is said, they were drugged and murdered, and buried in the copse adjoining the Church. The murderers are said to have then plundered and burned the vessel.

**18th century**
World trade increased greatly in the eighteenth century but navigation techniques were still unreliable. As a result there was a sharp increase in the number of wrecks and between Compton and Chilton chines alone there were 37 wrecks between 1749 and 1797 (this figure does not include those boats stranded but later re-floated).

William Slaney Lewis 1888 -1907

# Coastguard rescues

July 5th 1829
When the *Carn Brae Castle* split her hull on the rocks of Brook Ledge she had been bound for Bengal with a cargo of goods for the East India Company. The passengers were rescued by Lt Dornford in the coastguard cutter. Lt Dornford's part in the rescue was to save his life in 1836 when he was accused of collusion with smugglers. He was obviously guilty but he was acquitted when the Island's gentry and clergy defended him stoutly quoting the *Carn Brae Castle* rescue.
John Medland, *Shipwrecks of the Isle of Wight*.

January 18th 1856
The English brig *George Lord* had helped supply the British Army in the Crimea and was carrying a cargo of currants and raisins from Patras in Greece to London when she was driven aground in thick fog in Brook Bay, see the newspaper report below. The rescue again involved an ordinary boat with a crew made up of coastguards and fishermen. The heavy boxes of currants and raisins were eventually taken ashore and placed under police guard. See newspaper report below:

WRECK OF A SCHOONER OFF THE ISLE OF WIGHT.

We regret to announce the wreck of the *George Lord* schooner, which went on shore in Brook Bay, Isle of Wight, on the morning of Friday, the 18th of January. She was bound for London, and was laden with a valuable cargo of fruit from Zante. She encountered foggy weather in the Channel, and the master, being out of his reckoning, hailed a French vessel, the Captain of which informed him that he was off the Lizard Point. Altering his course in consequence, he ran his ship directly upon a reef of rocks which juts out into Brook Bay. The coast-guard, seeing a vessel approaching through the darkness, burnt a blue light and fired pistols, but it was too late for the master to alter his course. She struck heavily, and her back was soon broken, through the heaviness of the sea. The crew were got off by the boats of the coast-guard, and a portion of the cargo was saved on Friday and Saturday. Early on Monday morning the stern was beaten in by the sea, and she immediately became a complete wreck. A good deal of the cargo was then washed ashore, but it was much injured by the salt water. This will probably be sold by auction, as well as the wreck. The Captain had commanded her for seventeen years, and had been round the world in her. Last year she was sent to the Crimea with a cargo of provisions, &c. She was insured, and the greater part of the cargo also. The accompanying Sketch was taken in the afternoon of Saturday, the 19th.

December 5th 1859
When the schooner *Sentinel* of Carnarvon came ashore in a tremendous south-westerly storm, two of the crew were swept away and the others could be seen from the land, clinging to the rigging. When the wind moderated, a boat was launched from Brook Bay. The Rev. Pellew Gaze of Brook and others waded up to their waists in freezing water to push the boat clear over the incoming sea. Four survivors were brought back to the shore.

# Dauntless

## 1860 - 1867

### 30ft x 7ft self-righter, built by Forrest of Limehouse, London. Cost £148 9s 6d.

New Year's Day 1861
The first call for Brooke's first lifeboat the *Dauntless,* came at 7am on New Year's Day. The 32 pounder lifeboat canon on the cliff top boomed out over Brook and in a few minutes the whole village was alive with activity. The ship, *John Wesley*, was in danger in Compton Bay. The Captain, George Abbott, declined John Hayter's offer of help and twice the lifeboat returned to shore even though the crew could see that the schooner was doomed. The schooner finally went aground under the white cliffs and a cliff rescue was begun. Two coastguards reached the ship by ropes only to find it empty, the crew were safely on their way to Southampton on a tug. Sadly, when climbing back up the cliffs there was a cliff fall and coastguard McLeod was killed. It was an unnecessary tragedy and Widow McLeod was left with five children. The Trust Fund collected to support her was considered quite a sum for those days, with the RNLB and Charles Seely putting in ten pounds each.

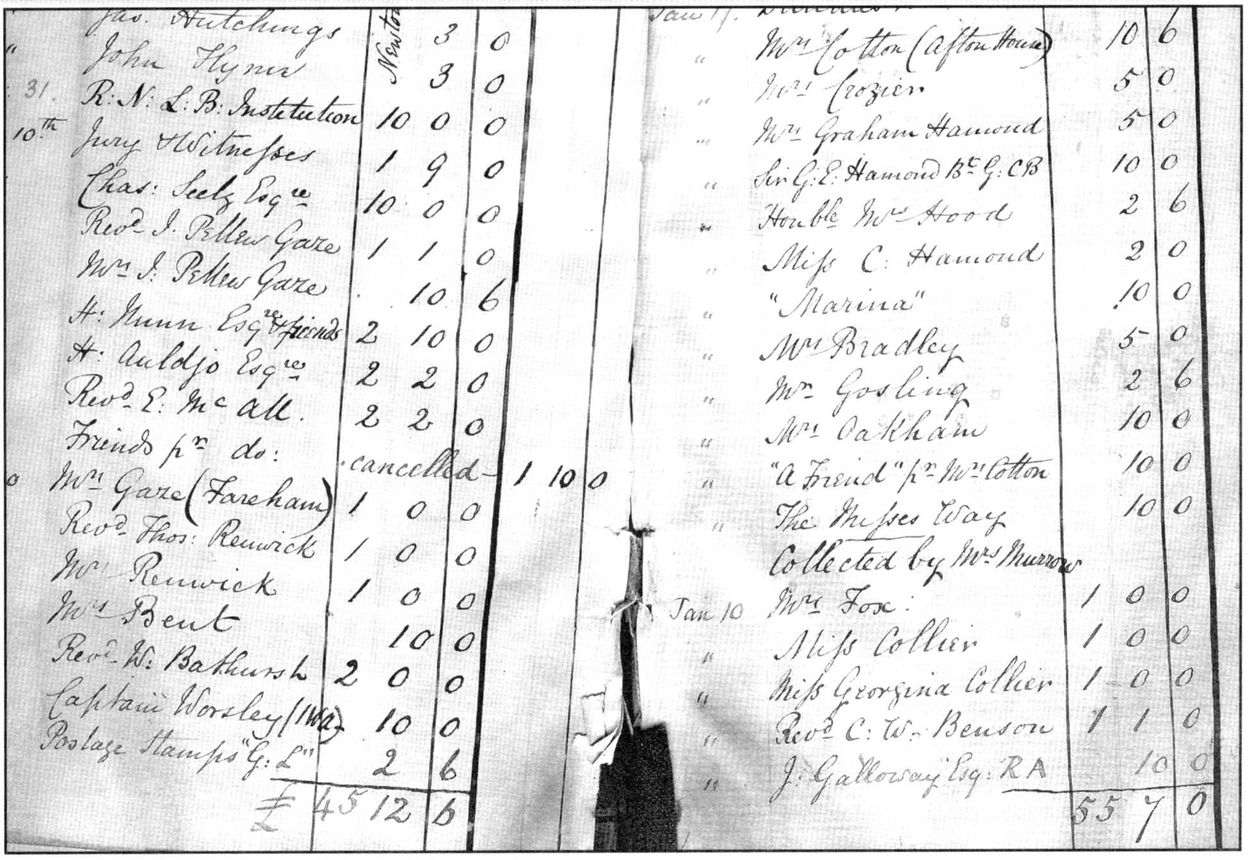

| | | | | | | |
|---|---|---|---|---|---|---|
| | Jas: Hutchings | Newton | | 3 | 0 | |
| " | John Flynn | | | 3 | 0 | |
| 31. | R: N: L: B: Institution | | 10 | 0 | 0 | |
| 10th | Jury & Witnesses | | 1 | 9 | 0 | |
| | Chas: Seely Esqre | | 10 | 0 | 0 | |
| | Revd. J. Pellew Gare | | 1 | 1 | 0 | |
| | Mrs J. Pellew Gare | | | 10 | 6 | |
| | H: Munn Esqre & friends | | 2 | 10 | 0 | |
| | H: Auldjo Esqre | | 2 | 2 | 0 | |
| | Revd. E. McAll. | | 2 | 2 | 0 | |
| | Friends pr do: | | cancelled | | | 1 10 0 |
| | Mrs Gare (Fareham) | | 1 | 0 | 0 | |
| | Revd. Thos: Renwick | | 1 | 0 | 0 | |
| | Mrs Renwick | | 1 | 0 | 0 | |
| | Mrs Bent | | | 10 | 0 | |
| | Revd. W: Bathurst | | 2 | 0 | 0 | |
| | Captain Worsley (RN) | | | 10 | 0 | |
| | Postage Stamps "G: L" | | | 2 | 6 | |
| | | | £45 | 12 | 6 | |

| | | | | |
|---|---|---|---|---|
| Jan 17 | | | | |
| " | Mrs Cotton (Afton House) | | 10 | 6 |
| " | Mrs Crozier | | 5 | 0 |
| " | Mrs Graham Hamond | | 5 | 0 |
| " | Sir G: E: Hamond Bt. G: CB | | 10 | 0 |
| " | Honble Mrs Hood | | 2 | 6 |
| " | Miss C: Hamond | | 2 | 0 |
| " | "Marina" | | 10 | 0 |
| " | Mrs Bradley | | 5 | 0 |
| " | Mr Gosling | | 2 | 6 |
| " | Mrs Oakham | | 10 | 0 |
| " | "A Friend" pr Mrs Cotton | | 10 | 0 |
| " | The Misses Way | | 10 | 0 |
| | Collected by Mrs Murrow | | | |
| Jan 10 | Mrs Fox: | 1 | 0 | 0 |
| " | Miss Collier | 1 | 0 | 0 |
| " | Miss Georgina Collier | 1 | 0 | 0 |
| " | Revd. C: W: Benson | 1 | 1 | 0 |
| " | J. Galloway Esq: RA | | 10 | 0 |
| | | 55 | 7 | 0 |

Widow McLeod's Trust Fund book established after her husband was killed following the rescue of the *Dauntless*. This was considered a substantial settlement for those days.

February 2nd 1867
The American ship *Fanny Larribee*, 1271 tons in ballast, went ashore off Brook Chine. In spite of a heavy ground swell, Captain Randall decided to stay with his ship until a tug arrived and eventually the vessel was re-floated.

# George and Anne
# 1867 - 1888

## 32ft x 7ft 6in self-righter, built by Forest of Limehouse, London. Cost £274.

November 15th 1871
The fine Liverpool barque *Cassandra* was sailing from London to Madras when she was caught in a particularly fierce gale in the Channel. On the night of the 15th November she was driven onto the long, rocky fingers of Brook Ledge. The *George and Anne* was pulled along the beach to the wreck and launched. The *Cassandra* was rolling heavily on the Ledge but was not in any immediate danger. Coxswain John Hayter wanted everyone to come ashore but the Captain thought they were safe enough and the lifeboat returned with only 7 of the 21 crew, including the injured.

The lifeboat was returned to the lifeboat house (not an easy operation) but an hour later the *Cassandra* was signalling for assistance and the whole lifeboat launch procedure had to be repeated. By now the tide had risen and the seas were breaking over the wreck and up the cliff over the exhausted launchers and horses. The re-launch was successful and the remaining fourteen men were saved.

In 1872 there were four rescues:

In January assistance was rendered to the *Sjorn,* a Norwegian ship which came ashore in Compton Bay.

-----------

Two efforts made to save the crew of the barque *Hope* proved ineffectual and the 'Vessel foundered in a hurricane with all hands'.

-----------

In May the brig *L'Etoile* with a cargo of salt came ashore at Sudmore Point in heavy ground swell. All eight crew were landed by the Brighstone Lifeboat assisted by the *George and Anne.* It is said that within four days there was no more trace of the *L'Etoile.*

--------------

On the January 13th 1872, the brigantine *Malcolm Brown* was reported ashore in heavy seas. Coxswain Hayter decided to get the lifeboat overland to Compton and launch as near to the wreck as possible. Things did not go according to plan however; the carriage sank into the soft clay at the foot of the cliffs and became immovable. By the time they had removed the lifeboat from her carriage and got her back to the firm part of the shore, the tide had risen to such an extent that the seas were dashing the lifeboat and its thirty local helpers against the cliff. After working waist deep in icy water retrieving the boat, they went back for the carriage. No damage was done to the lifeboat but when they finally launched, they found that the vessel had already been abandoned.

October 18th 1874
When the brig *Hermoso Habanero* struck on the rocks at Sudmore below Mottistone, the crew took to their boats, but as the sea was so rough they had to secure them to the anchor in the bows of the vessel. Eight people were rescued with much difficulty, in the heavy surf. In the afternoon of the next day her main mast was carried away and she broke up within half an hour. Her cargo of rum, sugar and mahogany,was strewn along the coast from Brighstone to Brook (no doubt this received a warm welcome when the coastguards were not around).

January 15th 1875
The lifeboat once more proved its worth when the barque *Blanche Margeurite* from Philipville, on her way to Dunkirk loaded with barley struck on the Sudmore ledge. A crew of ten lives were saved in spite of heavy seas in which no ordinary boat could have survived.

December 14th 1883
The *Castle Craig,* from Odessa in the Black Sea, was loaded with Russian grain, oil and feathers when she lost her bearings in thick fog and drove on to Brook Ledge. The crew of the *George and Anne* were summoned at 4am and launched into the heavy freezing seas. They had great difficulty getting alongside the vessel so as to take the crew off. Eventually, after two trips all 31 of the crew were saved. This porthole was found under the sea at Brook and is believed to come from the ship.

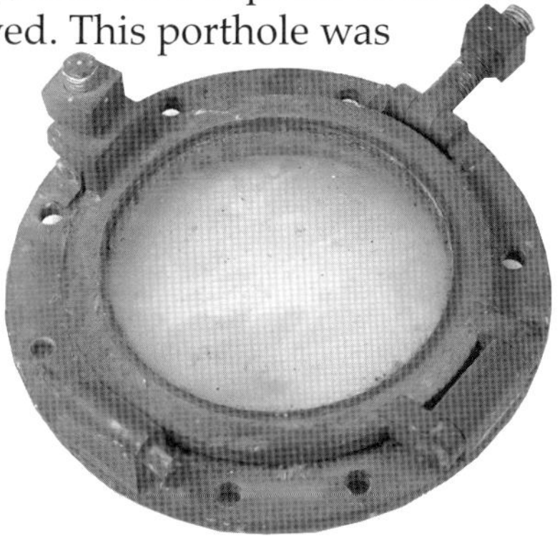

January 19th 1876
The Brooke lifeboat was launched to rescue fourteen men on board the barque *Mignonette* and succeeded in bringing all ashore in thick weather and a heavy ground swell.

January 30th 1886
A 100 ton schooner, *William Thornborrow,* bound from Teignmouth for London with a cargo of pipe clay, came ashore at Brook and soon became full of water and likely to become a total wreck. Captain Spiller and his crew took to their boats and abandoned her. She was afterwards boarded by the coastguards who took charge of her on behalf of the Receiver of Wrecks. The captain and crew rowed round the Needles and up through the Solent to land at Cowes.

November 1884
On a Tuesday morning at 1am a small schooner, *Princess of Thule,* owned by its captain and bound for Montrose, was laden with maize and came ashore on the rocks at Brook in very thick fog. With assistance from coastguards and fishermen she was lightened of some of her cargo and got off the rocks at 7.30pm.

# William Slaney Lewis
# 1888 - 1907

## A 34ft x 7ft 6in self-righter, built by Hansen and Sons of Cowes. Cost £347.

March 9th 1888
The 1,588 ton full-rigged ship *Sirenia* laden with a cargo of wheat was bound from San Francisco for Dunkirk when she ran aground on Atherfield Ledge. The Brighstone boat went out to help in the storm and thirteen crew members were taken off. In one tragic moment, however, the lifeboat capsized and two lifeboat men, Moses Munt and Tom Cotton and two of the rescued men were lost.
Unfortunately this was not the end of the disaster, as the Brooke Lifeboat had been launched to assist in the rescue and had to come down six miles through a, 'veritable hell of waters'. When they had almost reached the wreck, a huge sea broke into the lifeboat taking three of the crew overboard, Reuben Cooper and Ben and Phil Jacobs. The two Jacobs brothers managed to hang on to lifelines and were dragged back on board, but Cooper was swept away in the darkness, 'his cries for help being plainly heard both on the boat and the ship. The lifeboat was steered in the direction of the cries but he could not be found. ' By this time the Brooke crew were exhausted and could not beat back to the wreck. They anchored, drenched and hungry in Chale Bay to wait for daylight. As soon as dawn came up they hauled up the anchor and began the struggle back to the ship. Though their hearts were good, their strength was exhausted and they had to own themselves beaten, so they hoisted sail and beat back to their station. For his gallantry during this service, coxswain John Hayter was awarded his second silver medal by the RNLI.

In the WI Scrapbook (1958), Ella Hookey, who lived at Myrtle Cottage, recalls how: *Our most tragic moments were when there was a shipwreck and the lifeboat with our fathers and brothers had to go out to help rescue the unfortunate ones. I remember the Sirenia which was wrecked off Brighstone. The Brooke Lifeboat was called out to help the Brighstone boat. It was a very rough night and Brooke Lifeboat was launched at 9 pm. It was so rough they could not get near the ship... The lifeboat did not return until midday the next day and the crew including my father, were so exhausted they had to be helped ashore and carried to their homes. What a blessing that we now have more up-to-date lifeboats where the crews stand a better chance of survival.*

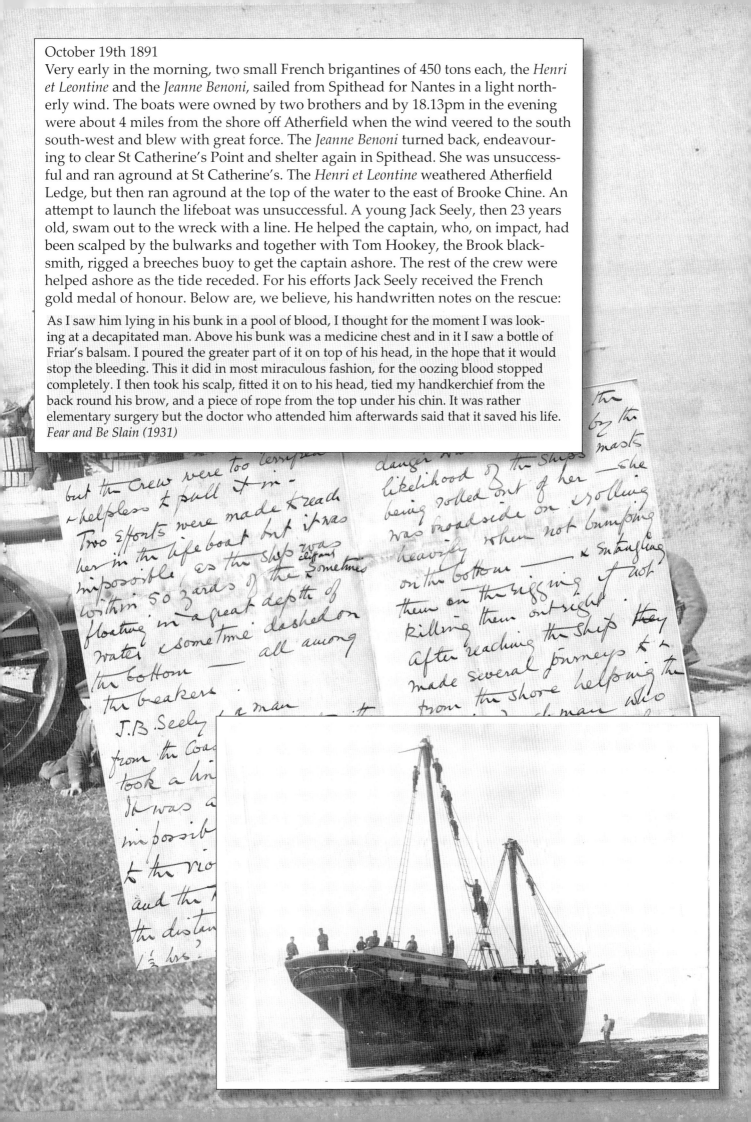

October 19th 1891

Very early in the morning, two small French brigantines of 450 tons each, the *Henri et Leontine* and the *Jeanne Benoni*, sailed from Spithead for Nantes in a light northerly wind. The boats were owned by two brothers and by 18.13pm in the evening were about 4 miles from the shore off Atherfield when the wind veered to the south south-west and blew with great force. The *Jeanne Benoni* turned back, endeavouring to clear St Catherine's Point and shelter again in Spithead. She was unsuccessful and ran aground at St Catherine's. The *Henri et Leontine* weathered Atherfield Ledge, but then ran aground at the top of the water to the east of Brooke Chine. An attempt to launch the lifeboat was unsuccessful. A young Jack Seely, then 23 years old, swam out to the wreck with a line. He helped the captain, who, on impact, had been scalped by the bulwarks and together with Tom Hookey, the Brook blacksmith, rigged a breeches buoy to get the captain ashore. The rest of the crew were helped ashore as the tide receded. For his efforts Jack Seely received the French gold medal of honour. Below are, we believe, his handwritten notes on the rescue:

As I saw him lying in his bunk in a pool of blood, I thought for the moment I was looking at a decapitated man. Above his bunk was a medicine chest and in it I saw a bottle of Friar's balsam. I poured the greater part of it on top of his head, in the hope that it would stop the bleeding. This it did in most miraculous fashion, for the oozing blood stopped completely. I then took his scalp, fitted it on to his head, tied my handkerchief from the back round his brow, and a piece of rope from the top under his chin. It was rather elementary surgery but the doctor who attended him afterwards said that it saved his life.
*Fear and Be Slain (1931)*

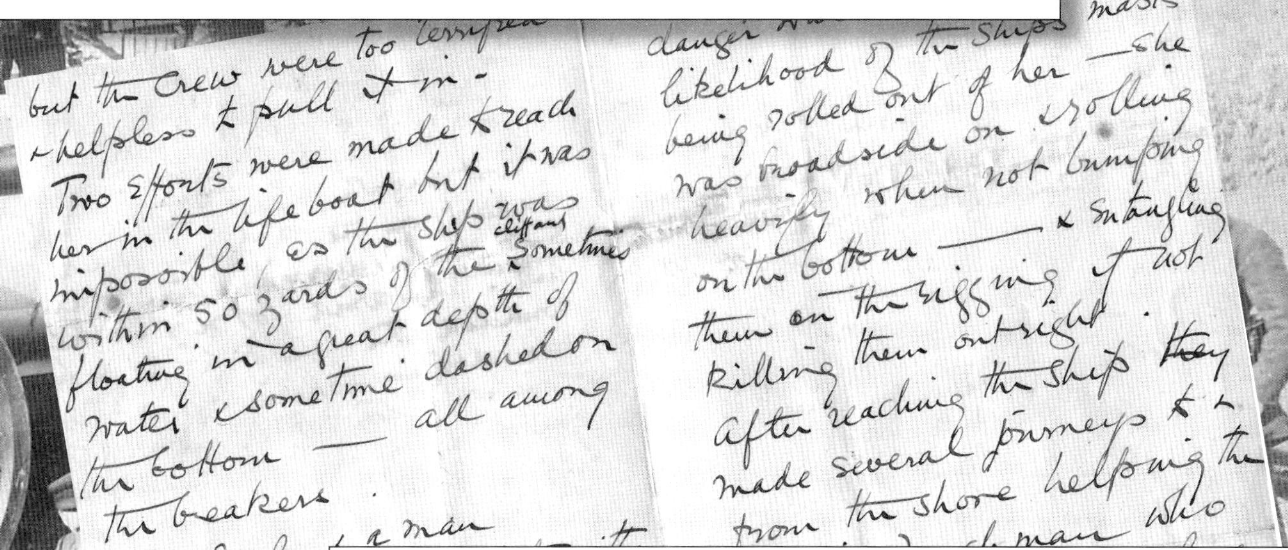

but the crew were too terrified
& helpless to pull it in -
Two efforts were made to reach
her in the lifeboat but it was
impossible as the ship was
within 50 yards of the cliffs and sometimes
floating in a great depth of
water & sometime dashed on
the bottom — all among
the breakers.
J.B. Seely & a man ... it
from the Coa...
took a lin...
It was a...
impossib...
to the rio...
and the ...
the distan...
1½ hrs?

the
by the
danger ... masts
likelihood of the ships
being rolled out of her — she
was broadside on & rolling
heavily when not bumping
on the bottom — & entangling
them in the rigging if not
killing them outright.
After reaching the ship they
made several journeys to &
from the shore helping the
... man who

January 31st 1892

The *SS Eider* of Bremen, a four-masted steamer of 4,719 tons was travelling from New York carrying 227 passengers and a crew of 167. There was thick fog and a stiff gale blowing but apparently it was only when the cut-glass of the chandeliers began to clatter that it was discovered the ship was hard aground on Black Slopper Rock. The Brooke Lifeboat along with the Brighstone Grange and Atherfield boats, were called out but the captain repeatedly refused help, expecting the ship to lift off the rocks with the tide. The next day it took the Brighstone, Atherfield and Brook boats eleven dangerous trips to save all the passengers and crew. The reason for the captain's reluctance to leave the ship became clear when it was revealed that there was £300,000 worth of gold and silver bullion on board. The lifeboats made 41 trips in all to retrieve all the bullion, silver plate and luggage. Heavily armed coastguards stood on the beach waiting to receive it. Expressions of admiration and thanks to the lifeboatmen came directly from Queen Victoria and the German Emperor Wilhelm II, who gave each coxswain a gold watch commending their outstanding courage. John Hayter, Brooke coxswain, was awarded his third silver medal by the RNLI. Punch magazine presented a citation and an especially written poem to each member of the lifeboat crews (see page 42). The lifeboats had been in action for four days landing passengers and crew and bringing ashore baggage and mail.

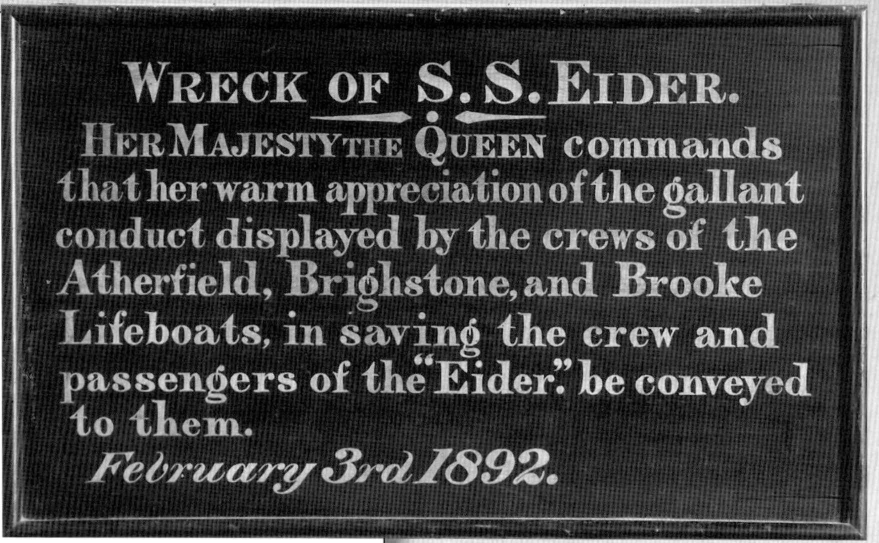

WRECK OF S.S. EIDER.
HER MAJESTY THE QUEEN commands that her warm appreciation of the gallant conduct displayed by the crews of the Atherfield, Brighstone, and Brooke Lifeboats, in saving the crew and passengers of the "Eider." be conveyed to them.
February 3rd 1892.

MR. PUNCH TO THE LIFEBOAT-MEN
[The President of the Board of Trade has, by command of the Queen, conveyed, through the Royal National Lifeboat Institution, to the crews of the Lifeboats of Atherfield, Brighstone, and Brook, Her Majesty's warm appreciation of their gallant conduct in saving the crew and passengers of the steamship *Eider*.]

January 17th 1894
The *SS Ossian* (387 tons) bound from Lisbon to Leith with a mixed cargo of wine, slates, sheepskins and cork shavings, came ashore in Brook Bay at 3am. As well as fog, there was a heavy ground swell. The lifeboat made its first trip bringing ashore seven of her crew. The Captain and eight men decided to remain on board until later when conditions would be more favourable. The boat was re-floated a week later by the Neptune Salvage Company.

February 13th 1899
When Norwegian barquetine *Moland* went ashore at Brook, the lifeboat was launched only to find the vessel breaking up and no sign of any crew. It was later learned that a French vessel had come across her and taken off the rest of the crew before she went ashore.

March 24th 1895
The *Noordstar*, an iron-hulled brigantine bound from Venezuela to Hamburg with a cargo of box wood and divi divi*, came ashore at Hanover Point, striking what was known locally as the Oil Rock. All seven lives were saved 'in a remarkably smart and able manner by the gallant crew'. A ring-tailed monkey miraculously escaped drowning by floating ashore in a sack and the rector's wife, Mrs Morris, took it in.

* 'Divi divi' are the pods (1 x 3 inches rolled up) of South American redwood trees and are used by tanners and dyers.

April 12th 1902
The *Kinfauns Castle* was stranded on Brook Ledge for a short time until she was pulled off by four tugs and her own engines.

November 18 1904
During thick fog, the Dutch steam dredger *Triton* went ashore at Hanover Point. The lifeboat was launched in heavy seas and the coxswain Ben Jacobs took the lifeboat alongside the ship. With heavy seas breaking right through the ship, the lifeboat took off her crew of ten. This was the last rescue of the lifeboat *William Slaney Lewis* which had been in service at Brook for 19 years.

# The Susan Ashley
# 1907 - 1937

## 35ft x 8ft 6in self-righter, built by Thames Ironworks. Cost £844

January 9th 1906
The *Briton*, a spritsail barge, came ashore at Sudmore Point left of Brook Bay.

November 27th 1910
The French ketch *Rene* went ashore at Sudmore. Brooke Lifeboat arrived in time to see her get off and sail away. A few hours later she was grounded again, just west of Freshwater Bay. This time the crew of four managed to get ashore but the Rene split up on the rocks and lost her cargo of valuable zinc ore.

1912
The engines of a steamer, *Poplar*, broke down 5 miles out at sea and Brooke lifeboat stood by until tugs arrived.

The five teams of horses and their carters who came from the local farms to pull the lifeboat.

February 4th 1916
During a south-west gale and heavily breaking seas, a Norwegian ship, the *Souvenir*, went ashore on Brook Ledge. The lifeboat launched at about 8am but was unable to get alongside owing to the violence of the seas. The crew of the vessel, seeing the difficulty of the lifeboat, decided to jump overboard and nine men were picked up from the water. Unfortunately the Steward died in the lifeboat from exhaustion and exposure. The *Souvenir* went completely to pieces before the lifeboat could turn round after landing the crew. The captain of the vessel, who had refused to leave his ship, was lost.

After the rescue, Ben Jacobs received the RNLI silver medal and second coxswain John Cook a certificate of thanks. It was during this rescue that lifeboatman, Joe Morris, had the unnerving experience of being grabbed around the throat and nearly strangled by one of the survivors who had temporarily lost his reason as a result of his terrible experience. The man was overpowered and lashed to the bottom of the lifeboat for the safety of everyone. The women of the village are said to have held out cups of soup laced with brandy to the mouths of the survivors and lifeboatmen alike. Some believe that this rescue was one of the finest, if not the greatest, rescue along the southern coastline of the Island. On the right is the crest of a Norwegian ship found in outhouses of Brook House in 1957 and believed to be from the *Souvenir*.

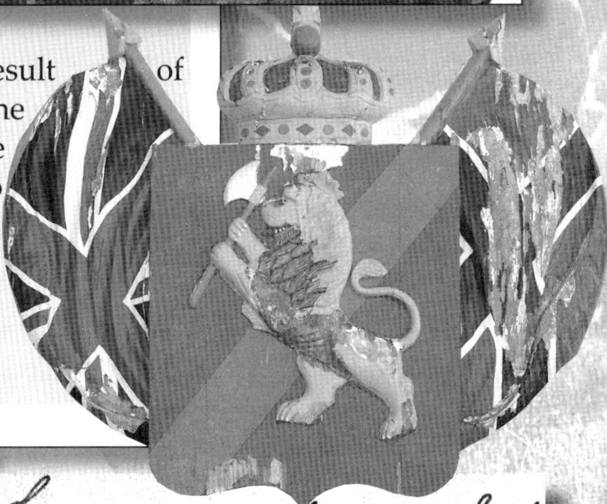

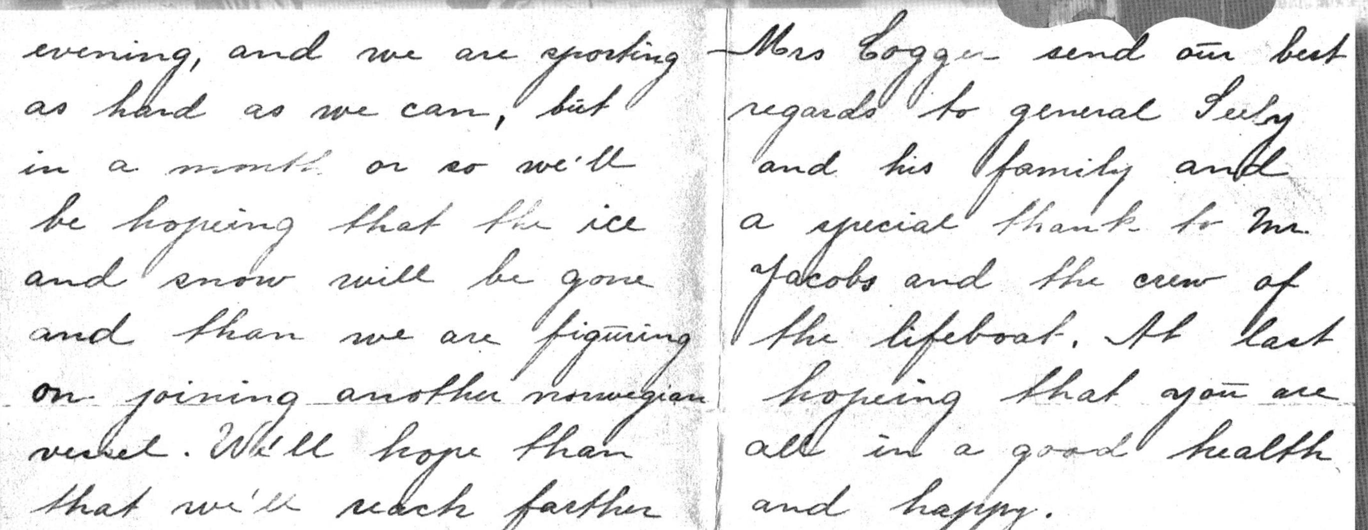

evening, and we are sporting as hard as we can, but in a month or so we'll be hopeing that the ice and snow will be gone and than we are figuring on joining another norwegian vessel. We'll hope than that we'll reach farther than we did last time. We should like to send your people a longer letter but we have not got very much to write about this time.

Mrs Cogger send our best regards to general Seely and his family and a special thank to Mr. Jacobs and the crew of the lifeboat. At last hopeing that you are all in a good health and happy.

Best regards
from
the crew of "Souvenir"

As this letter shows, a strong bond was established between the people of Brook and the Norwegian crew of the *Souvenir* who had been welcomed and put up by the villagers and at Brooke House.

Brook Church choir at a service of dedication for the Susan Ashley on the cliff top in the rain.

1926
The *Urkiole Mendi* was bound for Algeria from Middlesborough with a cargo of iron ore when it came ashore. Brooke lifeboat stood alongside with the Yarmouth motor lifeboat until she was re-floated.

1932
The 2600 ton steamer *Roumelian* of Liverpool collided with the *SS St Nazare* 24 miles south west of the Needles. The St Nazare continued her journey while the *Roumelian* limped towards the safety of the Solent. She had 56 crew and passengers and was taking in water fast. When the maroon went off the Sunday evening service in Brook Church was interrupted and abandoned and the lifeboat quickly launched :

…the rector is in the middle of an eloquent sermon – and very good sermons they are; he has preached many at St Martin's in the Fields. The windows suddenly shook with the reverberation of the maroon. The rector then said: 'I would suggest that we conclude the service. I have been in telephonic communication with the coastguard, and I know that the vessel in distress is being assisted by the Yarmouth lifeboat. Moreover, in any case, should our services be required it will take half-an-hour for the crew and horses to assemble, and I think it would be best for me to conclude my address, and give you a benediction.' Whereupon the faithful gardener who rows number three in the lifeboat (Joe Morris) started up from the choir in his surplice and said quite loudly: 'Well chaps, that be right enough, but I 'lows we five had better go now and see what is doing;' And without another word, out filed the whole of the adult members of the choir. I have been told, though I was not present, as I should have been, that the rector's closing words were of great eloquence, and that the benediction was delivered in record time.
*Launch*, JEB Seely

Launching the Brook Lifeboat June 10th 1933

Never before have the beach and cliffs at Brook presented such a scene of animation and interest as on Whit Monday afternoon, when a crowd, which must have numbered 2,000, saw what will probably be the last launch of the Brook lifeboat by horse power...the fact that our new Island Peer (General Seely) would be in charge as acting coxswain, and that Scouts from the All-Island camp at Brooke House would assist in the launch, aroused widespread interest. About 40 sturdy Rovers and Scouts clad in bathing costumes were waiting on the beach to play the part of shore helpers. Their duties were to push the carriage out into the water far enough to launch the boat and then to haul on the ropes to propel the boat into the water with her crew on board.

General Seely stood at the wheel as the launching operations commenced, but after getting into about three foot of water the carriage became fast in the blue slipper clay. General Seely descended and waded out to give the Scouts the 'heaves', but in spite of all their efforts the carriage refused to budge, and there was a wait until the rising tide gave a sufficient depth for the actual launch. The General climbed back on board, the Scouts hauled away lustily, and the *Susan Ashley* glided gracefully down the runners into the water, amid a roar of cheers from the crowd onshore. Meanwhile the Scouts had been disporting themselves in the water to the entertainment of the crowd, and after the cooling dip, they were ready for more hard work in hauling the boat ashore and getting her on to the carriage. The task was well and truly done, and without further incident the boat was safely re-housed.
*Isle of Wight County Press*

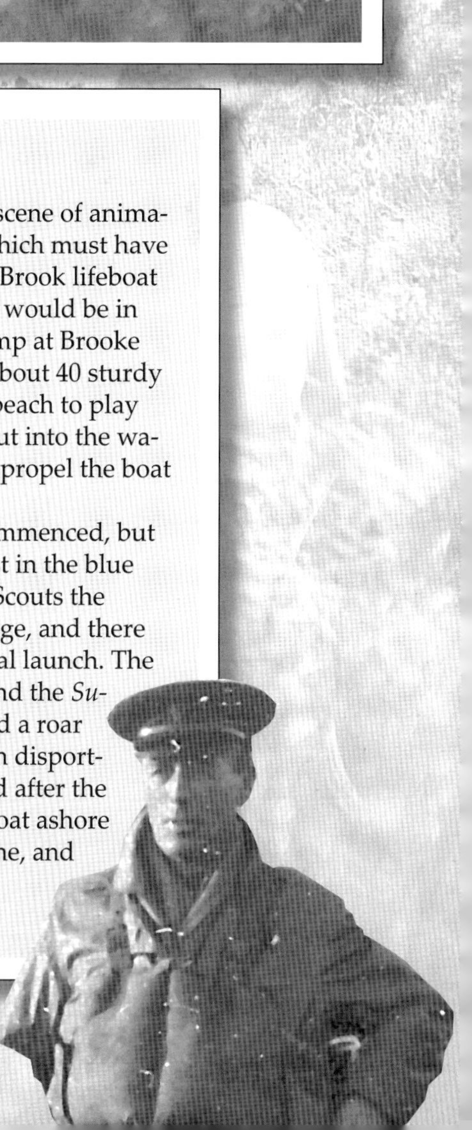

## MR. PUNCH TO THE LIFEBOAT-MEN.

[The President of the Board of Trade has, by command of the Queen, conveyed, through the Royal National Lifeboat Institution, to the crews of the Lifeboats of Atherfield, Brighstone, and Brook, Her Majesty's warm appreciation of their gallant conduct in saving the crew and passengers of the steamship *Eider*.]

YOUR hand, lad! 'Tis wet with the brine, and the salt spray has sodden your hair,
And the face of you glisteneth pale with the stress of the struggle out there;
But the savour of salt is as sweet to the sense of a Briton, sometimes,
As the fragrance of wet mignonette, or the scent of the bee-haunted limes.

Ay, sweeter is manhood, though rough, than the smoothest effeminate charms
To the old sea-king strain in our blood in the season of shocks and alarms,
When the winds and the waves and the rocks make a chaos of danger and strife;
And the need of the moment is pluck, and the guerdon of valour is life.

That guerdon you've snatched from the teeth of the thundering tiger-maw'd waves,
And the valour that smites is as naught, after all, to the valour that saves.
They are safe on the shore, who had sunk in the whirl of the floods but for *you!*
And some said you had lost your old grit and devotion! We knew 'twas not true.

The soft-hearted shore-going critics of conduct themselves would not dare,
The trivial cocksure belittlers of dangers they have not to share,
Claim much—oh *so* much, from rough manhood—unflinching cool daring in fray,
And selflessness utter, from toilers with little of praise, and less pay.

Her heroes to get "on the cheap" from the rough rank and file of her sons
Has been England's good fortune so long, that the scribblers' swift tongue-babble runs
To the old easy tune without thought. "Gallant sea-dogs and life-savers!" Yes!
But poor driblets of lyrical praise should not be their sole guerdon, I guess.

On the coast, in the mine, at the fire, in the dark city byeways at night,
They are ready the waves, or the flames, or the bludgeoning burglar to fight.
And are *we* quite as ready to mark, or to fashion a fitting reward
For the coarsely-clad commonplace men who our life and our property guard?

A question *Punch* puts to the Public, and on your behalf, my brave lad,
And that of your labouring like. To accept your stout help we are glad:
If supply of cheap heroes *should* slacken, and life-saving valour grow *dear*—
Say as courts, party-statesmen, or churches—'twould make some exchequers look queer.

Do we quite do our part, we shore-goers? Those lights could not flash through the fog,
And how often must rescuer willing lie idle on land like a log
For lack of the warning of coast-wires from lighthouse or lightship? 'Tis flat
That we, lad, have not done *our* duty, until we have altered all that.

Well, you have done yours, and successfully, *this* time at least, and at night.
All rescued! How gladly the last must have looked on that brave "Comet Light,"
As you put from the wave-battered wreck. Cold, surf-buffeted, weary, and drenched,
Your pluck, like the glare from that beacon, flamed on through the dark hours unquenched.

Nor then was your labour at end. There was treasure to save and to land.
Well done, life-boat heroes, once more! *Punch* is proud to take grip of your hand!
Your Queen, ever quick to praise manhood, has spoken in words you will hail,
And 'twere shame to the People of England, if they in their part were to fail.

PRESENTED BY THE PROPRIETORS OF "PUNCH"

To "Each Man of the Crew"

Of the Three LIFEBOATS, respectively stationed in the Isle of Wight,

AT BRIGHSTONE
**"Worcester Cadet."**

JAMES COTTON, *Coxswain.*
ROBERT BUCKETT, *2nd Coxswain.*
ROBERT SALTER.
WILLIAM BARTON.
FRANK EDMUNDS.
FRANK BUCKETT.
GEORGE NEW.
GEORGE MORRIS.
GEORGE SHOTTER.
GEORGE HAWKER.
EDGAR WHITE.
WILLIAM MERWOOD.
JAMES HEDGECOCK.

AT BROOK
**"William Slaney Lewis."**

JOHN HAYTER, *Coxswain.*
BEN JACOBS, *2nd Coxswain.*
ROBERT COOPER.
W. JACOBS.
J. COOKE.
G. WHITE.
W. CASSELL.
T. HOOKEY.
J. NEWBURY.
J. COOPER.
J. HOOKEY.
R. WOODFORD.
M. CASSELL.
WILLIAM HAYTER.
W. BLAKE.
W. HOOKEY.

AT ATHERFIELD
**"Catherine Swift."**

WILLIAM COTTON, *Coxswain.*
DAVID COTTON, *2nd Coxswain.*
JAMES COTTON.
THOMAS COTTON.
FRANK COTTON.
JOHN COTTON.
CHARLES COTTON.
WALTER WOODFORD.
WALTER WHITE.
CHARLES HARDING.
B. WHILLIER.

FOR DISTINGUISHED BRAVERY AND GALLANT CONDUCT WHILST ON DUTY

On the occasion of the Wreck of the S.S. "EIDER," January 31, 1892.

# Coxswains of Brooke Lifeboat

| | |
|---|---|
| John Hayter | 1860 – 1892 |
| Benjamin Jacobs | 1892 – 1917 |
| Thomas Hookey | 1917 – 1919 |
| Roland Hayter | 1919 – 1933 |
| Gen. Jack Seely and Alfred Woodford | 1933 – 1937 |

Between its establishment in 1860 and its closure in 1937 Brook Lifeboat had six coxswains. All were expert seaman and all, except for Jack Seely, were local longshoremen and fishermen. Living all their lives in Brook, they knew more than anyone the different sea states, the local weather and every detail of the coastline.

The coxswain's job was to judge the exact moment to shout 'Launch!' when the thirty or more helpers hauled on the two ropes which shot the boat from its carriage into the sea.

*The experience and knowledge required and the qualities of nerve and judgement are so exacting...It is an affair not of minutes but of seconds, and hesitation, vacillation, or weakness spells disaster.*

*Launch*, J E B Seely.

There are no known portraits of John Hayter, but this man standing in the stern of the *William Slaney Lewis,* alongside Ben Jacobs, is most likely to be him.

## John Hayter – coxswain 1860 - 1892

*'Brook's notable storm warrior,'* was what the Isle of Wight County Press called John Hayter. Over his 32 years as the first coxswain of the Brooke boat, John Hayter became the most decorated lifeboatman in the Island's history. He was awarded four silver good service medals by the RNLI and the German Emperor gave him a gold watch in gratitude after the rescue of the *Eider*.

Stories that survive about John Hayter, including the account of his tussle with the customs officer (see *Smuggling and the Coastguards*), show him as a tough, wise and unsentimental man. We also hear that in his younger days he 'did time' for smuggling. One story describes how John Hayter was working hard in the fields up at Dunsbury when a ship could be seen heading for trouble in Brook Bay. Hayter continued with his labour, and when asked why he wasn't rushing to the shore to man the boat he calmly, and famously, replied, 'She ain't hit yet...' Jack Seely remembers meeting the man he called 'old Hayter':

To me, and to all the lads in our villages of Brooke and Mottistone, he was the hero, and rightly so. Had he not commanded the successful launching of the lifeboat from a carriage pushed into the sea, in the teeth of a great gale? Had he not brought his tiny vessel alongside the wreck and rescued nearly all the crew before the vessel broke up into little fragments under the violent blows of the thirty-foot waves, driven forward by the wind of gale force? Yes, we admired him and loved him, but always from a distance, because while he would rejoice in talking to us about fishing or gardening, or even the art of catching a hare by the hand, he would never allow us to question him on his outstanding services as a saver of lives.
*Paths of Happiness,* J E B Seely

## Ben Jacobs - coxswain 1892 – 1917

Ben's father James Jacobs (born c.1827) was one of the first volunteer crew members of the Brook rowing lifeboat station when it opened in 1860. James served in the crew up until 1892 and continued to help launch the lifeboat from Brook beach up to his death, from pneumonia, aged 71 in 1898. Of James and Jane Jacobs' four surviving children, both Ben and Phil followed in their father's footsteps and volunteered for most of their lives on the Brooke Lifeboat with Ben elected coxswain for 25 years. On March 9th 1888, Ben and Phil as very young men were nearly drowned in the terrible rescue of the fully-rigged ship *Sirenia*, aground on Atherfield Ledge, and losing their fellow crewman Reuben Cooper overboard. Four years later and now second coxswain, Ben sat next to John Hayter in the rescue of 394 people aboard the German passenger liner *SS Eider*. After that extraordinary rescue, John Hayter retired and Ben was elected coxswain by the rest of the crew. In February 1916, Ben's last great lifeboat rescue was to save eight of the ten crew of the Norwegian barque *Souvenir* from Brook Ledge in horrendous conditions and he was awarded the RNLI Silver Medal. Ben and Phil never married, they remained living at Cliff Cottage, Brook Green, all their lives. Descended from a long line of longshoremen, the brothers fished and earned money working as gardeners and general labourers on the Seely Estate. Jack Seely

Ben Jacobs, coxswain, 1892 - 1917.

describes Ben as a remarkable man:

Ben was more than six feet high, and of immense strength. One of my older friends said to me the other day, 'Ben was as strong as a horse, braver than any lion, and gentle as a new-born lamb.' He was the most skilful man in getting a boat off the beach in a rough sea that I have ever known. Single-handed he would run a fifteen foot boat, stern on, to the water's edge. With a swift movement he would spin her round with her bow pointing seaward. He would then grip the stern, and bending forward till his body was almost horizontal, he would push her out to sea. He would hold her for a moment in a vice-like grip, keeping her bow pointing exactly to each oncoming wave, then, at what he judged to be the right moment – and he was rarely wrong – he would push her through the breaking wave, jump in over the stern, grab the oars, put them between the thole-pins, and standing up to his full height, push her with the weight of his whole body and his strong arms over the next wave and the next, and so out to sea. The combination of skill, nerve, balance, was wonderful to behold. *Launch!* JEB Seely.

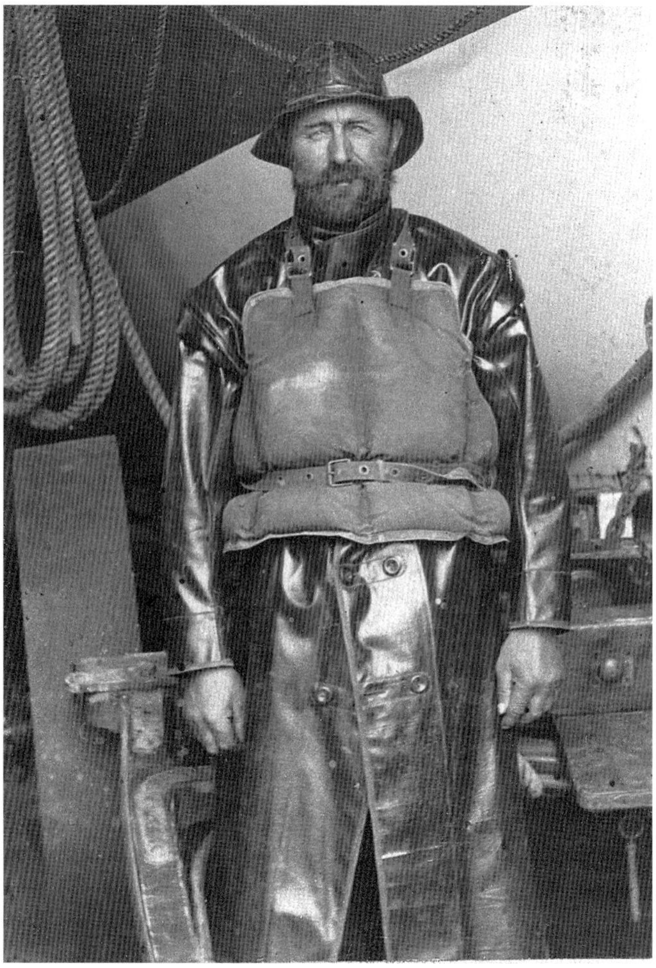

Ben Jacobs, Brook Coxswain, 1925. With the lifeboat behind him, this photograph is likely to have been taken inside the Lifeboat House on Brook Green, just yards from Ben's cottage. The size of his hands are evidence to his 'vice-like grip' when launching a boat into the surf as described by Jack Seely in *Launch!*

Ben grew up barely able to read and write. Perhaps because nominated by the Seely family, in later life the County Council appointed Ben as an Educational Representative to the local school at Hulverstone. He took immense pains with his task, teaching the children to row, play cricket, bait a line, spot a hare in its form – all the things of which he was a master. He would always add: *Now, you pay attention to your schooling. I never had enough of it, and I've been sorry ever since.* Stories passed down by those who knew Ben describe how, at a full moon in Spring, Ben was known to suffer extreme mental disturbance. We are told it took five men to hold him down.

In hindsight, it may be worth considering that this timing coincided with the anniversary of the tragic *Sirenia* incident when he, his brother and fellow crewman, Reuben Cooper, who was washed overboard. Reuben drowned in the dark while Ben and Phil managed to get back into the lifeboat. Jack Seely and Ben became lifelong friends despite their completely different backgrounds. Ben's great niece, Dot Lobb, recalls: *Once when Uncle Ben was ill he had a letter from General Seely saying 'we said we'd always tell each other if we weren't well'. Our grandmother kept and treasured that letter.*

The death of Ben Jacobs marked the passing of an era. His funeral cortege in 1929 files through Brook and up to the Church.

**Thomas William Hookey – coxswain 1917 – 1919**

Tom Hookey was the son of James and Harriett Hookey of Downton Farm. He became a farmer and blacksmith and was also a churchwarden. Tom was in the crew of the *William Slaney Lewis* when it rescued the *Eider* in 1892. Tom married Ella Way and two of their children, Barbara and Dora, went on to be very successful teachers at Hulverstone School. Jack Seely describes arriving at a wreck:

We all shouted together, but could get no reply, so two of us had to go on board. It had always been arranged that these two should be Tom Hookey, the blacksmith, and myself, because we were the lightest, and supposed to be the most agile. Tom was exactly the same age as myself, and we were lifelong and intimate friends. We both jumped into the rigging as the ship rolled over towards us, and managed to get on board. Down below was a strange and melancholy sight. Three lanterns were burning in the large fo'castle. There was nearly three feet of water, and floating about were coats, shirts, trousers, oilskins, caps and tobacco pouches, but not a sign of human life. We clambered out, dodged a wave and managed to get down the afterhatch. There the ship was more than half full of water, a light was still burning, but not a soul to be seen. Above the crash of the breakers we heard a shout from the lifeboat, and ran to the side. Tom jumped in first and I was about to follow when she swayed out about twenty yards from the side. I climbed up the rigging to escape a big wave which swept along the deck below me, then ran down again and as the boat sheered alongside, jumped. She was only about six feet below me when I jumped, on the crest of a wave, but she sank into the trough almost as fast as I fell, so that I should guess that I must have fallen quite fifteen feet before I reached her. I fell on an unfortunate man, and really hurt him quite badly. Just at that moment the grapnel parted and we were swept away to leeward. All our oars on one side had been smashed to splinters, but we got enough spares to pull her a bit to the east. Then we threw out the drogue over the stern, hoisted a jib and flew home before the wind at a wonderful speed. What had taken us two hours to accomplish on the way out took us twenty minutes on the return. As we sailed home we bemoaned our melancholy fate in having no survivors to bring ashore, and vowed, amidst laughter, that on future occasions we would take a few with us. *Adventure,* J E B Seely (1930)

At 56 years old, Tom died relatively young from Hodgkin's lymphoma, a type of cancer, and was ill for a while. He moved into his aunt's home, Chine Villa, on Brook Green, 'to get some peace and quiet'. His grandson, Paul Cutmore describes how Tom was referred to a specialist doctor - who later became King George VI's surgeon and in *Adventure,* Jack Seely goes on to say: *I have always thought that Tom Hookey's untimely death some years afterwards was hastened by the hardships of that terrible night.*

We hear that Tom had always wanted to go to sea and he joined the Royal Navy and served on the King of the Belgians' yacht. His mother Harriet however, influenced him to return home to run the farm when his father died. Tom's younger brother David 'Daf' Hookey succeeded Tom at the farm and smithy.

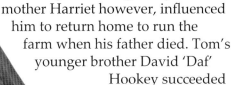

**Roland Hayter - coxswain 1919-1933**

Roland Hayter, below, lived in Brook Villa. He was a carrier and nephew to John Hayter, the first coxswain of Brooke Lifeboat.

'Rol' Hayter as coxswain c.1935; and above as best man at a Hookey wedding. On the right, his RNLI pension arrangements.

**Alf Woodford (right) and General Jack Seely, Lord Mottistone, joint coxswains - 1933-1937**

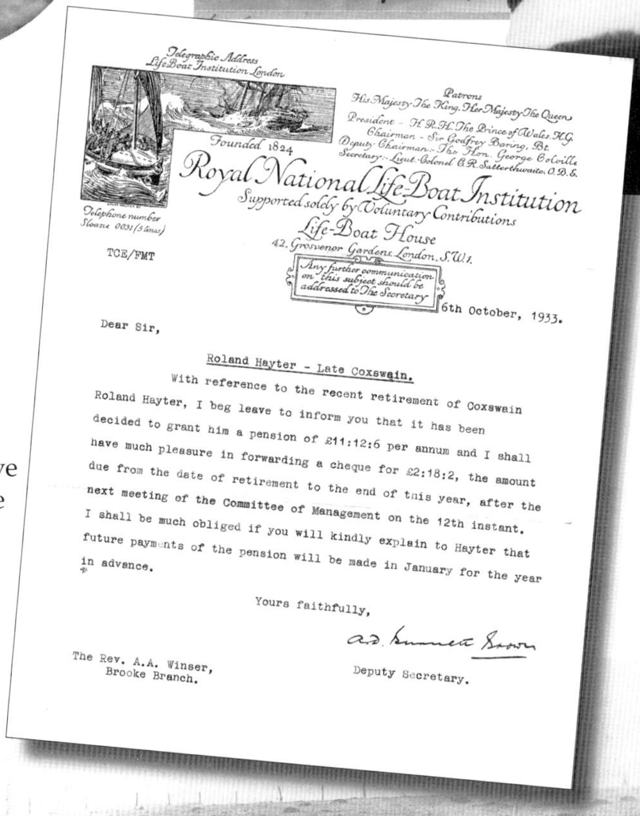

Telegraphic Address
Life-Boat Institution London

Patrons
His Majesty The King. Her Majesty The Queen
President - H.R.H. The Prince of Wales. K.G.
Chairman - Sir Godfrey Baring, Bt.
Deputy Chairman - The Hon. George Colville
Secretary - Lieut.-Colonel C.R. Satterthwaite. O.B.E.

Founded 1824

Royal National Life-Boat Institution

Supported solely by Voluntary Contributions

Life-Boat House
42, Grosvenor Gardens, London, S.W.1.

Telephone number
Sloane 0031 (5 lines)

TCE/FMT

Any further communication on this subject should be addressed to The Secretary

6th October, 1933.

Dear Sir,

Roland Hayter - Late Coxswain.

With reference to the recent retirement of Coxswain Roland Hayter, I beg leave to inform you that it has been decided to grant him a pension of £11:12:6 per annum and I shall have much pleasure in forwarding a cheque for £2:18:2, the amount due from the date of retirement to the end of this year, after the next meeting of the Committee of Management on the 12th instant. I shall be much obliged if you will kindly explain to Hayter that future payments of the pension will be made in January for the year in advance.

Yours faithfully,

A.D. Burnett Brown

Deputy Secretary.

The Rev. A.A. Winser,
Brooke Branch.

Service of dedication for the *Susan Ashley*, 1907.

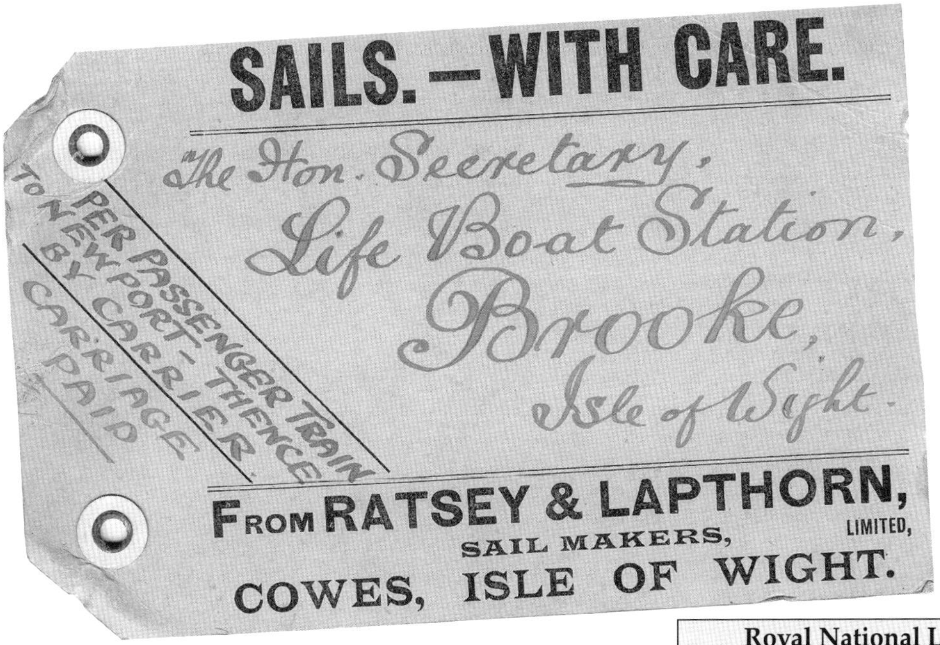


## Raising funds

Then as now the lifeboats were supported by public donations. We see that in Brook there was a tradition of raising money for the lifeboat in both entertaining and instructive ways:

> An entertainment was given in the Hulverstone School Room yesterday, the profits of which were donated to the Lifeboat Disaster Fund. During the evening a Second Service Clasp was presented to Mr John Hayter, the brave Coxswain of the Brooke Lifeboat. The Misses Gaze, Mrs Dean, Miss Selby, Miss Haygate, Mr Corte and Mr Connell took part in the programme, which was excellently performed throughout.
>
> *Isle of Wight County Press* April 21st 1888

> **Royal National Lifeboat Institution – Brook**
>
> On Tuesday evening a lantern lecture was given in the Parish Room by the Rev. R.L. Morris (Rector), entitled 'The men who face death, or our storm warriors'. Views of lifeboat services and wrecks around Britain were followed by illustrations of the rocket apparatus and other life-saving appliances, and caused much interest. There was a very good attendance, and the net proceeds amounted to 15s. 9d. We may add that a notable 'storm warrior,' Mr John Hayter, ex-coxswain of the Brook boat, still resides there and will complete his 68th year next month. He served for 33 years, and, received his pension in 1892; he holds the Institution's silver medal and clasp and four honorary distinctions, as well as being the proud possessor of the gold watch presented to him by the German Emperor after services rendered at the wreck of the *Eider*.
>
> *Isle of Wight County Press* March 19th 1904

Brook Lifeboat presentation, from left: Charlie Newbery, Bill Ballard, Roland Hayter, Albert White, General Jack Seely, Joe Morris, Charlie New, Phil Jacobs, Alf Woodford, Frank 'Safe' Edmonds and an unknown crew member.

*The lifeboat crews had to be psychologists as well as skilled boatmen, the Brook boat, for example, had to deal with crew members driven demented by their experiences, reluctant lady passengers and desperate ships' captains.*
*Launch,* J E B Seely

It was often extremely difficult to get survivors to jump into the lifeboat at the right moment. The great waves lifted the boat level with the rails of a ship and then dropped it 15 to 20 feet when the wave fell.

The chief carpenter in our neighbourhood, and a wonderful carpenter he is too, was one of three brothers (Newberys) belonging to our lifeboat crew. He had caught a number of men as they jumped at the top of a wave, when to his astonishment, as the boat rose for about the twentieth time, he saw a handsome young lady dressed in black satin, with a baby in her arms standing by the rail…he shouted 'Jump, ma'am,' but she did not seem ready to jump. As the boat disappeared he heard her voice saying: 'Am I to trust myself to you?' The lifeboat rose to the deck again, and he said: 'Yes, ma'am, throw me the baby for a start. She answered, 'No, I will stick with my baby. Can I trust you?' Down went the boat again. A brief interval and my friend the carpenter showed his face at the deck level and shouted: ' I am a family man with two children. Come along, ma'am.' She replied with these astonishing words as the lifeboat began another descent: "Well, you look like a respectable man and I will trust you, but can you promise me we shan't get wet, with the baby's best clothes?" …at the next chance …our gallant carpenter grabbed the lady and baby and hauled them into the boat."
*Launch* JEB Seely

Many found it hard to believe that it was safer to leave a big ship for such a little one as the lifeboat…

A vessel was stranded on the outer ledge in a heavy ground swell. We could hear the crash as her bottom struck …we saw, too, a gaping wound where the rivets had broken…the crew knew very well what had happened and almost before we were alongside had jumped into the boat. The last man stood at the rail and shouted loudly: 'I am not going to leave my ship. I will be better in here than in your little cockle-shell.' 'Come on,' shouted Ben Jacobs, our coxswain, 'we can't leave you there all alone.' 'No,' he cried, 'I will stand by my ship.' Ben shouts out, as we rise again: 'Do you want to drown the lot of us? If you don't get aboard we will come and fetch you, but it will be your fault if we are all swamped.'… finally he jumped , for a moment the lifeboat was right under water…'we came out of it as we knew we would, and there was the captain, in the early dawn, with bloodshot eyes, sitting in the stern with his feet entangled in mine, shouting out: 'Put me back on my ship, your boats are not fit to ply the sea…' The poor man was so grieved at the loss of his ship that we knew we must humour him, but when he stood up to protest still further, Ben Jacobs put an enormous

Brooke Lifeboat crew c.1933 on left from back: Charlie New, Bill Ballard, Hedley Barnes, Walter Newbery. On right from back: David Hookey, Joe Morris, Frank Edmonds, Albert White.

hand on the top of his head and pressed him down with irresistible force, as a man might press down a rebellious puppy trying to escape from its basket.
*Launch*, JEB Seely

Bert Morris had a fund of stories about the Brooke lifeboat, one went back to the First World War when a destroyer came ashore in fog on the bar at Brook. The old parson asked the coxswain to take him out in a 14 foot beach boat so that he could investigate what was going on. He rowed round the stern of the warship. A sailor leaned over the rail and shouted down, ' Good God we don't want a parson, we want a tug.' Another story concerned Phil Jacobs, who like his brother, Ben, was a large man, tall and upright in his trademark bowler hat (see Lifeboat presentation photograph). *One day on a lifeboat practice Phil's bowler came off. It was quite rough and the coxswain was loath to recover the hat in spite of Phil's urgent requests. 'Bugger your hat' he said, but in the end he went about and picked it up. Phil's concern was soon clear to all - inside the hat band was a large number of pound notes.* He will certainly never have been allowed to forget that incident...
Charles New was another loyal member of the crew. Charlie helped with the lifeboat from the age of 16 until the 1914-18 war when he joined the Hampshire Regiment. His daughter Marjorie Clark tells us that: *Soon after his demob he filled a vacant seat in the lifeboat. He became the lifeboat's signaller and when the Susan Ashley was sold he went with her to Yarmouth and was the last man to step ashore.* Charles New lived at Chessell and worked at Dunsbury Farm. He was also sexton and grave digger at Brook Church. Charlie died in 1977 and his signallers' flags are now in Carisbrooke Castle Museum together with a certificate for his seventeen and a half years' service with the RNLI. The last launch using horses is featured in a 1933 Pathe News film 'For the Last Time,' and subtitled 'The Picturesque must give way to the Practical!'
When the final inspector's report was made in the late 1930s, he could not shy away from the truth, that these gallant men were over-age and under-equipped for the job they were still so very proud of doing. Sold out of service in 1937 and converted into a motor yacht, the *Susan Ashley* had her second starring role in 1978 when she played the part of *Dulcibella* in the feature film of the novel, 'The Riddle of the Sands,' pictured right.

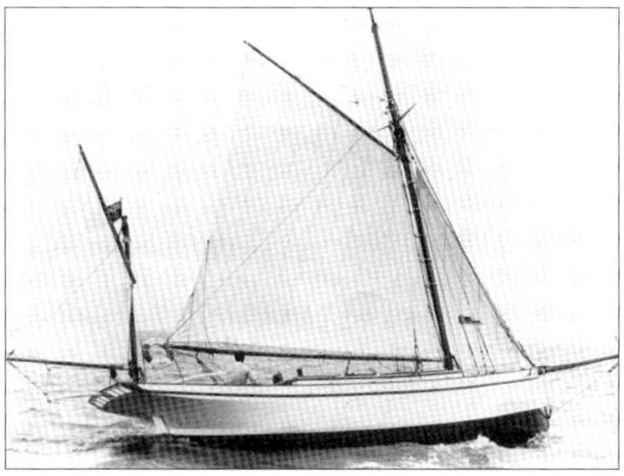

*The days of the rowing lifeboats were over, while the Yarmouth motor lifeboat (BASP) roared across the sea to the stricken steamer Roumelian, in 1932, the Susan Ashley returned to Brook station after 2 hours.*

*When Brook Lifeboat was sold in 1937 we rowed her all the way round to Yarmouth. The local preacher Reverend Winser came along with his son. Unbeknown to us he had put in a bottle of beer for each of us. We stopped off at the Needles waiting for the tide to come in and had this bottle of beer, like, before going on.*

*Brook Lifeboat*, Robert Cassell

November 9th 1947
The tug *Carbon* (left) was being towed from Portland to Southampton for salvage when the towing line broke off the Needles. The *Carbon* drifted into Compton Bay and went aground on the rocks. It appears it was not worth anyone's while to recover her and so, known as, 'the wreck', she has remained a familiar landmark and source of adventures for successive generations.

Above is what still remains of 'the wreck' in 2010.

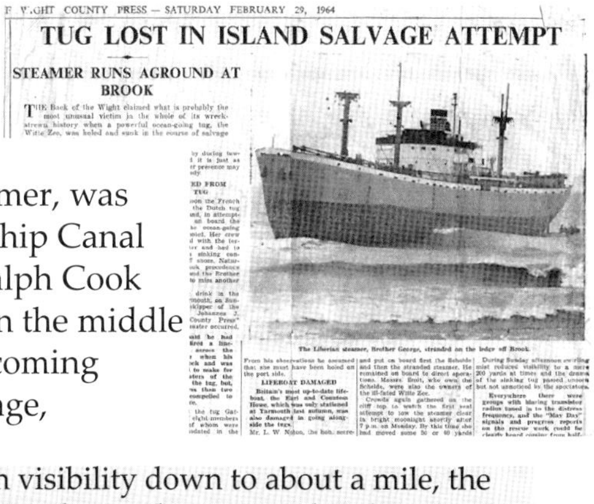

I.W. COUNTY PRESS — SATURDAY FEBRUARY 29, 1964

**TUG LOST IN ISLAND SALVAGE ATTEMPT**

**STEAMER RUNS AGROUND AT BROOK**

THE Back of the Wight claimed what is probably the most unusual victim in the whole of its wreck-strewn history when a powerful ocean-going tug, the Witte Zee, was holed and sunk in the course of salvage

The Liberian steamer, Brother George, stranded on the ledge off Brook.

February 23rd 1964
The *Brother George*, a Liberian steamer, was on her way from the Manchester Ship Canal to Rotterdam with a crew of 28. Ralph Cook remembers as a teenager waking in the middle of the night to see blinding lights coming through the windows of Red Cottage, Brook Green.

At 1.45am with visibility down to about a mile, the coastguard at Brook saw the steamer heading for the Ledge. He fired a rocket to warn her to change course but it was too late. Once aground, the Yarmouth lifeboat and the coastguards set up a line-carrying rocket to the ship. One of three tugs which answered the calls for help was the Dutch tug *Witte Zee*. In the process of trying to free the *Brother George*, the tug was holed by a rock and her crew had to abandon her two miles off shore. The tug's crew were saved by the Yarmouth lifeboat and the Red Funnel tug *Gatcombe*. The *Witte Zee* was towed away from the shore but eventually sank four miles off Compton Bay. Meanwhile the *Brother George* was still aground, and a salvage master from Holland was finally put on board to direct operations. In bright moonlight at 7pm on Monday crowds gathered on the cliff top to watch the first real attempt to tow the steamer clear. The stranded vessel proved to be one of the biggest open air attractions on the Island for many years and the police had to control the traffic on the Military Road, normally deserted at this time of year. Groups everywhere were tuned in to the distress frequency on their transistor radios and the 'May Day' signals from the tug could be clearly heard coming from several directions. Mr H. Morris, one of the auxiliary coastguards at Brook recalled that in 1915 the three-masted barque the *Souvenir* was lost about 50 yards west of the point struck by the *Brother George* and just about the position where the tug *Witte Zee* was holed.
Courtesy of the *Isle of Wight County Press*.

Rita Whitewood of Brook in front of the *Kingsbridge* stranded on Brighstone Ledge in January 1955.

This chapter is dedicated to the memory of the Brooke Lifeboat crews. We are grateful for the material collected over the years by a number of local people including Bob Buckett, Bert Morris, Bob Cassell, Geoff Cotton and Chris Bull. We are also very grateful to John Medland's *Shipwrecks of the Isle of Wight* (1986).

# Farms and farming

Stook-making in the 1930s with Dunsbury Farm, Brook Hill House and Mary's Cottage behind.

For centuries, farming was at the heart of village life, and Brook was no exception. There were at least 11 working farms in the area for many hundreds of years: Downton, Hanover, Brook, Chessell, Shalcombe, Dunsbury, Compton, Hulverstone, Longstone, Mottistone, Pitt Place and two smallholdings, Seaview Dairy and Grange Farm (see map at front of book). Up until the 1960s most farms were run by tenant farmers. Today there are just three farms working the same land: Dunsbury, Chapel Furlong and Compton, two owner-occupied and one owned by the National Trust. While increased mechanisation and intensified farming in the 1960s and 70s resulted in the removal of hedges and enlarged fields across the country, this area has remained relatively unchanged and many fields in the tithe map of 1838 (see end of this chapter) are the same today. For a comparatively small area, the soil types in the area are suprisingly varied. Mrs Connie Jackman wrote in the WI Scrapbook: *While the high chalk down is mostly uncultivated and used for limited grazing, the lower ridge of greensand to the south of this forms a narrow belt of fertile sandy loam, past this and on to the coastal cliffs is an undulating area of alluvial soils which, while fertile are difficult to handle as arable land because within practically every field the soil varies from medium loam to stiff red and yellow clay. It is a favourable climate and soil for grass in particular and while today sheep and some beef cattle are the main herds, in the 1950s dairy cows were most*

A group of men and boys pose for the camera as they collect milk from Brook Farm. Those on the right of the picture are in their Sunday clothes. Recognisable faces here are Dick Whitewood, a young Jack Hayter, Arthur Newbery and Joe Morris. The postbox saved a walk up to the post office at Hulverstone.

*common and each farm employed a cowman, carter, ploughman, and often more.* The 1891 census for Brook and Mottistone shows approximately 25 agricultural labourers, by 1901 this has increased to 34 and in 1911 reduced to 29. The men and women who worked on the farms felt a strong attachment to the land and to the animals they worked with. In such a small, interdependent community the quality of any work, be it ditching, hedging, or carting, had an impact on everyone and was a responsibility keenly felt. Each team of horses attached to a farm was well-known to the village and had to be harnessed and ready for action at any time of day or night in case the lifeboat maroon went off. Until well after the Second World War horses were vital to the work of every farm. Mrs Alice Morris, aged 87, writing in the WI Scrapbook in 1958, recalled the days when: *On the farms there were horses only and they were trained by word of mouth. The men only had to say, 'Bither' or 'Hoot' for them to go right or left. They never led them by hand.* By the late 1950s there was not one agricultural horse left in Brook or Mottistone.

Harvesting at Compton Farm in 1901.

All over the country, but particularly in the south, where farmers did not have to compete for labour with large manufacturing towns, agricultural wages were extremely low throughout the 19th and early 20th centuries. Robert (Bob) Cassell remembered how: *In the early days we used to get harvest money in August. That was when all the farm people would buy all their clothes because they would have a bit of money to spend. Usually a farm worker was paid eight pence an hour but in harvest time it was nine pence an hour.* During the Second World War, government intervention pulled agriculture away from the severe depression it had suffered in the 1920s

*It was a hard physical working life. They say hard work never hurt anyone - just crippled you for the rest of your life...*

*In 1960 a pay rise for farm workers to seven guineas a week compared with nineteen pounds a week take-home pay for builders*

and 1930s and, in return for government guaranteed prices, farmers provided maximum levels of home-grown food. After the war the Agriculture Act of 1947 was drawn up with farmers to ensure stability by guaranteeing minimum prices for key products. The aim was to ensure adequate pay and living conditions for farmers and their workers and to encourage investment in equipment. Until the Agricultural Holdings Act of 1948 a worker's home was often tied to his job. As George Thompson puts it: *The majority of village people worked in the village, like any village, you either lived in an Estate cottage or a farm cottage and if you lost your job you lost your house.* When Bob Cassell's father needed to retire at seventy he could only stay in his home, The Elms in Hulverstone, if his son took over his job as carter at Hulverstone Farm. The greater sense of security provided by these Acts of Parliament encouraged the movement towards more owner-occupied farms. Compared to other types of work, agricultural wages remained low however. David Stephens was working at Chessell in 1960 when a rise from seven pounds a week to seven guineas a week was given to farm workers. This compared with nineteen pounds a week take-home pay as a builder. As he says: *often a family man couldn't afford the luxury of choosing to do a job he liked over providing for his family.* Before he moved into the building trade, Bill Ballard from Brook Green walked to Compton early in the morning to feed the horses, then walked home for his breakfast before going back again to start his day's work. George Thompson remembers when he started work he couldn't afford a bicycle to get from Calbourne to Dunsbury and back each day and that his father's words were, 'Well you've got a pair of legs.'

*The horses were trained by word of mouth. The men only had to say, 'Bither' or 'Hoot' for the horses to go right or left. They never led them by hand.* Alice Morris, Brook WI Scrapbook

The Brook and Hulverstone farm horses called on to launch and pull up the lifeboat. Six horses were needed for the launch while ten horses were needed to haul the boat up from the beach when it had taken up water.

Left: Dunsbury Farm horses readied for a special occasion such as the County Agricultural Show.

*By the late 1950s there was not one agricultural horse left in Brook or Mottistone.*

Will Morris and Jim Hookey with Punch on Brook Green 'South fields' (known locally as South hills) in the 1930s.

Tom Hookey (above left) holds Wizard, Captain and Poppet, while A. Barnes steers the plough. This picture was taken in 1918, when Tom Hookey was coxswain of Brooke lifeboat.

National Agricultural Union,

.. THIRD ANNUAL ..

Ploughing Competition

Held at BROOKE FARM, I.W.,

By kind permission of Sir Charles Seely, Bart., and Col. H. G. Browne, V.C.,

On TUESDAY, OCT. 15th, 1901.

CLASS 1.

First Prize, £2.

Awarded to

Chairman of the Rural Council:—Mr. W. J. Barrington, Thorley, Yarmouth.

Vice-Chairman:—Mr. G. E. Coombes, Little Budbridge, Merstone.

Judge:—Mr. John Rand, Boufre Farm, Beaulieu.

Stewards: Mr. I. M. Hendy, Brooke Farm, I.W.; Mr. James Attrill, Waytescourt, Brighstone; Mr. G. E. Coombes, Little Budbridge, Merstone; Mr. J. P. Harvey, Chale Abbey, Chale; Mr. Seymour Pittis, Hale Manor, Arreton.

Hon. Stewards: Mr. Thos. Way, Limerstone, I.W.; Mr. Henry Way, Pyle, Chale, I.W.; Mr. J. R. Fisk, Brighstone, I.W.

Hon. Auditor:—Mr. W. Hooker, Langbridge, Calbourne, I.W.

RURAL COUNCIL:—

Dr. Groves, J.P., Carisbrooke
Mr. J. R. Fisk, Brighstone
" Thos. Way, Limerstone, Brighstone
" Henry Way, Pyle, Chale
" Stephenson R. Clarke, The Cliff, Shanklin
" Robert Urry, Hill Farm, Gatcombe
" Jas. Attrill, Waytescourt, Brighstone
" J. Linington, Atherfield, Chale
" Andrew Morris, Chillerton
" Seymour Pittis, Hale Manor, Arreton
" J. P. Harvey, Chale Abbey, Chale
" L. C. Attrill, Bowcombe Manor, Carisbrooke
" W. E. Loe, Heasley Manor, Arreton
" H. Russell, Roslin, Carisbrooke
" H. Morris, Kingston, Shorwell
" R. Woodward, Rookley
" J. Mearman, Salween, Newport
" R. Harvey, Great Afton, Freshwater

Mr. T. Taylor, Bembridge
" Oliver Hayles, Pagham, Rookley
" Wm. Souter, Wootton
" H. Barton, Mersley, Newchurch
" F. Linington, Parsonage Farm, Newchurch
" Baker Harvey, Ningwood Manor, Ningwood.
" Geo. Heal, Fullholding, Calbourne
" H. E. Warder, Idlecombe, Carisbrooke
" W. J. Nash, Lessland, Godshill
" A. Hearn, Sen., Niton Manor, Niton
" S. Berden, Whitwell Farm, Whitwell
" Mullett, Northwood
" R. Y. Morgan, Ramsdown, Chillerton
" J. W. Fisk, Brighstone Mills
" G. King, Newnham Farm, Binstead
" Richard Mew, Fairlee, near Newport
" J. R. S. Blake, Stone, Blackwater
" I. M. Hendy, Brooke Farm, Brooke

Hon. Sec.:—Mr. Robert Fisk, Apes Down, Carisbrooke.

Asst. Sec.:—C. Horlock Way, 148 High Street, Newport.

## Ploughing

Ploughing skills make all the difference between a successful or unsuccessful crop and today ploughing matches continue to be strongly fought in the Brook area. George Humber tells how: *In about 1901 there was a big ploughing match in the large field by Hanover House. The ploughman from the Royal Estate at Whippingham came over (he and his horses would have walked all the way, he in hobnail boots). Everyone noticed he had gold-topped (probably brass) pegs to mark out his acre - while everyone else would have used sticks. My great grandfather, George Humber, beat the Royal ploughman!*

The local farms were not slow to take on modern machinery. Carol Worrall (Woolbright) remembers being woken up early in the morning in Briar Cottage by an almighty bang as the tractor was started by a cartridge which made a huge noise like a shotgun going off. David Hookey of Downton Farm restored the tractor and used to fire it up by hitting the cartridge with a hammer.

The tractor is kept in prime condition today by Jim Abbott of Calbourne.

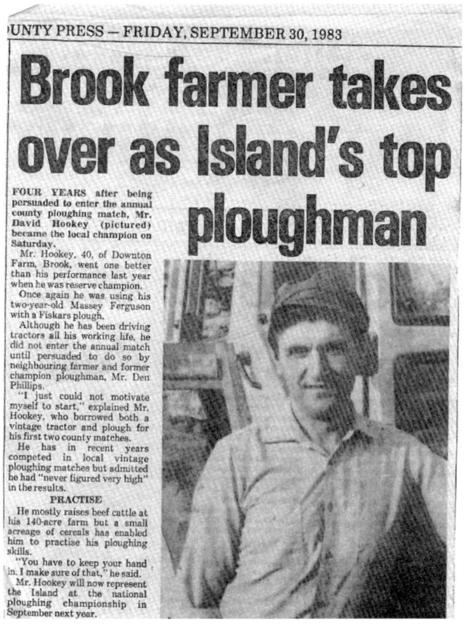

COUNTY PRESS — FRIDAY, SEPTEMBER 30, 1983

**Brook farmer takes over as Island's top ploughman**

FOUR YEARS after being persuaded to enter the annual county ploughing match, Mr. David Hookey (pictured) became the local champion on Saturday.

Mr. Hookey, 40, of Downton Farm, Brook, went one better than his performance last year when he was reserve champion.

Once again he was using his two-year-old Massey Ferguson with a Fiskars plough.

Although he has been driving tractors all his working life, he did not enter the annual match until persuaded to do so by neighbouring farmer and former champion ploughman, Mr. Den Phillips.

"I just could not motivate myself to start," explained Mr. Hookey, who borrowed both a vintage tractor and plough for his first two county matches.

He has in recent years competed in local vintage ploughing matches but admitted he had "never figured very high" in the results.

PRACTISE

He mostly raises beef cattle at his 140-acre farm but a small acreage of cereals has enabled him to practise his ploughing skills.

"You have to keep your hand in. I make sure of that," he said.

Mr. Hookey will now represent the Island at the national ploughing championship in September next year.

Continuing the Brook tradition of ploughing a straight furrow, Den Phillips (top) of Compton Farm; David Hookey (right) of Downton Farm and Ralph Cook of Brook Green (above) have won the Isle of Wight Ploughing Competition a number of times in recent years.

## Downton Farm

For 159 years, from 1851 to earlier this year (2010) Downton Farm has meant the Hookey family. Originally owned by the Hookeys, the farm and smithy was bought in the mid-1850s by Charles Seely and became part of the Seely Estate for nearly a hundred years. Jim Hookey was able to buy the farm back in the Estate sale of 1957 and today the farm is owned once more by Charles Seely's descendants. The last Hookey to farm at Downton was David Hookey, who took over from his father Jim and grandfather David, who was also the village blacksmith (see *Village Trades and Occupations*). Downton was no doubt a farm long before the 19th century and possibly had a different name. A field behind the farmhouse is called the 'Round O' and appears on the earliest maps of the area. Despite much speculation about an early settlement, corral for animals or circuit for leading horses to grind corn, there is no definite interpretation of this distinctive circular field. Jim Hookey's notebook shows that his research found it to be similar in shape to early human settlements in Cornwall.

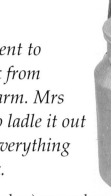

*I sometimes went to collect the milk from the Hookeys' farm. Mrs Hookey used to ladle it out into my can. Everything smelled of milk.*

Barbara Heal (Hookey) remembered her childhood on the farm between the two world wars: *A large Jersey herd gave rich milk and cream. It was often my task to turn the handle of the butter churn until the cream turned to butter and this before school in the morning! The women in the family made the butter. In the heat of the summer the butter was made in the cool of the evening and suspended in buckets in the garden well to be made into half pound pats in the morning. Most of the butter was sold to Mr Cooper of Brighstone Stores, but enough was kept for the village folk who came to the farm with cans for milk, as well as buying butter and eggs. A pint of milk was given daily to the labourers.*

As a child, Priscilla Hamlin, grand daughter of Tom and Ella Way Hookey, lived in Myrtle Cottage in the early 1940s: *Uncle Jim was at the farm and he used to milk the cows by hand. I used to walk there twice a day to collect the fresh milk in a small metal churn. Back at home the top of the milk was skimmed off into a dish to set, ready for your porridge or cereal to be added the next morning for breakfast. Before milking, the cows would be herded up from the fields to the farm, twice a day.*

Anne Ham (Hookey) remembers growing up at the farm in the 1950s:

One of my earliest memories (at about 3 years) was the birth of my brother David, Nurse Rann coming and going, my Mother upstairs for some strange reason and me being looked after by Granny Hookey and Aunt Lizzie. I was taken for a walk, to keep me out of the way and down Sheepwash Lane a big man with a long white beard gave me a bunch of daisies for my mother and little brother. Of course in those days I only remember sunshine and the animals. There were usually about three dogs on the farm; greyhounds were a favourite of my Father with perhaps a terrier or spaniel. Cats were a-plenty, the dogs had names but not the cats. There were also some very fierce cockerels! My Mother used to leave an old broom out by the front

gate so that people coming to collect their cans of milk could defend themselves. We had two Clydesdale horses called Duchess and Poppet. Poppet used to bolt and I can still see her taking off along the Military Road with a cart load of mangles with Father standing in the middle of the road waving his stick and expressing his annoyance!!! Duchess, our remaining horse (Father sold Poppet the bolter) eventually died. I remember sitting beside her big head, stroking it and crying. Favourite animals came and went as is the way of life to this day. I still cry and remember old Duchess. Cows were originally milked by Father, 'Granfer', occasionally different helpers and sometimes by me (once learned, never forgotten!). The milk was then carried in buckets from the

*Poppet used to bolt and I can still see her taking off along the Military Road with a cart load of mangles...*

stable to the dairy, which adjoined the house. It was strained, then cooled through a corrugated cooler (water cooled) into churns which were then placed on the churn stand outside the front gate on the opposite side of the lane. At approximately 11am a lorry from Isle of Wight Creameries would collect our milk together with that from Brook Farm. Now and again, during a heat wave, it would all come back to us having soured. Mother would then turn it into cheese. When the hens were in full-lay, the eggs, after a good scrub (one of my jobs) were preserved in an isinglass solution, the surplus sold at the door with milk (sold in cans in pre-bottle days), cream and butter.Summer WAS Brook to me, down the shore, harvest, relations arriving and various scout and church camps coming and going, not forgetting Uncle Alf Woodford's prawns, I have never tasted better. We used a binder for cutting the corn. When I was very little it was pulled by horses, but later converted for a tractor. My brother had a stick with a knob on the end, which he used enthusiastically to knock rabbits on the head with. This was always referred to as a "Nobby Jo" and only ever used at harvest time. Us girls, probably Janet (Stone) from Hanover Tea Rooms and me, used to rescue as many as possible! In the spring the men would shoot at the rook nests killing as many rooks

*I remember some very fierce cockerels! My mother used to leave an old broom out by the front gate so that people coming to collect their cans of milk could defend themselves.*

as they could, the plan being to keep the birds off the crops. Once again Janet and I went to the rescue. As soon as all the men had gone we would go into the copse and collect baby rooks, wounded rooks and traumatised rooks. These would be taken to our "hospital" (which was the loft over the pig sty) and force fed worms and left for the night. The next morning we had funerals. Shallow graves were dug, the bodies interred and a little cross constructed, to the best of our ability. We then sang Onward Christian Soldiers! I have wonderful memories of a very happy childhood. The sun did not shine every day and when it was cold and wet we got cold and wet. Perhaps an animal's life was more brutal than it is for farm animals today but I am inclined to think probably not. The rooks most certainly were much worse off!

*Of course in those days I only remember sunshine and the animals.*

Barbara Heal (Hookey) also remembered summer on the farm: *It was great fun at harvest time to help make the hay pooks and later the corn stooks. Tea was taken out to the fields in a wine bottle covered with an old sock to keep it hot! The children enjoyed riding on top of the waggon loaded with hay or corn back to the farmyard where the ricks were made and later thatched.*

In the 1960s, Pat Tyrrell would cycle from Chessell to work at Downton Farm on an old bike. He would race down Brooke Shute and use his boots as brakes so that the hobnails created sparks! He remembers everything about those days:

My job was to get the cows in from the field for milking. One cow I was especially fond of was 'Brown Cow'. She was very crafty, and a bit of a character. She was always waiting at the gate, and rushed to get to the milking shed first, where she ate several portions of cowcake before the others arrived, then ate her own! There were heifers out on the clifftop most of the time, and calves in the pen. The cows were artificially inseminated. On one occasion there was a cow out that was due to calve, so we brought her in. She was very agitated and blared all night, but no calf arrived. Mr Hookey was puzzled. I thought maybe she'd already calved, but there was nothing to indicate that she had. After another night of blaring, Mr Hookey told me to take the tractor and trailer up to the field to have a look around. Sure enough, there was the calf, curled round a grass hillock! She was very weak, but I loaded her gently into the trailer, and took her back to her mum. She recovered well, and I had a couple of shillings bonus that week!
On one dark winter morning when getting the cows in, I noticed there were several cows clustered in a group around the electricity poles. When I looked to see what was going on, I found that there was a cow lying against the stay-wire. I picked her head up by the horns, and saw that her head was partially severed, and that there was smoke rising from the wound! I reported back to Mr Hookey, who used the public phone box to call the engineers. When they arrived they instructed that no-one should approach the area closer than 30 yards. I was lucky to be alive, as there were thousands of volts coming off the wire, and it was wearing Wellington boots that had saved me from being electrocuted like the cow.
Spring really was a re-awakening of life on the farm. We would roll meadows, then chain-harrow. Land that had stubble ploughed in from previous harvests would be ploughed in again, then disc-harrowed. Spring corn was drilled and sown (mostly barley)

*I was lucky to be alive, it was wearing Wellington boots that had saved me from being electrocuted, like the cow...*

*Working hours depended on the weather conditions, rather than on the clock.*

and mangels and kale re-sown. All this was done from April. Maybe half a dozen heifers were put to calf, by courtesy of the AI (artificial insemination) man. The rickyard would be tidied up, ready to start all over again...
Late summer saw the beginning of the harvest. There was no combine harvester then, at least not at Downton! We used a binder, which cut the corn and produced the sheaves, which were stacked into stooks

David Hookey feeds the calves

*One cow I was especially fond of was 'Brown Cow'. She was very crafty, and a bit of a character. She was always waiting at the gate, and rushed to get to the milking shed first*

and left to dry out in fields for a couple of weeks or so. They were then collected by trailer and taken to the rickyard, where they were built into ricks. When the time came to use the corn, Den Phillips would bring his thresher over from Compton. When it was time for Den to do his own threshing, Dave and I went over to Compton to help him out. I particularly remember Jane Phillips feeding us well with sandwiches and cake. During the winter months there was kale to cut to feed the cows, also mangels to pull. These were not jobs that were nice to do in cold, wet conditions. The equipment then was very basic and heavy. Mangels and kale would be planted in spring, then later flat-hoed and thinned out. The mangels would be pulled in late autumn and the foliage cut off. They were piled up in the fields, then put into a clamp covered first with straw, then with soil. Kale was left in the fields and cut as needed during the winter months. There was always a lot to do on the farm, with ploughing, sowing, harvesting, also maintenance of fields, hedgerows, fences, and equipment as well as the dairy side of things.

Anne remembers that during the Second World War: *We had prisoners of war on the farm; the Italians were great with children and made us toys. One German prisoner called Richard seemed to be with us the longest. My Father paid him a bit and he kept the money in an old tobacco tin on a beam in the scullery. He kept in touch with us after he returned to Germany where he joined the police force.*

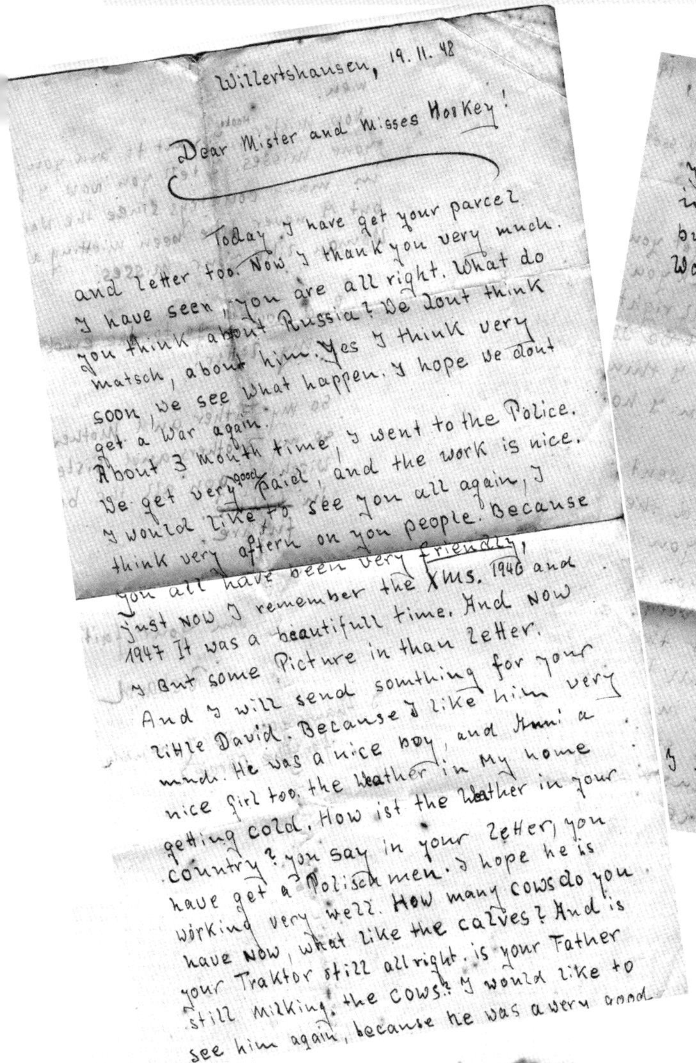

Willertshausen, 19. 11. 48

Dear Mister and Misses Hokey!

Today I have get your parcel and letter too. Now I thank you very much. I have seen, you are all right. What do you think about Russia? We dont think about him. Yes I think very matsch, soon we see what happen. I hope we dont get a War again.

About 3 month time, I went to the Police. We get very good paid, and the work is nice. I would like to see you all again, I think very aftern on you people. Because you all have been very friendly.

Just now I remember the Xmas. 1946 and 1947 It was a beautifull time. And now I put some Picture in than letter.

And I will send somthing for your little David. Because I like him very much. He was a nice boy, and Anni a nice girl too. the Weather in My home getting cold, How ist the Weather in your country? You say in your letter, you have get a Polisch men. I hope he is working very well. How many cows do you have now, what like the calves? And is your Traktor still all right. is your Father still milking the cows? I would like to see him again, because he was a very good

men.

Now Mister Hookey I want to ask you How is your Misses. I tell you now I have been in many countrys since the War startet, but I never have been mietting a so good Woman like your Misses.

And now I go to the end of my letter.

So my Father and Mother, so my Brothers and Sisters wisching you all the best in future.

I am your faithfulli

Richard

I thank you very much for the parcel

Richard, the German prisoner of war who worked at Downton Farm for two years during the war. He had happy memories of his years in Brook, as his letters (left) testify.

## Dunsbury Farm

Dunsbury Farm, with one of the best views in the world

Dunsbury Farm was owned by Sir Charles Seely as part of the Seely Estate in the late 19th and early 20th centuries and farmed by the Brown family for many years. In the 1950s Dunsbury was owned and farmed by Harry and Bunty Minchin (Bunty's family the Dockerells had farmed Brook Farm). Following the Minchin family was Mr Hedley Flitton, who lived and managed the farm in the 1960s and 70s. Dunsbury is owned today by Sir Charles Seely's great grandson Patrick and his wife Susannah. The farm continues to be a successful working farm producing and selling its own lamb with shepherd Steve Fruin looking after 800 breeding ewes and a flock that reaches 2,000 sheep at any one time.

*When asked how he constructed the magnificent ricks at Dunsbury, Ned was famous for never saying a word*

Dunsbury Farm between the wars, with its impressive collection of hayricks. Ned Woodford (above) was famous for his rick-building and lived with his wife Elizabeth and nine children in the small cottage (above left) now Mary's Cottage. Their children included Alf Woodford, fisherman and coxswain of Brooke Lifeboat (see *Fishing*).

*Brian was a big lad and he'd say 'Stand on the shovel and I'll see if I can pick you up.'*

Dunsbury farm buildings and pond. The rick is so neatly built it could be mistaken for a barn.

Fred Price, sheep shearer and steam enthusiast, recalls: *Harry Minchin that was at Dunsbury, he was a marine commando in the war. I know he had a famous donkey there. They put an advertisement in the newspaper, "Jill donkey needs a Jack donkey, apply Mrs Minchin Dunsbury Farm"!* Robin Shepheard (Newbery) who grew up at Meadow Cottage in Brook, recalls: *Colonel Dockerell had two daughters, Bunty and Jill, who married into large farm-owning families. Bunty married Harry Minchin who owned Dunsbury Farm and welcomed me as a casual working lad at weekends and school holidays. I spent many hours at the farm and remember very well two of the workers – George Thompson and Eric Sheath. I recall the old green tractor, a Field Marshall, which I think had to be started by a cartridge. Mr Minchin used to give me a small brown wage packet on a Friday, which I treasured.*

George Thompson worked on the farm from the 1930s and took the photo on the left: *I did like that photo…how it use to be done years ago. Brian loaded it, Hilt pitched it and I drove the tractor. Old Fred Barnes, he worked there at Dunsbury, used to say, 'What does a boy know about loading sheaves on a wagon?' I said 'he's had good tuition.' We started off with an under-hand prong, a short-handled half-pitcher prong and then moved on to a full-pitcher, an over-hand long pitcher. They all had different length handles. We took it back down to the farm to be threshed in the Dutch barns, they're not there now. The sacks in the trailer were sacks of barley, weighing two cwt. We would carry them up the steps on our backs, it was the only way you could carry them. It was hard work and Brian Sheath and me had little bets on who could carry the sacks farthest. Brian was a big lad and he'd say 'Stand on the shovel and I will see if I can pick you up.' I am a little bit heavier now than I was then when he would pick me up on the shovel.*

Farming at Dunsbury in the 1950s. Farmer Harry Minchin with Hilton ('Hilt') Snow and Brian Sheath

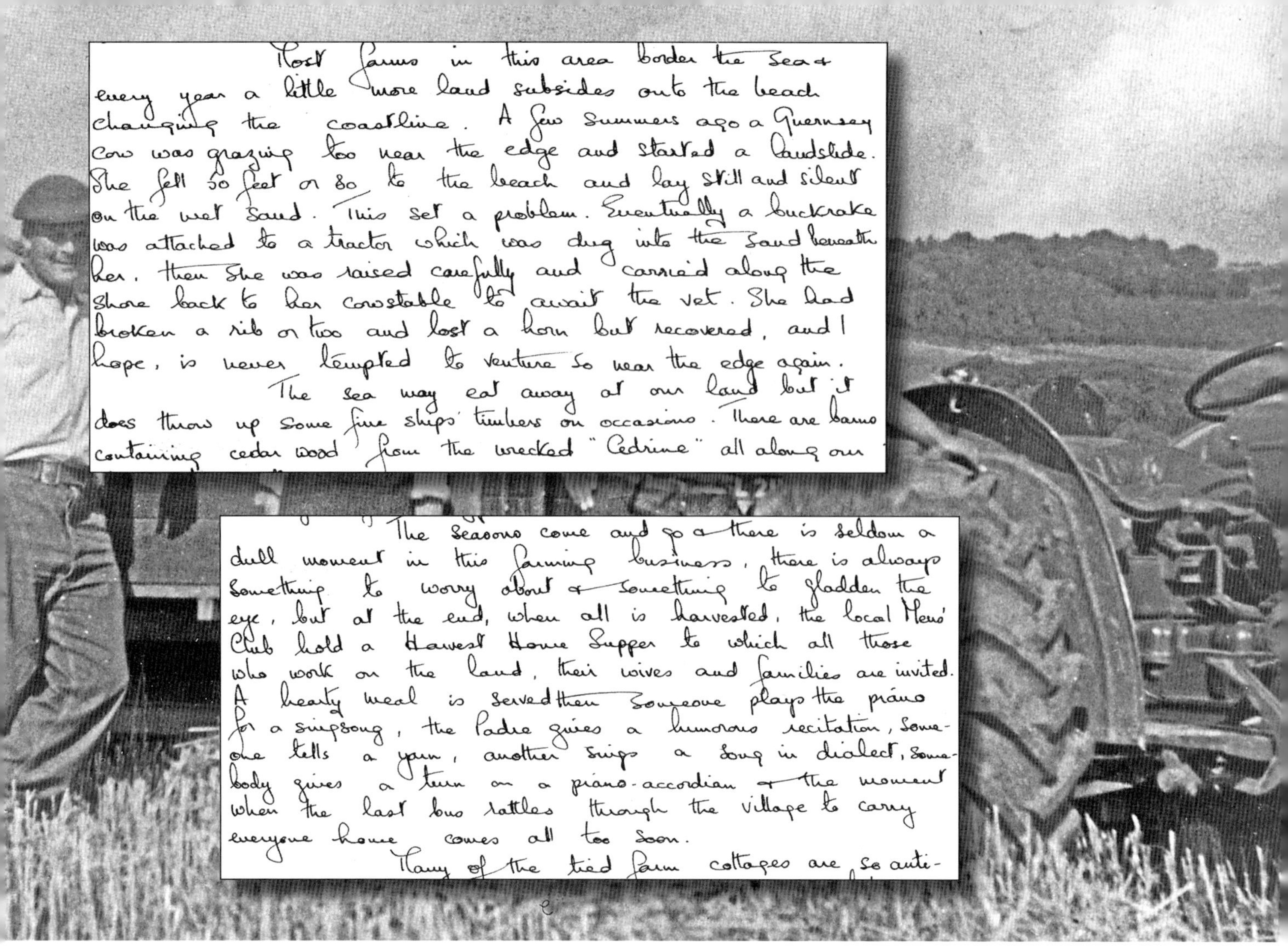

Most farms in this area border the sea & every year a little more land subsides onto the beach changing the coastline. A few summers ago a Guernsey cow was grazing too near the edge and started a landslide. She fell 50 feet or so to the beach and lay still and silent on the wet sand. This set a problem. Eventually a buckrake was attached to a tractor which was dug into the sand beneath her. Then she was raised carefully and carried along the shore back to her cowstable to await the vet. She had broken a rib or two and lost a horn but recovered, and I hope, is never tempted to venture so near the edge again.

The sea may eat away at our land but it does throw up some fine ships' timbers on occasions. There are barns containing cedar wood from the wrecked "Cedrine" all along our

The seasons come and go & there is seldom a dull moment in this farming business, there is always something to worry about & something to gladden the eye, but at the end, when all is harvested, the local Men's Club hold a Harvest Home Supper to which all those who work on the land, their wives and families are invited. A hearty meal is served then someone plays the piano for a singsong, the Padre gives a humorous recitation, someone tells a yarn, another sings a song in dialect, somebody gives a turn on a piano-accordian & the moment when the last bus rattles through the village to carry everyone home comes all too soon.

Many of the tied farm cottages are so anti-

In 1958 Bunty Minchin wrote an engaging account of her life as a farmer's wife at Dunsbury for the WI Scrapbook. The extracts above give a flavour of the piece.

**Home (Hooam) Harvest**

In the WI Village Scrapbook, we hear how in the old days, after the exhausting work of harvest:

The last load of corn was adorned with a floral wreath and a puncheon of 'nammet beer' was drunk before setting off to the ricks. The harvesters came to the supper straight from the fields and the 'meyster' carved the large legs of mutton or ham and they ate mutton pies or a chine followed by a huge plum pudding and even larger apple pies. When the meal was over and the tables cleared, jugs of real 'Hooam Harvest Stingo' (best brew), were brought out and pipes and tobacco placed before the men who were called upon for a song and a yarn alternately, with often one having bearing on the other. All stood for a toast to the 'Meyster, the founder of the feast' and gave three cheers to 'Missus.'
The stories often made fun of fellow labourers or were ghost stories. The songs included, 'Lumps o' pudden,' 'Come all you jolly harvest men,' 'I'm seventeen come Sunday' and 'As I walked out one May morning'. There was also always a love song, like 'Said John to Joan.'

George Thompson meets Richard Minchin outside the Seely Hall at the *Brook - A Village History* 'Get together ' in 2009.

## Compton Farm

In 1086 the manor of Compton, which Earl Tostig had held before the Conquest, belonged to the king, William I. The overlordship was granted to Richard de Redvers in 1100. From then on the farm's ownership followed that of Carisbrooke Castle. The tenants were the Compton family and in the 13th century we see that Odo de Compton owned a knight's fee in Compton and Atherfield.

Compton Farm in 1906. Left: a photograph found in a 1901 album of walkers on holiday taking a rest in the sun outside the farm

In about 1431 the tenants were the de Compton family. The farm was later passed to the Lisle family and many others. Throughout this time the abbotts of Quarr Abbey held land at Compton.

The Phillips family, who have farmed here for over 70 years, arrived in 1926. Jack Phillips, was living on the Yar at Wilmingham. He had bad lungs and was told he needed a drier environment. A land agent who recognised the popularity of country holidays between the wars, suggested Compton would be perfect, saying: *For God's sake, Jack, get some campers in for an income.* The farm was owned by the Seely Estate until it was bought by the National Trust in 1957 with money bequeathed by Amy Salter in memory of her son Edmund who was killed in Italy during the Second World War. Jack and

*For God's sake, Jack, get some campers in for an income.*

Minnie Phillips (Cheek) brought up their nine children on the farm, Gwen, Ron, Doris, Bill, Isobel, Marjorie, Bernard, Min and the youngest, Den, who was born on the farm in 1928. From that day to this, the Phillips family have run Compton differently to many other farms, welcoming campers and encouraging them to help out and take an interest in farm life. In the 1930s and 40s, Huntley and Palmer's factory workers came to camp, as did the Elim Gospel Group and the Rev Daniels brought large groups of boys in relays from the East End of London throughout the summer months. Jane Phillips recounts how: *They had a ton of coal delivered each fortnight for use in their cast iron range which cooked hundreds of meals (the range lived at Compton full time so it*

The farmhouse in the 1920s, with long tables set for thirsty holiday makers. The tea garden was popular for its proximity to Freshwater Bay.

*One cow was called Twist, because she fell down the cliff and survived, from then on she would throw her leg sideways and waddle down the lane.*

*Summers were summers in those days.*

*was ready for use every summer). Gallon loaves were delivered from Lithgows in Freshwater. They had their own cooking tents and latrines. The Rev Daniels stood no nonsense from the boys, they were very disciplined and had to march to the beach. Some of the boys still come back today as adults with their families. Summers were summers in those days. The cows at Compton were Guernseys and they all had names, usually flower names, Primrose, Daisy, Bluebell and such like. One cow was called Twist, because she fell down the cliff and survived, from then on she would throw her leg sideways and waddle down the lane. You could put an arm around her neck, she was so friendly.*

In the wartime pig-killing was illegal, but the Phillips' were friendly with a sergeant at Yarmouth Police Station who would somehow tip them off when things were all clear. One day they were in the middle of a killing, when word of a police raid arrived. Everything was quickly packed away and cleaned up, but no one came, which was apparently just as well as a huge bucket of entrails had been forgotten and would have given the game away... Another family story tells how, in the war Den's mother heard a great crash and thought a bomb had dropped on Compton, but on going outside she saw that an outside wall of the farmhouse had suddenly collapsed.

Left: Minnie Phillips with Den in 1933. Below: the Phillips family involve the holiday makers in haymaking in 1949. Jack Phillips is on the tractor and Den is standing on the right on the haycart.

Jane also remembers how: *In winter when they were snowed in at Compton and the milk lorry didn't come, they would need to use the milk and so set to work on making butter using scotch hands (butter pats) and making clotted cream.*

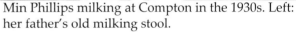

Min Phillips milking at Compton in the 1930s. Left: her father's old milking stool.

Den and daughters, Mary, Anna and Lucy, in 1971.

Den and Jane Phillips kept up the traditions of welcoming people to Compton with their own daughters, Mary, Anna and Lucy. Since Den died in 2008, Jane and Anna now manage the farm. Each Easter Monday, come rain or shine, the traditional 'Steam Up' takes place at Compton. Crowds gather in this idyllic spot and are transported back to the age of steam power and old country ways. From then on starts the busy time at Compton; as well as the usual farming jobs it is the beginning of the camping season. As in 1926, all are made very welcome, many returning year after year.

As well as being a champion ploughman, Den was a wizard at converting and renovating old farm machinery and cars.

Below: Anna with Ron the bull at Compton in 2010.
Photo: Rosy Burke

Left: Jane and Den Phillips on their 50th wedding anniversary.
Courtesy of Isle of Wight County Press.

## Chessell Farm

Chessell is known today for its thriving Pottery Cafe. It is perhaps a coincidence that in early history it was a Jutish settlement, where instead of weapons, archaeologists found jewellery and cooking pots. From the late 1930s Chessell Farm was a renowned stud farm for prize-winning Suffolk Punch heavy horses. Tony Pettitt was born at Chessell in 1937 and remembers the farm in those days: *Summer holidays were spent around Chessell and Brook. The farms were more interesting then. Chessell Farm was owned by Sir Hanson Rowbothom who lived in Brook Hill House. His estate took in Afton, Wellow and Ningwood farms and also some land at Newtown. They were mixed farms with sheep, dairy and beef cattle. He also had a Suffolk Punch horse stud, not just a hobby, but as working horses on the farm. As kids, we would watch Alec Ballard and Hilt Brett making hurdles for sheep pens and spars for thatching hay and straw stacks. They did this in a shed down the cinder track at Little Chessell.* In 2009 David Stephens spoke about how he left school to work for Sir Hanson Rowbotham in 1945. Sir Hanson was a successful business man and High Sheriff in Birmingham, before moving to the Island in 1934 where he lived at Brook Hill House until 1946 when he died suddenly. David worked at Afton with the Suffolk Punch horses bred at Chessell stud. One of these show horses, Beyton Duchess, won the title of National Suffolk champion twice. David's duties ranged from grooming to feeding, mucking out and cleaning harnesses. He often had to lead the great horses along the road between Afton and Chessell. There were 52 horses at Chessell; they worked on various farms sowing, harrowing, carting, rolling and hay-turning. The local farms were also well known for Red Poll cattle which could be seen in many fields in the area. David remembers how: *As youngsters on Friday afternoons we had to sweep from the Causeway to Afton Manor Farm as Sir Hanson was coming back from Birmingham. He doffed his hat as he passed us.* After Sir Hanson's death, David and fellow workers accompanied the horses on their sad journey to a sale in Suffolk: *A special ferry and train were put on to take the horses from Yarmouth to Ipswich. They travelled two to an especially prepared box designed*

NOTED SUFFOLK BREEDER

Sir Hanson Rowbotham's Dea—: a Great Loss to Breed Supporters

Sir Hanson Rowbotham

SIR HANSON ROWBOTHAM, the noted breeder of Suffolk Punch horses and Red Poll cattle, died suddenly at his home at Brooke, Isle of Wight, on Thursday, at the age of 66.

His death will prove a great loss to supporters of these Suffolk breeds, and of Suffolk sheep, for not only was he an enthusiastic breeder but also a successful exhibitor with many firsts and championships to his credit.

On his 3,000-acre estate at Brooke, Sir Hanson had a Suffolk horse stud, and at Suffolk shows he took the mare championship two years running. His herd of over 200 Red Polls he started just before the war.

Left: obituary for Sir Hanson Rowbotham, October 1946. Below: Chessell stud farm in the 1940s.

Bert (driving), John, Roy and Paul Tyrrell with Jean Storie at Chessell in the early 1950s

*to minimise stress. It was a long journey - on the ferry at 10am and not arriving until 2am the next day. The men bedded down on straw, with the horses in stalls.*'Even now there's a lump in David's throat as he recalls the horses' pet names - Polly, Valiant, Sandy, Scamp (with a bump on her forehead), Jewel, Lucille... David's son took him up to a show in Suffolk recently where he met a gentleman who was able, many years after the event, to send him a copy of the sale catalogue of the Chessell horses. David of course had been there, and remembered it well, but he hadn't been able to face seeing his old friends go...

The sheep shearing gang that travelled the West Wight are seen here working in a barn at Chessell in the 1950s.

## Chapel Furlong Farm

In 1989 Pat and Dick Carder and family bought farmland that had originally been Hulverstone and Brook Farms, but which, in the 1970s and 80s had been amalgamated into Dunsbury Farm with hedges and pastures taken out. Chapel Furlong Farm came into being with the Carders inheriting 60 acres of cauliflowers but no farm-house or outbuildings. Since those early days the farm has reverted back to traditional mixed farming and pastures and hedges have been replaced. Tod, Jackie and their sons John and Phillip now also farm Mottistone Manor Farm and run the farm shop selling their own beef, lamb and pork.

*In 1989 when Chapel Furlong Farm, Hulverstone, came into being it consisted of 60 acres of cauliflowers with no farmhouse or outbuildings.*

The Carder family harvesting below the Sun Inn in 2010. Photo: Dudley Bryant

Hanover's barns when it was still a working farm. Brook Green can be seen in the background.

## Hanover Farm

Like most farms in those days, Hanover Farm was a dairy farm. From the census we know that in 1861, farmer Benjamin Jacobs was the tenant, in 1871 the Blakes, in 1881 Fred Priddle and in 1891, Ellen A Way, a widow, was living there on her own. By 1911 James Wheeler was the last dairy farmer to farm there.

Right: the barns of Brook Farm in the 1960s, later to become Brook Farm Close. Below right: Joliffe Kingswell, who farmed there in the 1950s and 60s and famously kept his pigs on what is now the village green. Below left: William, or 'Old' Selby as he was known, whose family farmed Brook Farm in the second half of the 19th Century.

## Brook Farm

The 1841 and 1851 censuses show Brook Farm was farmed by brothers William and James How. In 1861 it was farmed by William Selby and remained in that family until 1901 when it was farmed by Ira Hendy, it was still being farmed by them in 1911. It then passed to the Walmsley-Dockerell family and onto the Browns and finally to Jollife Kingswell in the 1960s who left much of the land to Cancer Research.

## Seaview Dairy

The Phillips' at Compton Farm were on good terms with their neighbours, the Cheeks, on their smallholding Seaview Dairy (what remains of the buildings was High Grange, now known as Compton Grange). The Phillips' helped out with the dairy herd and one of their daughters, Marjorie Phillips, lived in for two shillings and sixpence a week. Jane Phillips tells how one day in the 1920s Mrs Cheek's husband was tragically killed by a bull at Compton: *Bulls were treated roughly in those days, they were chained on to a bracket attached to the wall and only able to stand up or lay down; they were only let loose to go out into the yard to 'serve' the cows and then back to be chained up. Understandably, through frustration, they got a bit 'annoyed'.* Another person who had memories of Seaview Dairy was Robert (Bob) Cassell. Bob left school aged 13 in 1926 and went straight to work for the widow, Mrs Cheek. The only work locally for boys leaving school in those days was farm work and Bob remembers he was lucky to get that: *I had fifteen cows to look after, three horses and about fifteen pigs. The horses' names were Chale Diamond and Joe. The cows had flower names like Primrose and Cherry. Some were Fresians, but most were Guernseys. We would start the milking at half past six in the morning and I milked them by hand. The butter was made in a great wooden end-over-end churn every Wednesday. One day, I remember, when I took the cover off I found a blessed great rat in the butter with its tail sticking out. I went along to the widow and said, 'I shan't want no butter this week.' 'Oh why,' she said, 'Whatever's the matter?' So I said ' You'd better come out and look.' When she saw the rat she said, 'I don't want no butter either.' I said 'Well, leave it to me now.' I just got some butter pats and scooped around the rat and got him out with a little bit of butter all around him and dealt with him. I gave the churn an extra good wash after. A local grocer used to take the butter. He had a butter round at Freshwater. The following week he came and he said, 'Whatever did you do to your butter last week, Mrs Cheek?' She said, 'I don't know, what did I do?' 'Well,' he said, 'I couldn't get enough of it. Everybody was crazy for it.' I can see that rat's tail now...'*

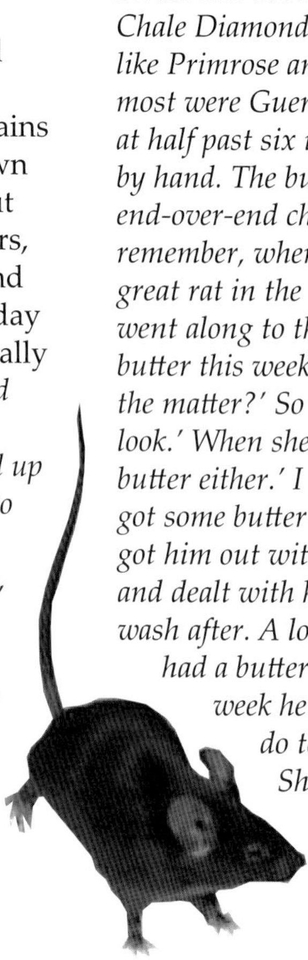

## Hulverstone Farm

Hulverstone Farm, above, was managed as a working farm until 1957 by Mrs Heal (left). When her husband died she ran the farm alongside Hilton Snow, seen right milking at Hulverstone, and above right: Bob Cassell who tells his life story in *'An Eventful Life.'*

*The horses I had most to do with at Hulverstone were Captain, Colonel, Nelson and Smiler.*

While Bob Cassell enjoyed the work at Seaview Dairy, on his fifteenth birthday in 1928 his wages went up to twelve shillings a week and Mrs Cheek could no longer afford to pay him. Later when he was eighteen, and she had lost another worker, she was able to offer him 'a man's money' of thirty shillings a week and this enabled him to marry and live with his wife in their own tied cottage (Ivy Cottage, Brook).

When Bob's father needed to retire at seventy, he could only stay in his home, The Elms in Hulverstone, if Bob took over his job as carter at Hulverstone Farm. Bob was glad to be back working with horses: *I was brought up with horses. Even from when I was about six year old the farmer very often came to the door to ask the schoolmistress if she would let me out to get a certain horse to the blacksmith...The horses all had names. The horses I had most to do with at Hulverstone were Captain, Colonel, Nelson and Smiler. Colonel was a great big horse but gentle as a lamb. You can talk to horses. Of course I had to go tractor driving during and after the war, but I missed the horses.They're alive and all have their own personalities.* Bob also recalled what the daily work involved: *Soon after five in the morning I would be over to feed and clean out the horses. By seven o'clock we would be ready to do whatever we had to do. It was a bit difficult in the war though because with double daylight saving it would still be dark at seven o'clock. I would use three horses for ploughing, sowing and harvesting with the binder. That was hard work for the horses - there was no let up, they would be at it seven or eight hours a day. To plough a big field like Chapel Furlong would take about three weeks. Before the war we had about forty acres of ploughed land, then during the War I ploughed up two or three meadows and we ended up with about a hundred acres in which we sowed wheat, barley and oats alternately, with a few acres of roots for cattle feed. Sometimes I used to take a cart into Newport with pigs and calves all in together, to sell at the market. Mostly I walked alongside the cart, to keep myself warm. After Mrs Heal died, the people who took over the farm brought their own men with them and I worked at Dunsbury Farm on the tractors. Hulverstone Farm has always seemed like home to me, especially with the horses.*

*I had a two and a half mile walk to work, so in the winter it was well and truly dark. I would have a candle in a lantern or a hurricane lantern - you really wanted another one to see that one...*

Farm workers in the 1920s in Mottistone; from the length of their shadow it must have been at the end of a working day.

## Mottistone Farms

In 1926 Jack Seely sold Brooke House to his brother Charles and worked with his son John on bringing Mottistone Manor back to the condition it was in before the great landslip in 1703. Mr Jackman and his family, who, up until then had worked and lived in the Manor as tenant farmers, were moved to Mottistone Manor Farm. Babs Barton (Jackman) remembers living at the Manor as a child: *I was frightened. It was so big and full of black beetles and mice. The black beetles were so thick on the floor you crunched as you walked through the oldest part of the Manor.*

The barns that remained of Longstone Farm in the 1950s

Mottistone Manor Farm, formerly Little Mottistone Farm.

## Longstone and Pitt Place Farms

Of Mr Jackman's children, Peter took on the tenancy of Pitt Place Farm and his brother Bill took on Longstone Farm. Bill was the first person to live in the wooden house at the bottom of Strawberry Lane (now the National Trust offices and designed by the second Lord Mottistone). Like a number of houses in the area, Longstone Farmhouse still had no electricity in the 1950s and everything was done by candle light and paraffin lamp. Bill did not find the land productive and stopped farming altogether, while his brother Peter and his wife Connie continued to farm 165 acres around Mottistone, Longstone and Hoxall for 36 years. They kept beef and dairy cattle as well as up to 500 pigs out in the open. One of their Jersey cows, Josie, became a local celebrity, living to the grand age of 21 years and gaining an obituary in the IOW County Press.

*The black beetles were so thick on the floor you crunched as you walked through the oldest part of the Manor.*

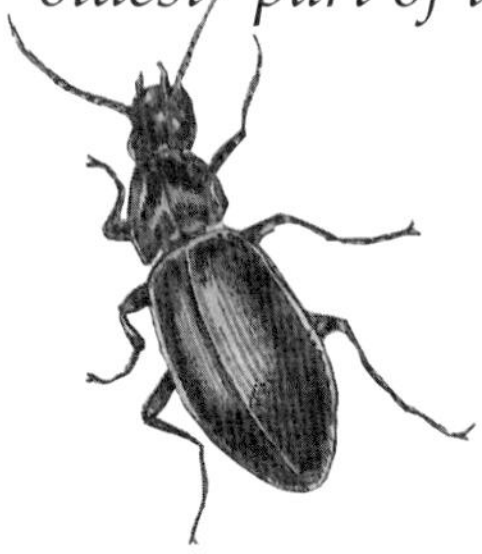

Outside Rose Cottage, Mottistone, a car that Jack Jackman and sons adapted to get animals to market in the 1920s.

SAD news this week from Peter and Connie Jackman. Josie, their 21-year-old Jersey cow pictured in this column in March, died in the early hours of Monday at Pitt Place Farm.

Like his father, Peter Jackman worked from dawn to dusk, taking no holidays. A tall and striking figure, he was never without a broad brimmed hat and was known at the Tuesday farmers' market in Newport as 'the man who always wears the trilby'. He got his hats from Dunn & Co. in Regent Street and always had three on the go. As they became worn the hats were demoted from 'best' to 'market' and then finally to 'work', before being thrown away when a new one was bought. Like the Hookeys at Downton Farm, the Jackmans became lifelong friends with a German prisoner of war, Willie, who worked for them from 1945 to 1948. Peter and Connie's eldest son John, decided against farming and joined the police force. He learned to drive a tractor at 5 years old and when he returned to Mottistone on leave he could still win the IOW ploughing championship. The land of Pitt Place Farm is today divided up between neighbouring farms.

P.C. BECOMES PLOUGH CHAMP

A Hampshire policeman has become champion ploughman of the Isle of Wight.

P.C. John Jackman (27), stationed at Gosport, left his father's farm at Brighstone, Isle of Wight, five years ago to join the Force.

Since then he has kept his hand in at ploughing while helping his father on his days off.

His previous success was when he became reserve champion in 1964.

P.C. John Jackman: champion ploughman

The Pitt Place farmland farmed by Peter Jackman for 36 years from the 1940s to the 1970s. Peter and Connie Jackman at their home at Pitt Place in the 1980s.

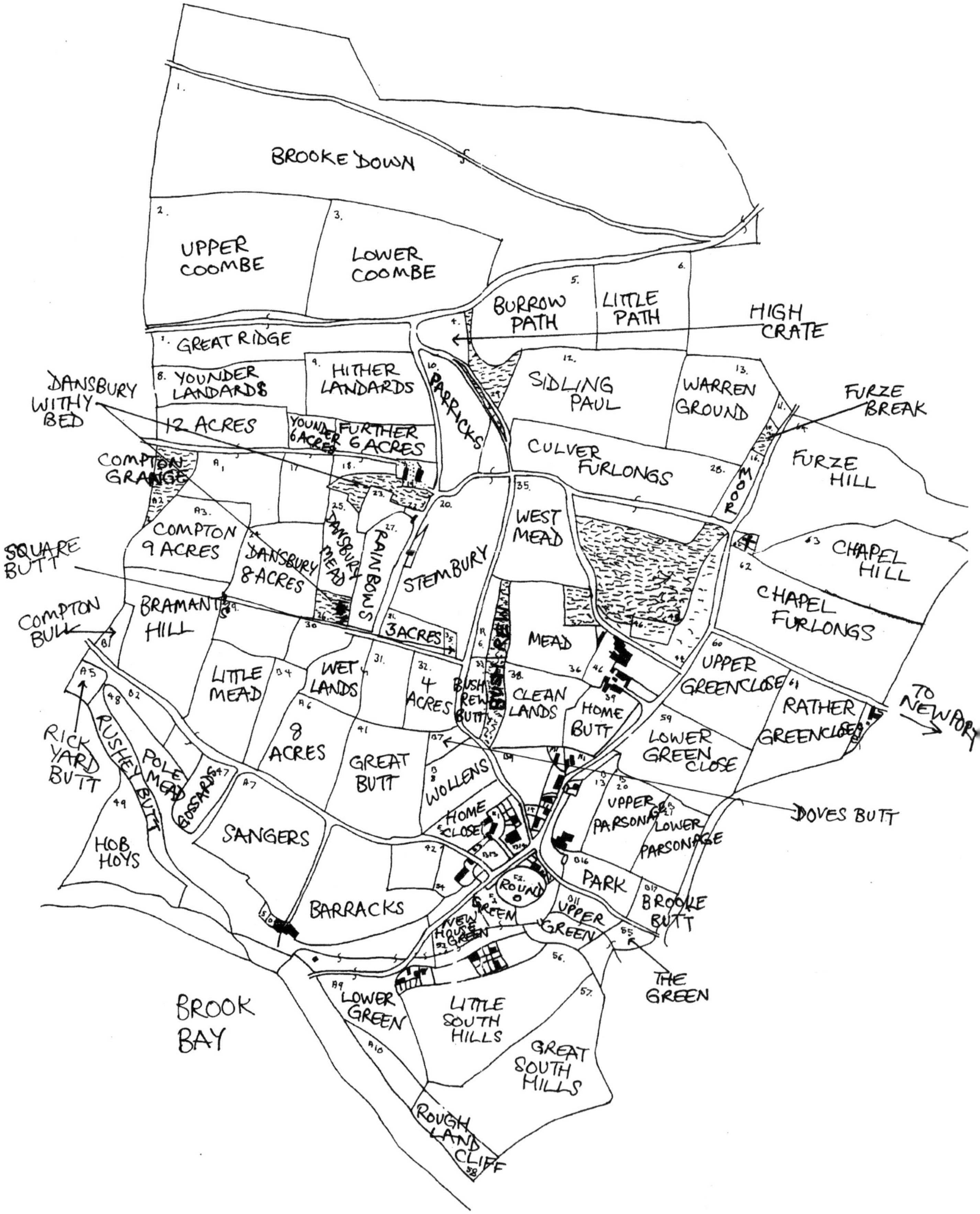


Field names in the parish of Brooke from the Tythe map of 1838.

Drawn by Kevin Trott

Mottistone Field Names
From
Estate Map 1820
Tythe Map 1838

# Brook Church

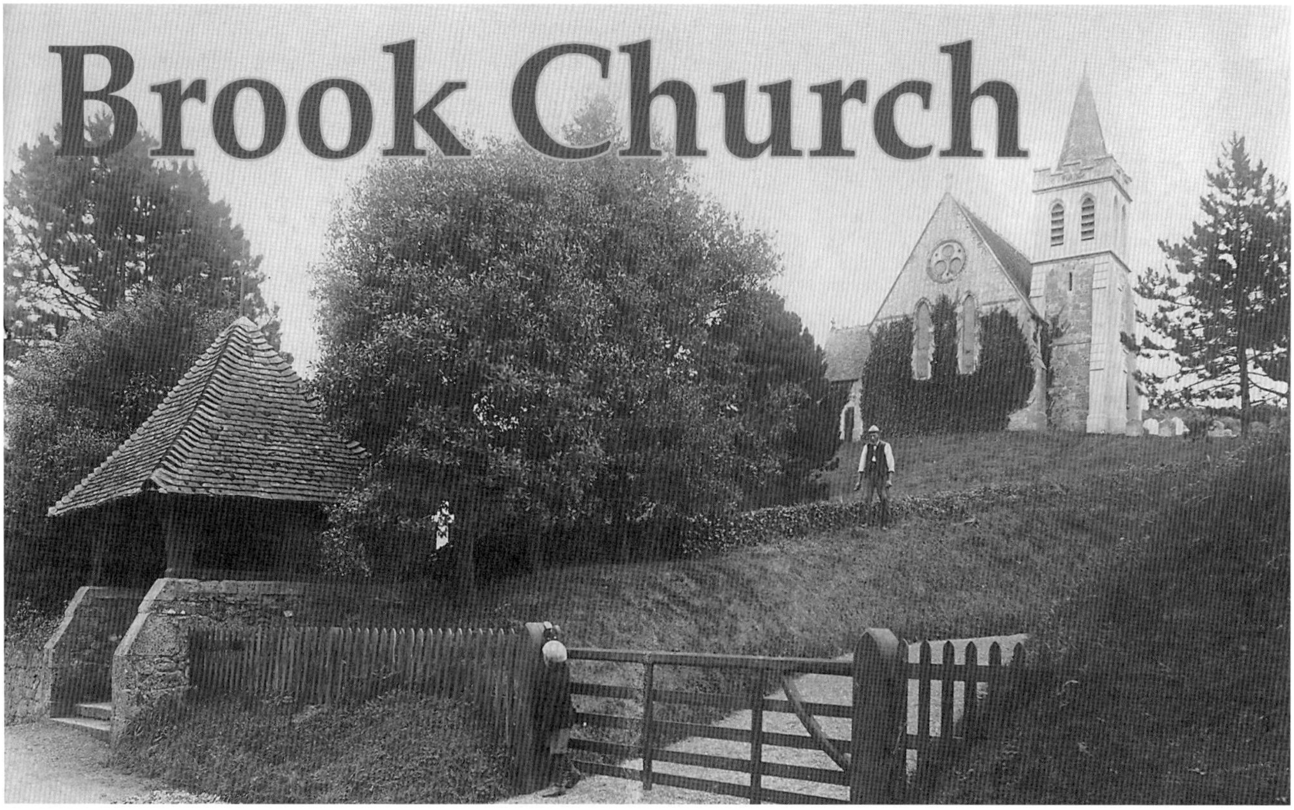

The church in the 1880s. The man walking down the path is said to be James Jacobs, longshoreman, of Cliff Cottage.

The church of St Mary the Virgin, Brook, is set on a small knoll in a gap between the downs on Brook Shute. It stands rather more than a quarter of a mile from the centre of the village and from the church porch there is a most beautiful view over the surrounding countryside and out to sea.

*The curate from Freshwater came over the Downs to take services. When the sexton at Brook could see him coming over Five Barrows he would begin to ring the bell and the villagers knew that a service would take place.*

An engraving of Brook Church with a square tower in 1794. This church was destroyed by fire in 1862.

## The old church

The date of the original church is uncertain, but in the thirteenth year of the reign of Edward III (1325) the local dean's return to Bishop Woodlock names Brook as a chapel endowed with the tithes of the Manor of Compton and charged with a pension of seven shillings to the mother church of Freshwater. The church was originally a 'chapel of ease' to Freshwater church, and during the 13th century there was a long dispute and lawsuit between St John's College Cambridge, the patrons of Freshwater and the Bowerman family, the lords of Brooke Manor. The Bowerman family claimed the patronage of Brooke, maintaining it was a separate parish. The rectors of Freshwater maintained Brooke was within their parish and that all tithes and rights belonged to them. This dispute rumbled on into the 16th century occasionally breaking out into court actions.

A small card made of the newly-built church.

*Some of the older people slept unashamedly during most of the service, it was difficult not to...*

In the aftermath of the Civil War, Thomas Bowerman, Lord of Brooke Manor, was one of the Committee that governed the Island from 1643. This meant Bowerman wielded considerable power over most matters throughout the Island and he seized the chance to establish Brooke as a parish by endowing it with parochial trappings. He railed in a piece of his ground as a churchyard, provided a register book, encouraged the inhabitants of Brook to bury their dead in Brook burial ground, allowed them to hold christenings and marriages and to receive the sacraments there and, finally, demanded that people living in Brooke 'parish' pay their tithes to the person that he, Bowerman, had presented as 'rector'. The dispute between Freshwater and Brooke erupted again after the Restoration of the monarchy in 1660 and continued for many years until it was finally terminated in favour of Brooke.

In 1728 the church had a small porch and the parishioners agreed to replace it by building a tower for one bell which would be paid for by a parish rate. This forms the basis of the present tower which was later strengthened and raised to house eight bells.

## Brook Church today

In 1862 Brook Church was totally destroyed by a fire. Mr Seely, then the lord of the manor, offered to give a piece of land and rebuild the church more in the centre of the village. At a meeting of the villagers to discuss the matter, his plan was turned down, as they all wanted it rebuilt on its

*Rebuild your own church!*

original site. It is said that he was so hurt that he there and then tore up the expensive architect's plans and threw them into the fire, saying: *rebuild your own church!* Charles Seely must have recovered from his pique however, as we know the church was rebuilt and 'beautified' at a cost of nearly £2,000 and his wife, Mary Seely, laid the foundation stone of the new church on the 30th September 1863. Mentioned in Emily Tennyson's diary as 'kind Mr Cotton ... a country squire of the old type', Benjamin Cotton, of Afton Manor, generously donated all the stone required from his quarries. He was also Charles Seely's son-in-law. The new church was completed and consecrated by the Bishop of Winchester in 1864. Charles Seely also presented an additional piece of land to enlarge the churchyard. *Many people these days wish his offer* (of moving the church into the village) *had been accepted, as they plod up the long hill to the church, culminating in the very steep path from the lych gate.*

Design notes made before building the new church in 1863.

**Harvest Festival, 1896**

The Annual Harvest Festival at St Mary's Parish Church was celebrated with Holy Communion at 8 am and Choral Evensong at 7 pm. The chants and harvest hymns were heartily joined in by a large congregation, while Maunnatt's 'Deus Misereatur' and Makers anthem 'The Lord is my Shepherd' were carefully rendered by the choir. As usual, the Church was tastefully decorated. The harvest text, 'The earth is the Lord's and the fullness thereof' with sheaves of corn and other fruits, appeared o'er the altar, which with the vases, standards, and the Chancel Screens was beautifully treated with scarlet and white dahlias. The font, with its white datula cross and delicate ferns and the central pillar wreathed in corn and red berries, were greatly admired. After the evening service, Mrs Renwick (housekeeper), in the absence of Sir Charles Seely and Miss Seely, entertained the various church workers and members of the choir at Brooke House.

*... at 3pm came choral evensong and sermon, when the church was crowded to overflowing and the vestry and the porch had to accomodate the latecomers.*

Miss Emmie Dalbiac remembered: *The church contained an old-fashioned pew, square in shape and curtained off, for the use of the lord of the manor and his family, this was most comfortable, the curtains only being drawn back during the sermon; some of the older people slept unashamedly during most of the service, it was difficult not to.* This soporific pew was in use until early in the 20th century after which it was transformed into the vestry. It was unlikely that there was any sleeping at Harvest Festival in 1900, when the newspaper reported a 'true blending of the holy day and the holiday spirit.' The importance of the event in the village calendar is reflected in the newspaper report:

**Harvest Festival, 1900**

The music throughout was very hearty, and the choir, who sing in unison, acquitted themselves well. The decorations, as usual, were very tasteful and effective. The altar and font were treated with white asters, dahlias, and maiden-hair; magnificent bunches of grapes and the many fruits of the earth appear everywhere, while the reredos was surmounted with sheaves of corn and the text "I am the Bread of Life." A well-designed screen was composed of oats and wheat, relieved with scarlet dahlias... the eight bells rang out merry peals before and after the services. By half past 4 the Park (Brooke House grounds) was rapidly filling with parishioners, old and young ... A large tent was provided with a substantial tea for all the adult parishioners, numbering some 150, while about 50 children had a separate entertainment to themselves on the tennis lawn. An excellent band from Freshwater discoursed sweet music out in the open grounds, and with plenty of dancing, and many an exciting race and round game, the glorious evening passed all too quickly, and after regretful looks at the setting of the sun and many a cheer for their kind friends, the party broke up and dispersed, well pleased with their efforts to keep Brook harvest home.

*It always seemed that the wind blew at the church and if the rain was from the south west – watch out!*

The East window serves as a memorial to those who fell in the 1914-18 war with their names carved in the glass of the window. Two slender pillars in front of the East window are said to be made of polished stone from the fossilised forest in Brook Bay. The pulpit and font are of marble and were given by Miss Bowerman, in memory of her sister and her father, a former rector. The reredos (the ornamental screen at the back of the altar), was presented by Mrs Fenwick in memory of her husband, rector from 1833-1856. The church was originally lit by candles, but after the Second World War, Hugh Seely, Lord Sherwood installed electric lighting in memory of his brother, Nigel. He also gave an additional piece of land adjacent to the churchyard in celebration of the Coronation of Queen Elizabeth II. The altar rail was given by the Dalbiac family in memory of their parents, in 1957.

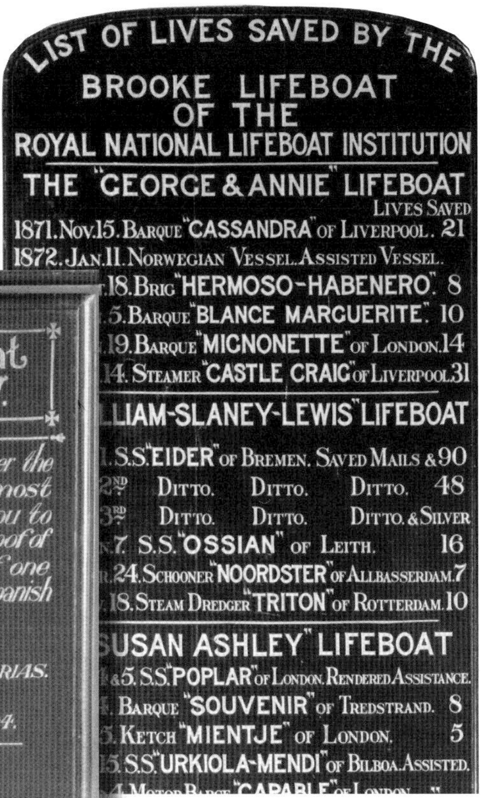


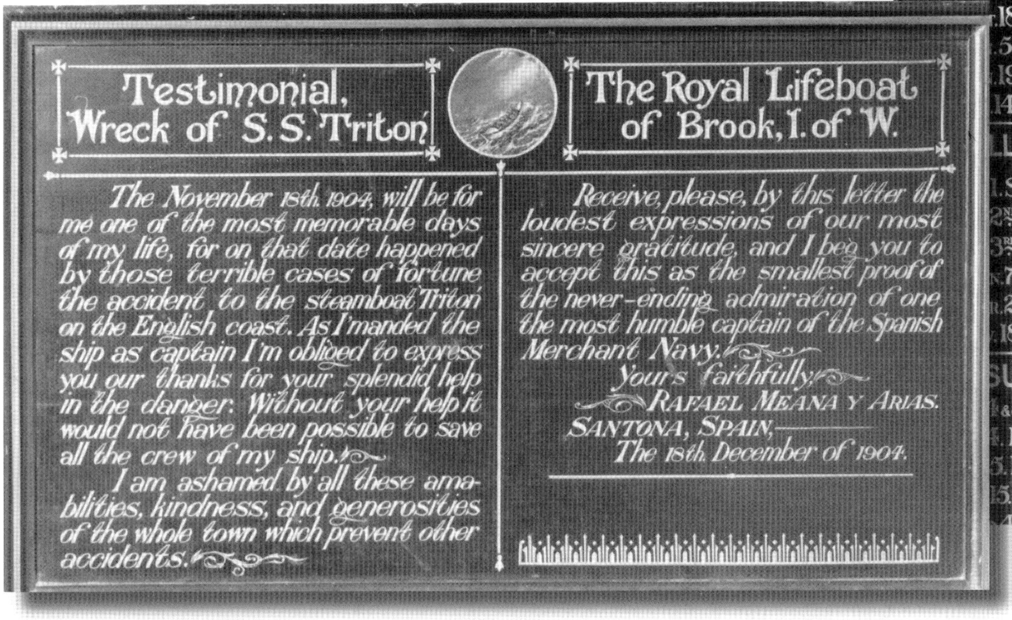


The lifeboat memorial plaques in Brook Church (above) show the pride the community had in their role in saving lives on the often treacherous strip of coast off Brook and Compton. The Testimonial, from the Captain of S.S.Triton, 'one the most humble captain of the Spanish Merchant Navy,' is moving in the strength of its appreciation for the lifeboat crew and the whole village.

A sewing party at Mottistone Manor Farm in the 1880s. In the photograph the rector appears to be reading from the scriptures as the ladies work.

Right: a sewing party photographed in the same place in the 1960s; back row: Mrs Summerfield, D.Smith, Miss Johnson and far right, Miss Dora Hookey, past Hulverstone schoolmistress; front row: Mrs Roberts, Mrs Smith, Mrs Stone, Mrs Morris, Mrs Austin and Mrs Sheath.

The striking view out to sea framed by the Church doorway.

Avice Mariner (French) lived in Ivy Cottage and remembers attending Brook and Mottistone churches as a young girl in the 1950s and 60s: *We attended Sunday school in various locations, Hulverstone School, The Elms, Brook Church and the Seely Hall. We were members of the Brook Church choir and even had robes. These consisted of a dark grey button-through gown with long sleeves and a red skull cap and belt. The church in winter was so cold we wore the robes over our ats and ended up looking like hessian sacks! Our first choir mistress and organist at Brook was Erica Newbery and sometimes we would sing for services in Mottistone Church. When Erica married and left Brook, Mrs Stone, Janet's mother, took over. I regret to say we didn't always behave ourselves as we should and Mrs Stone would glare at us in the mirror above the organ. Sometimes we would get the giggles, sometimes we would invent actions to the words of the hymns and occasionally we would not stop whispering. I cannot recall Reverend Bowyer ever telling us off, but I think Janet used to be told off for her behaviour.*

Children's memories of their more eccentric elders are always vivid. Ann Male's (Hailey) memories of going to church include one of: *Mrs Farrah, who lived in Badgers Lane, wore a fox skin around her neck with head and dangling feet on it. She also had fur covered shoes and a matching hat. When I saw her going up to her front pew (the one with cushons on) if it was raining her fur covered shoes looked like two wet rats shuffling along.*

Sue Mears (Stone) remembers how: *Grandad Joe Morris always sat at the back of the Church, which probably dated back to when he was in the lifeboat and meant that if there was 'a call' he was always ready to go. He was a bit deaf in later life and when he sung 'Eternal Father strong to save,' he would sing every word, but just a bit behind everyone else.*

In the 1950s and 60s the children would collect primroses from the fields and woods around Brook and, using lengths of wool they would make small bunches for decorating the church on Easter Sunday. Avice remembers the reward for helping: *All the children would receive a shilling and one of Mrs Morris' brandy snaps from Hanover Stores. The church was always wonderfully decorated, the font by Bunty Minchin and the altar by the older members of the village, Mrs Joe Morris, Mrs Daisy Newbery and Mrs Ella Hookey.*

Robin Shepheard was in the choir and rang the bells for a number of years: *All my (Newbery) ancestors on my mother's side of the family are buried here. It always seemed that the wind blew at the church and if the rain was from the south west – watch out! Burials in the wet weather were grim affairs. There was very much an order of seating in the church, seats were not reserved, but sitting in a pew of another family was frowned upon. In the early days the front pew was reserved for the Seely family, the only pew to have cushions and kneelers.*

Erica Newbery was organist at Brook Church, when the children of Margaret Stone, the regular organist, were young. Her sister Myrtle, remembers: *We had quite a good choir: there was myself, my sister Rosemary, Robin Shepheard, David Hookey, Gladys Morris and Joe Morris. I remember one Harvest Festival and in the sermon hearing a loud munch from an apple – was David Hookey guilty?*

*I regret to say we didn't always behave ourselves as we should and Mrs Stone would glare at us in the mirror above the organ.*

*The church played a big part in all our lives and most people went to a service at sometime each Sunday - and never, ever, missed Harvest Festival.*

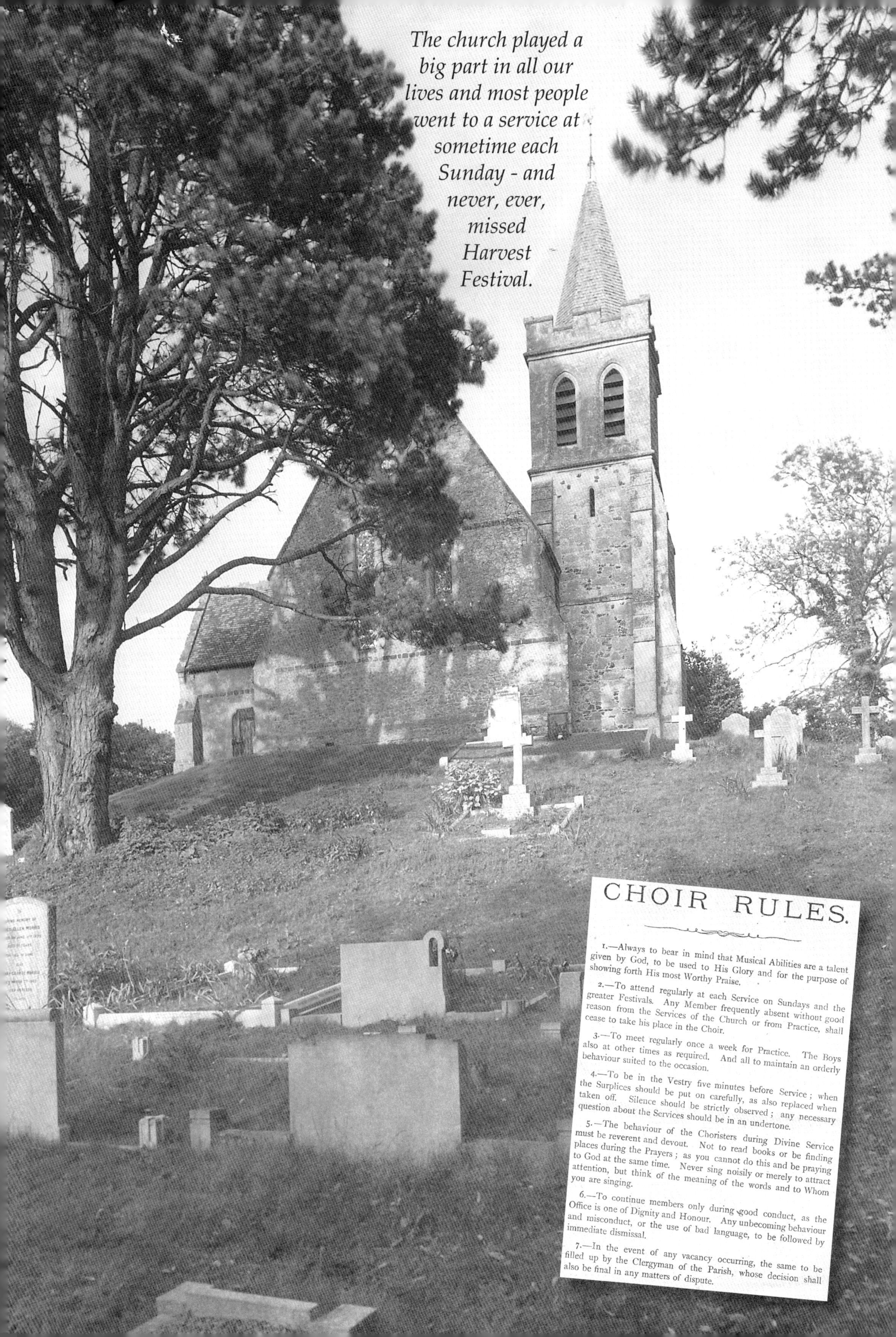

# CHOIR RULES.

1.—Always to bear in mind that Musical Abilities are a talent given by God, to be used to His Glory and for the purpose of showing forth His most Worthy Praise.

2.—To attend regularly at each Service on Sundays and the greater Festivals. Any Member frequently absent without good reason from the Services of the Church or from Practice, shall cease to take his place in the Choir.

3.—To meet regularly once a week for Practice. The Boys also at other times as required. And all to maintain an orderly behaviour suited to the occasion.

4.—To be in the Vestry five minutes before Service; when the Surplices should be put on carefully, as also replaced when taken off. Silence should be strictly observed; any necessary question about the Services should be in an undertone.

5.—The behaviour of the Choristers during Divine Service must be reverent and devout. Not to read books or be finding places during the Prayers; as you cannot do this and be praying to God at the same time. Never sing noisily or merely to attract attention, but think of the meaning of the words and to Whom you are singing.

6.—To continue members only during good conduct, as the Office is one of Dignity and Honour. Any unbecoming behaviour and misconduct, or the use of bad language, to be followed by immediate dismissal.

7.—In the event of any vacancy occurring, the same to be filled up by the Clergyman of the Parish, whose decision shall also be final in any matters of dispute.

# Rectors of Brooke

If there are threads that connect the past rectors of Brooke they appear to be a love of music, of learning, and, especially, of cricket. Mrs Morris, who was 84 years old in 1958, said: *I can remember six rectors but it seemed to me their wives ran the parish bar the sermon.*

**Rev. Collingwood Fenwick (1833- 1856)** appears to have been one of the last of the hunting and land-owning clergy. The estate map of 1856 shows that he owned most of the farmland in Brook. He is recorded as the man who first brought foxes to the Isle of Wight. He also appears to have been vicar of the parish of Blidworth, near Charles Seely's home at Mansfield, Nottinghamshire. George Humber who lived and worked in Brook knows by heart a rhyme about Fenwick which concludes with the line....*'the parson who sold the common land.'*

Photographic portrait of Rev. John Pellew Gaze (1856-1892), courtesy of the National Portrait Gallery. Below: the diary notes of Rev. R. Leslie Morris (1892-1909)

**Rev. Pellew Gaze (1856 - 1892).** Few records survive about the tenure of this long-standing rector who must have been appointed just before Charles Seely bought Brooke House. Newspaper reports reveal his daughters played a significant role in the village and that in the 1880s: *Ethel and Helen Gaze, daughters of the Rector, produced a capital programme of sketches, songs and piano and violin solos; and the school was literally packed with people of all ages.* The Rectory must have been a lively place at this time. In the 1881 and 1891 census 15 and 13 people respectively, are recorded living there, including cousins, a governess and at least three female servants.

From newspaper clippings we can see that **Rev. R. Leslie Morris (1892-1909)** and his wife worked hard for the village community. They clearly enjoyed music and singing as their names crop up at several village entertainments and outings. He was praised for his singing of duets like the 'Two Gendarmes' and she for her

The Rev. Robert Leslie Morris with his wife Frances at their Golden Wedding when he was 78 years old. An accomplished school master, the Rev. Morris was invaluable as Sir Charles Seely's right-hand man on the Reading Room Committee and as a trustee of the Chale and Brooke Shipwreck Fund.

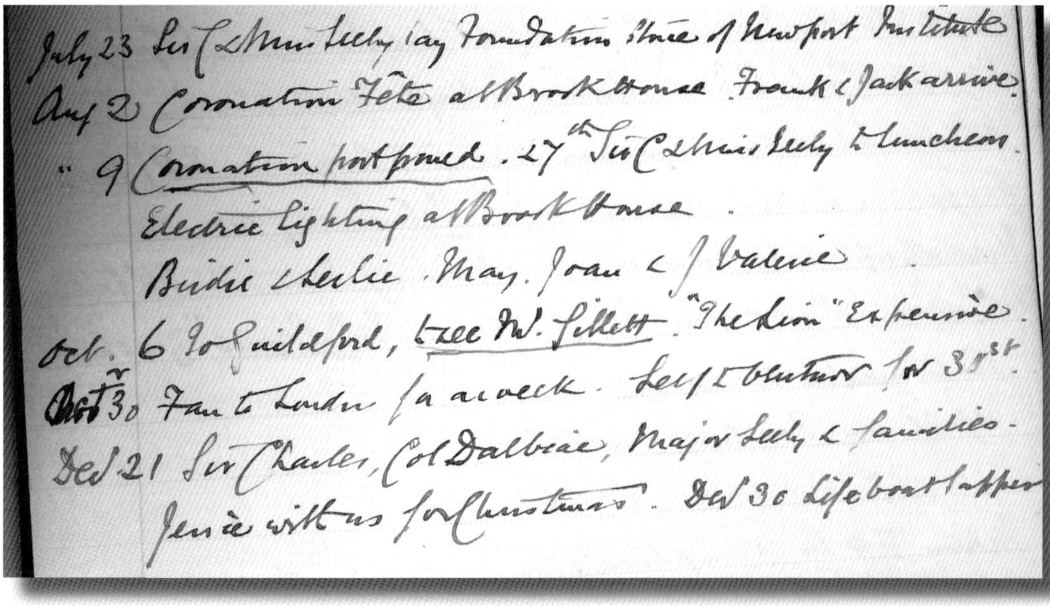

July 23 Sir C & Mrs Seely lay Foundation Stone of Newport Institute
Aug 2 Coronation Fete at Brook House. Frank & Jack arrive.
" 9 Coronation postponed. 27th Sir Charles Seely to luncheon.
Electric lighting at Brook House.
Birdie & Leslie. May. Joan & J Valerie.
Oct. 6 To Guildford, to see W. Gillett. "The Lion" Expensive.
Oct 30 Fan to London for a week. Self & [illegible] for 31st.
Dec 21 Sir Charles, Col Dalbiac, Major Seely & families.
Jessie with us for Christmas. Dec 30 Lifeboat supper

accompaniments on the pianoforte.

While the Rev. Morris' diary confines itself to dates and facts, we learn that Winston Churchill visited Brook at least three times between 1903 and 1907, that electric lighting was installed at Brooke House in 1902 and that his bees died in the same year as Queen Victoria (and have an equal mention in his journal). We also hear that in March 1895, the *Noordstar*, a brigantine bound from Venezuela to Hamburg, came ashore at Hanover Point. A ring-tailed monkey miraculously escaped drowning by floating ashore in a sack and the Rector's wife took it in. Examples of the kinds of entertainments at the time include:

The Annual Harvest Festival was held on Thursday, September 16th 1886 at 8.30 am. Holy Communion and 3 o'clock Festival Evensong. Grapes were sent to the inmates of the Hospital and workhouse. Tea and amusements were at the Rectory after. The party broke up at 10.30pm.

**January 1st 1898 - Lantern slide show**
An entertainment arranged by the Rector and Mrs Morris in the Parish Room for children of the village. A series of fine lantern slides illustrating the story of 'Alice in Wonderland' from the original pictures by Tenniel, caused much delight and various other humorous pictures followed.

**4th August 1900 - Brook Church choir outing**
The Church choir made a very enjoyable excursion to Sandown and Shanklin. The day was perfect, and the drive by way of Shorwell and Godshill in a four horse brake, was much appreciated. The Rector and Mrs Morris were of the party which numbered twenty in all. A capital dinner at Seagrove, lessons in diving from the pier, wanderings by shore and cliff to leafy Shanklin, and a glorious drive home after tea made a programme not soon to be forgotten.

**Rev. Shaw (1909 - 1930).** Although vicar for 21 years, the only record we have found of the Rev. Shaw is the glimpse of him in the photograph at the foot of this page.

The **Rev. Winser (1930 - 1942)** is remembered for his love of cricket, even his sermons had a cricketing theme. He lived in the Rectory with his wife and daughter Mary. He could be seen walking around the village with a shepherd's crook and Audrey Rann (Barnes) recalls that: *The Rev Winser was known not to like children even though he had children of his own. On one occasion he threw a Bible at a boy.* This may or may not link with Ron Emmett's memory from the same time: *Mr Winser was keen on cricket and he tried to get us youngsters keen on cricket, but without much success.*

The **Rev. Kirkbride (1942 - 1949)** was appointed next. He came from Canada and was Rector for a comparatively short time. He, too, liked cricket. He did like children, however, and particularly encouraged them in gardening. Audrey Rann remembers: *Rev. Kirkbride, put me on the road to Christianity, which, like my love of gardening, has been with me all my life.*

After this came **Rev. Appleton** (1949 - 1953). He had already retired and was 'priest in charge.' He was everyone's favourite. His family lived at Buddlebrook, Brighstone and he later lived at The Lodge in Brightone until he died in 1963. Supplies were short after the war and his great nephew remembers as a child, *'being very impressed by a device which Fred and his elderly sisters had for splitting matches lengthwise - so one match became two! Fred had the room at the top of the house and he used to sit there with his telescope watching the ships coming up to the Solent entrance. We used to attend the church where he conducted services, even though he was profoundly deaf. The congregation would be in one part of the service and Fred, quite oblivious to this, would be in another!*

Rev. Frederick Appleton (1949-1953)

Rev.Shaw (1909-1930) leads the mourners up to Brook Church at the funeral of the second Sir Charles Seely in 1926.

The **Rev. Robert Bowyer (1953 - 1978)** is remembered with great fondness by many who lived in the area when he was vicar of Brook with Mottistone. He came to the Island from Derby with his wife Elisabeth and in those days the Rectory was a wing of Mottistone Manor (see the article he wrote for a Derby newspaper, right). The Bowyers' arrival is remembered by Robin Shepheard (Newbery) sixty years later: *When I was young, the Rev Appleton was the vicar and on his retirement a young "with it" vicar took over. The Rev Bowyer was modern, much to the annoyance of some of the older parishioners, as he changed many staid traditions, but boy was he good! He encouraged families to come back to the church and his sermons were always interesting, seldom boring.* As well as giving memorable sermons, Robert Bowyer was a keen writer, teacher and amateur artist. His wife, Elisabeth, also painted and wrote poetry. Erica Browitt (Newbery) recalls: *There was a portable stage in the Seely Hall and Mrs Bowyer tried her hardest to turn us into actors - without much success! She did, however, manage to produce a highly successful passion play which she had written. It took place at Mottistone in the village, in the Manor grounds and in the Church and almost everyone in Brook and 'Mott' had a part to play. She was a forceful lady and I expect most people would have found it difficult to refuse to take part!* Ann Male (Hailey) recalls the fun involved: *We went carol singing around the village each Christmas with the rector and lots of other people, it was great as we were invited into big houses - we had mince pies and nibbles and the adults had an alcoholic drink or two.*

*The Rev Bowyer was modern, much to the annoyance of some of the older parishioners, as he changed many staid traditions, but boy was he good!*

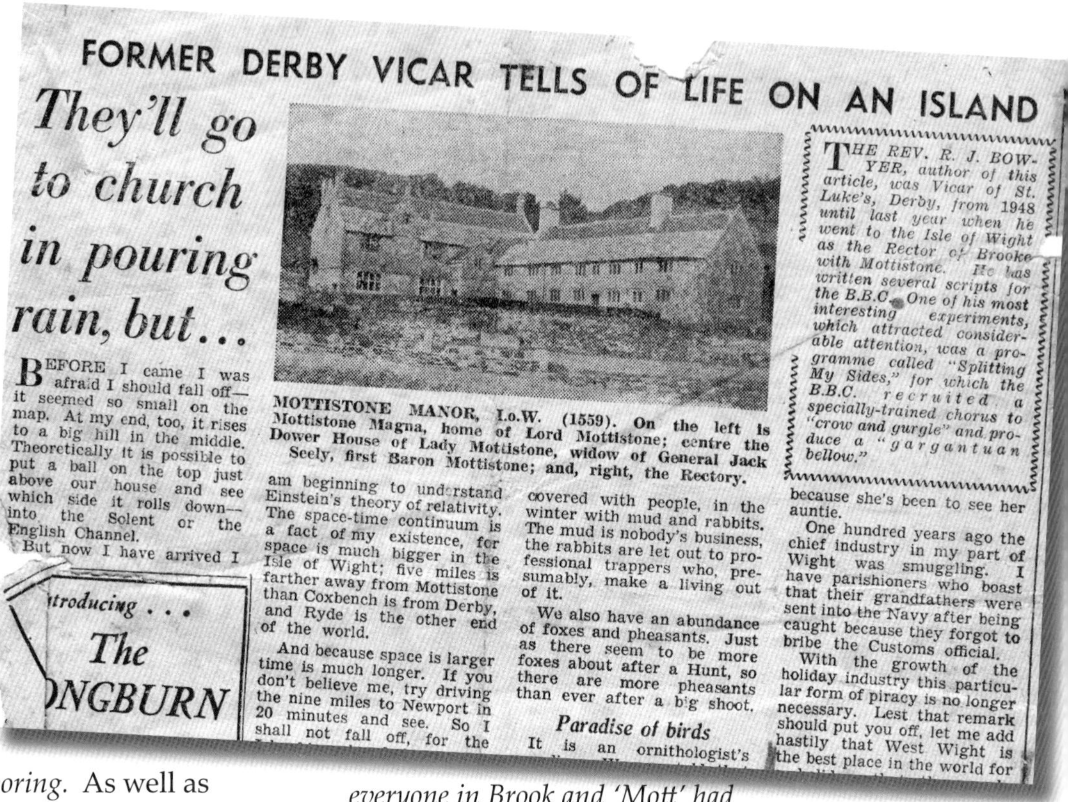

FORMER DERBY VICAR TELLS OF LIFE ON AN ISLAND

*They'll go to church in pouring rain, but...*

BEFORE I came I was afraid I should fall off—it seemed so small on the map. At my end, too, it rises to a big hill in the middle. Theoretically it is possible to put a ball on the top just above our house and see which side it rolls down—into the Solent or the English Channel.

But now I have arrived I am beginning to understand Einstein's theory of relativity. The space-time continuum is a fact of my existence, for space is much bigger in the Isle of Wight; five miles is farther away from Mottistone than Coxbench is from Derby, and Ryde is the other end of the world.

And because space is larger time is much longer. If you don't believe me, try driving the nine miles to Newport in 20 minutes and see. So I shall not fall off, for the

**MOTTISTONE MANOR, I.o.W. (1559). On the left is Mottistone Magna, home of Lord Mottistone; centre the Dower House of Lady Mottistone, widow of General Jack Seely, first Baron Mottistone; and, right, the Rectory.**

covered with people, in the winter with mud and rabbits. The mud is nobody's business, the rabbits are let out to professional trappers who, presumably, make a living out of it.

We also have an abundance of foxes and pheasants. Just as there seem to be more foxes about after a Hunt, so there are more pheasants than ever after a big shoot.

*Paradise of birds*

It is an ornithologist's

*THE REV. R. J. BOWYER, author of this article, was Vicar of St. Luke's, Derby, from 1948 until last year when he went to the Isle of Wight as the Rector of Brooke with Mottistone. He has written several scripts for the B.B.C. One of his most interesting experiments, which attracted considerable attention, was a programme called "Splitting My Sides," for which the B.B.C. recruited a specially-trained chorus to "crow and gurgle" and produce a "gargantuan bellow."*

because she's been to see her auntie.

One hundred years ago the chief industry in my part of Wight was smuggling. I have parishioners who boast that their grandfathers were sent into the Navy after being caught because they forgot to bribe the Customs official.

With the growth of the holiday industry this particular form of piracy is no longer necessary. Lest that remark should put you off, let me add hastily that West Wight is the best place in the world for

*...troducing . . .*

*The ...NGBURN*

It is perhaps notable that at Robert Bowyer's funeral in Mottistone Church there were a number of women who, when young mothers in the area, had been tutored by him to take English Literature A-Level and without his support would not have gone on to higher education. With a group of friends, including Jack and Johanna Jones, Robert and Elisabeth Bowyer were the founding members of the Island's cultural lifeline, the Quay Arts Centre. Robert was also a founder member of the Apollo Theatre and drama critic for the IOW County Press. Erica Browitt (Newbery) remembers: *When Reverend Bowyer became our Rector, he set up a youth-cum-social club which met once a week in the Seely Hall. This was a big leap forward for the young people and for some of the adults too, who came along to play billiards and table-tennis.John Betjeman, a close friend of the Bowyers, made several visits and*

Above: Rev. Robert Bowyer, christening Philip Mears, Brook Church 1970.

*found 'sheer delight' in the two villages. He loved Mottistone Church.* In 1970, after nearly 20 years as Rector of Brook and Mottistone, Robert Bowyer was asked to be 'vicar' to the Isle of Wight Pop Festival at Afton. He put his heart and soul into helping many young people left worse for wear and penniless after the event. He even married two 'hippies' in Mottistone Church - again, much to the astonishment and displeasure of some of the older members of the congregation. It is hard, today, to understand the change Robert represented from previous village vicars. The Bowyers welcomed foreign students to the Rectory each summer, they enjoyed parties and, more scandalously, in their retirement, hosted life drawing classes (see *The Sunday People*, above). The affection felt by many for the Bowyers was mutual and on their retirement they settled in a flat in part of Brook House where they read, painted and brought the sunken garden back to its former glory. As President of the Tennyson Society Robert attended one of their events the evening before he died, peacefully in his armchair at home.

SUNDAY PEOPLE, September 30, 1979 19

# PARSON PAINTS A NUDE

## It's just heavenly, he says

THE REV. Robert Bowyer would be delighted if any shapely young ladies would care to pop around to his home to take off their clothes.

He will pay £6 if they will stay that way for an hour and a half.

And while he eyes the form of things bright and beautiful, his wife will pop on the kettle for a cuppa.

"We even have a gas fire to keep them warm," said Mr. Bower, 65-year-old retired rector of Mottistone, Isle of Wight.

His wife, Elizabeth, added: "We really enjoy our little sessions. "They've brought a whole new depth to our lives."

For Mr. Bowyer has a new hobby . . . painting.

"It's meant a new lease of life for me and Elizabeth," he said.

"I can't think why we didn't start doing this before. I'm having a marvellous time."

The models seem to enjoy it, too—although Mr. Bowyer says he cannot find enough of them.

Carmel Rooney, who has had £24 worth of posing sessions with the Bowyers, said: "It makes a change to model for a Parson. He's a real gent.

Does he have any anxieties about his hobby? Certainly not.

"The human form is a thing of beauty," he said.

The Rev. Robert Bowyer, a dab hand with nudes, and model Carmel Rooney, as nature intended. "He's a gent," she says.

## DRUMMING UP A SCARE

POLICE and firemen sealed off a council dump during an atom scare.

It was like a scene from a space film as white-coated men with geiger counters examined a mystery canister.

The drama began when a night watchman spotted the drum marked "dangerous, radioactive" on a tip at Slough, Berks.

Scientists carefully lifted the canister into a special van and drove it back to the atomic research station at Harwell for closer examination.

Then the mystery was solved—it WAS from a space film. The canister was a left-over prop from the TV series Space 1999 filmed at near-by Pine-

WOMAN SENSE

LEFT-OVER paint should keep better if you seal the surface of the paint in the tin with foil before

A collage celebrating the inauguration of the new Millennium bell at a family service on April 18th 1999. It features the Rev. Tim Eady (1991 - 2008) with Mrs Barbara Heal (Hookey) on the left, Thomas and Patrick Seely trying out the bell and Erica Browitt (Newbery) at the organ.

# Rectors of Brook

The church registers escaped the fire and are complete from 1653. The list of incumbents goes back, with some gaps, to 1297:

| | | | |
|---|---|---|---|
| 1297 | William | | |
| 1305 | Gulielmus de Compton | | |
| 1320 | Johannes Lodecote | | |
| 1350 | Robertus de Eversden | 1638 | Joannes Percival |
| 1351 | Johannes de Middleton | 1643 | John Barnard |
| 1356 | William Whytheres | 1647 | John Grizlie |
| 1362 | Richardus Rouz | 1650 | Daniel Rolls |
| 1362 | Joannes Symond | 1657 | Joshua Tomkins |
| 1376 | Nicholas Ellyot | 1675 | Joannes Ellis |
| 1382 | Thomas Milton | 1694 | Daniel Dickenson |
| 1386 | Willielmus Urry | 1701 | Joseph Creffield |
| 1394 | Johannes Bennet | 1728 | John Woodford |
| 1418 | Joannes Ledys | 1760 | William Gother |
| 1425 | Robertus Knight | 1766 | Robert Gibbs |
| 1449 | Richard Canon | 1797 | Thomas Bowerman |
| 1450 | Willielmus Newport | 1833 | Collingwood F. Fenwick |
| *Intermission of 66 years* | | 1856 | John Pellow Gaze |
| 1525 | Willielmus Botyll | 1892 | Robert Leslie Morris |
| 1529 | Joannes Bust | 1909 | Courtney Arthur Shaw |
| 1538 | Robertus Dixon | 1930 | Arthur A. P. Winser |
| 1539 | Richardus Ellyot | 1942 | Thomas Kirkbride |
| *Intermission of 21 years* | | 1949 | Frederick Appleton (priest in charge) |
| 1586 | Robert Birch (curate in charge) | 1953 | Robert Joselyn Bowyer |
| | | | Gordon Broom |
| 1586 | William Hayes (curate in charge) | 1980 | Stephen Palmer |
| *Hayes was ejected the same year and* | | 1992 | Tim Eady |
| *the parish annexed to Freshwater.* | | 2008 | Malcolm Williams |

# The Church of St Peter and St Paul Mottistone

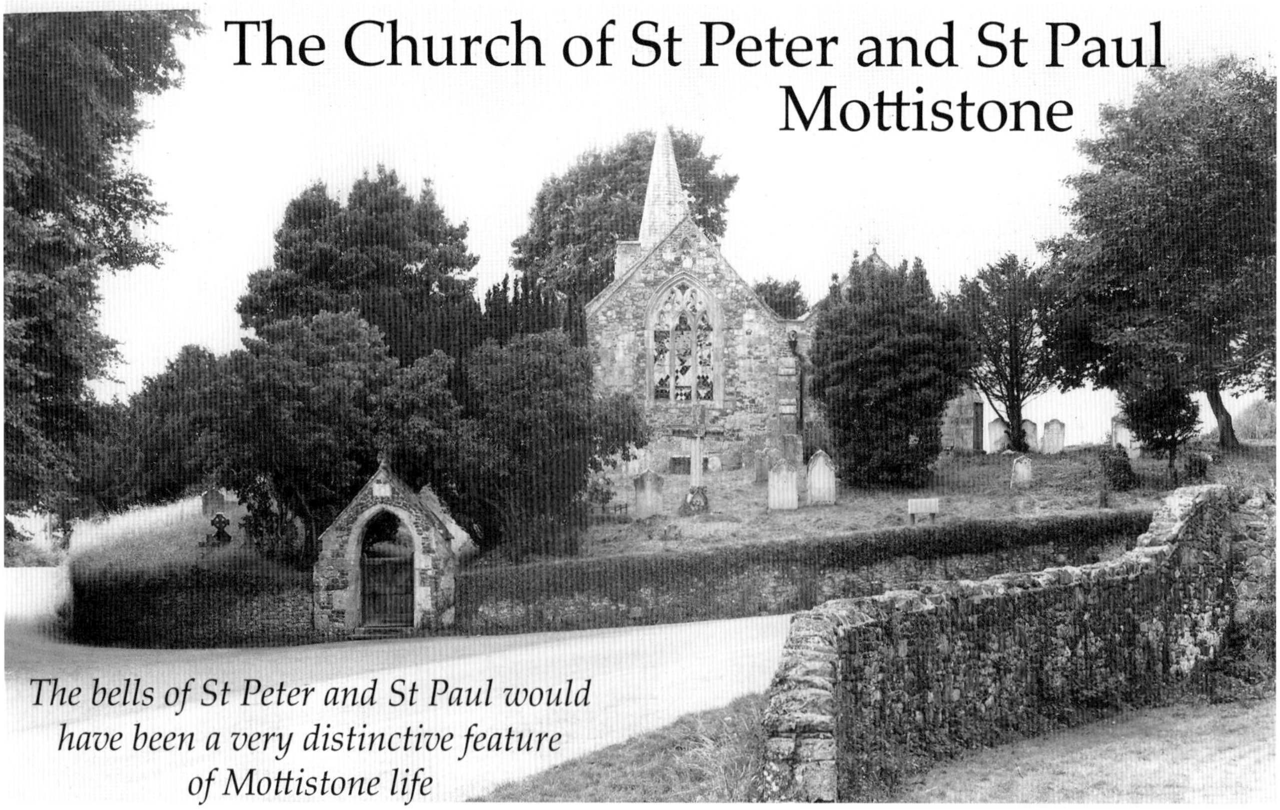

*The bells of St Peter and St Paul would have been a very distinctive feature of Mottistone life*

The Church of St Peter and St Paul dates from the 12th century. It was a private chapel to the Manor and a 'daughter' to the church of Calbourne. The church stood within the manor grounds with the public highway curving to the west of the church where the lane is today. It was only in 1846 that the road was re-routed to the north of the Church. The Chekes were one of

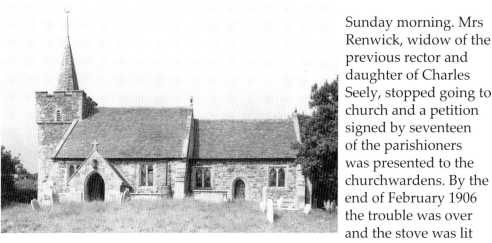

several great families to own Mottistone Manor and took possession in the mid-14th century. On the north side of the chancel is the manorial chapel, known as the Cheke chapel, originally built by Robert Cheke during the 15th century when the Church was restored. Over the years there have been many alterations and very little of the original medieval church still remains. The nave was rebuilt and the tower added in the 15th century. The tower is built of small slate-like stones found on the beach nearby. In 1553 it is recorded that there were three bells in the tower, plus the sanctus bell which would have been rung at the moment of the consecration in mass.  Now there is only one bell dated 1664. The bells of St Peter and  St Paul would have been a very distinctive feature of Mottistone life, calling the parish to church, giving news of joy and sorrow and, most importantly, warning the village of possible invasion. The bells were also rung when a parishioner was on the point of death, so that those who heard it might offer prayers. The tolling for a man's funeral was three bells thrice repeated, for a woman, two bells thrice repeated and for a child one toll thrice repeated. As with a number of churches on the south coast of the Island the larger tomb in the churchyard was a convenient place to stash smuggled tubs. When the chancel roof was repaired it was lined with cedar wood salvaged from the wreck of the Cedrine in 1862. The Hookey family's blacksmith mark of two crossed pipes can still just be seen in the ironwork on the gates. In 1870 heating was added in the form of a coal stove. In 1906 a village row erupted when the stove was no longer lit on Saturday but early on Sunday morning. Mrs Renwick, widow of the previous rector and daughter of Charles Seely, stopped going to church and a petition signed by seventeen of the parishioners was presented to the churchwardens. By the end of February 1906 the trouble was over and the stove was lit on Saturdays once more. Church lighting presented a problem and it was not until the 1850s that 'candles for lighting the church' feature in the churchwardens' accounts. The church is still lit by candles at evensong and at the Christmas midnight service when the soft glow of nearly 100 candles is most beautiful. In 1916 the church interior was altered to make Seely family pews in the Cheke chapel. The little chamber organ was built by George England in 1770 but was, interestingly, not installed until 1957.  However, an organ is recorded in the Cheke chapel in 1849. Previously an orchestral group must have provided the music as the church purchased cello strings in 1843 and in 1845 a new clarinet for six shillings. Miss Hollis, the school headmistress, until 1909, was church organist for many years. Avice Mariner (French) recalls the challenge of playing the organ at Mottistone in the 1950s: *I had to pump with one foot and play at the same time. This took some getting used to, as concentration was required for both hands and foot. Later, the organ was made electric which made playing easier. I used to struggle through services and disliked playing for weddings and funerals. I remember one of the services was recorded on the radio, but someone else was invited to play for this!*

*In 1906 a village row erupted when the stove was no longer lit on Saturday but early on Sunday morning.*

Drawing of Mottistone Church. the view from the north-west in 1891.

# Methodist Chapel

*When the foundation stone was laid in 1848 people came from all over the Island...*

The Bible Christians commenced preaching at Brook in 1835. Services were held fortnightly on Sunday evenings in barns and members' houses. There were clearly concerns about Brook and the following account was used to prove how necessary the preaching of the gospel was at this time. A Brook minister was said to be:

> very anxious to keep the young men out of mischief after church service and, in order to accomplish this, he would get them together at all kinds of sport – trap, bat, cock-fighting etc. – and so enamoured was he with this kind of sport, that on one occasion, becoming a little drowsy in church, he so far forgot himself as to be thinking more about cocks than aught else, he cried out, 'Half-a-crown for the white one'!
> *A History of the Bible Christian Churches on the Isle of Wight*, Rev J Woolcock 1897.

During the pastorate of Rev. James Way, we hear that the Bible Christian services were held in the house of Farmer Hart. The first enrolled member was George Hendy and the first class leader was George Whitmore. Despite opposition to their meetings from those who looked down on non-conformists, Farmer Hart gave the Bible Christians a plot of land 23 by 31 feet which formed part of a field called Sheepwash in the Parish of Brook. The chapel was built in 1848. When the foundation stone was laid, we hear that people came from all over the Island and about two hundred people took tea in the Old Malt House (unknown today). Many farmers, even though not connected with 'the little cause', helped with building materials and by the time the Chapel was opened only about £40 was owing. This debt was soon 'discharged by the generosity of friends of the Chapel.'

In the 1890s we hear that the minister was Josiah Datsun, who, in 1898 gave a talk on *Radical Diseases Require Radical Remedies* and *Big Doors Turn on Small Hinges*. Miss H. Newbery presided at the harmonium. In 1870 the Yarmouth Circuit was formed, which included Brook. The circuit held quarterly meetings with each chapel taking turns to host the occasion. Any alteration in Bible Christian members was recorded under one of the following headings: *New members, Removals, Deaths, Emigration, Backsliders,* and finally, *Backsliders through drink.*

In *Forever England* (1932), Jack Seely looks back a hundred years to 1832: *The life of a 'Chapel man' was incredibly hard in those days; he was regarded by most of his neighbours as a pariah...* He describes with admiration a man who was: *born in an inland village where the clergyman was a drunkard and a wastrel, and who, with his friends had 'out of their meagre earnings, raised enough money to build a small chapel, where, as they phrased it, 'the simple words of Christ should be read each Sunday'. He had then lost his job as a weaver and had had to move away, but every Sunday morning, winter or summer, rain or shine, he walked to and from his chapel 16 miles away.* At the end of this story, Jack Seely shows his disgust at the bitter differences between Church and Chapel at the time (1830s): *though his conduct compelled admiration, he was never quite forgiven for being a 'Chapel man.'* In 1907 the Bible Christians joined with the United Methodists and in 1932 they were known simply as Methodists. David Hollis remembers in the 1930s: *the Chapel was in full sway then. The Seelys gave a piece of land for the preacher to park his horse by the Chapel. There was Lance Barnes (2 Old Myrtle Cottage), he was one of the mainstays. I remember going with father to a Harvest Festival service. It was chockablock with people, they raised the roof when they sang.*

As described in the WI Scrapbook (1958): *The interior of the Chapel is fitted with part pews and open seats to seat about one hundred persons.* In 1959 the Rt Hon Hugh Seely, Baron Sherwood of Calverton, gifted a parcel of land on the north-east side of the Methodist Chapel for the preacher's car. Maps show that a lodge for the back drive to Brooke House had previously stood there. The last service was held in 1998 and the Chapel was sold. Sadly in 2001 the Chapel was demolished, to no-one's advantage, as part of a planning application.

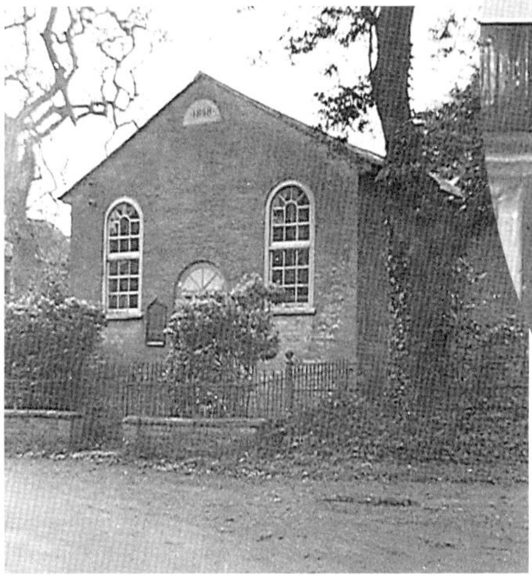

The Chapel at the turn of the 21st century.

The Methodist Chapel in Brook in the 1950s.

**Chapel Trustees, March 1848:**

| **Name** | **Occupation** | **Origin** |
|---|---|---|
| Henry Hart | Cordwainer | Brook |
| Barnabus Grove | Carpenter | Brook |
| Isaac Lowe | Blacksmith | Brook |
| Edward Ward | Yeoman | Shalfleet |
| James Guttridge | Labourer | Shalfleet |
| George Hendy | Labourer | Mottistone |
| Peter Plumbley | Labourer | Mottistone |
| Mark Fallick | Labourer | Mottistone |
| Andrew Jackman | Bricklayer | Brixton |
| Charles Jackman | Bricklayer | Brixton |

Isle of Wight County Press, 5 April 1998:

*It has been reported that Brook Methodist Chapel is to close, the last service will be on Sunday at 3pm conducted by Mr Keith Winn, Superintendent Minister of the West Wight Circuit. The chapel has been standing for 150 years but the maintenance of the building has become too much of a burden for the small congregation. Mrs Doris Barton has been worshipping in the chapel since her childhood and has recently carried most of the responsibility for keeping it going. Another member is Mrs Rosa Rushin, whose late husband did much dedicated work to maintain the interior of the building.*

# The flying-boat crash at Chessell, 1957

At the time it was the second worst air crash there had been in the United Kingdom yet until recently there was no local memorial to the 43 people who lost their lives. In 2007 a 50th anniversary service was organised by Nick and Lou Dorley-Brown and in 2008 a permanent memorial was dedicated at St Mary's Church, Brook. Conducted by the Archdeacon of the Isle of Wight, Caroline Baston, the services were attended by relatives of the deceased, police officers, firemen, casualty staff, local rescuers and colleagues of the crew.

On the 15th November 1957 the Solent flying boat, *Sydney*, owned by Aquila Airways and bound for Madeira via Lisbon took off from Southampton Water at 10.46 pm. Ten minutes into the flight the crew reported trouble with the engine and in its attempt to return to base it crashed into the chalk pit at Shalcombe and burst into flames. Local farmer Mr Harry Kitson heard the plane roar low overhead, then he heard a loud bang. He said he pulled on his boots and ran out of the house half-clothed. Quick as he was, Mr Bert Tyrell, a local shepherd, was already on the scene getting people away from the blaze which he described as, 'like a volcano.' Harry helped Bert carry away the living and dead on sheep hurdles. By chance a party of junior NCOs were on a night exercise a few hundred yards away and were quickly on the scene. Ambulances took the fifteen survivors to St Mary's and Fairlee hospitals. Soldiers from Golden Hill Fort, Freshwater, were sent to help and used their greatcoats and tunics as padding for the hurdles and for covering the injured. The Berryman family whose land the plane crashed on

said they would never forget that night and were thankful that they stayed up later than usual as, 'if our lights had not been on, it might have been a different story and the plane might have come down on the farmhouse. The Berryman's kitchen was used as an emergency casualty ward. A Newport police officer descried the scene: *In a big area of blasted trees, some still alight, all I could recognise of the plane was the tail standing up over the flames.* J B Priestley and friends were returning home to Brook Hill House after an evening out with friends in Freshwater when they heard the plane and then the crash and saw a red glow in the sky. When they reached the scene, the wreckage was blazing furiously with flames shooting high into the air. The Reverend Bowyer who was with J B Priestley, described how he knelt and prayed for the dead and injured in the light of the blazing aircraft. Tom Priestley remembers how it brought back Jack Priestley's memories of World War One when there was nothing to ease people's pain and that he was horrified that there was no morphine on hand. Few survived, of the fifty passengers and eight crew, all the crew died and thirty-five of the passengers, amongst whom were three honeymoon couples. Many victims could only be identified by their jewellery and other personal items. Those who did miraculously survive told their horrific story. Two of the survivors described the short flight was like being on a 'big dipper'. 'We dropped and climbed throughout the short journey.' One survivor said, 'the whole flight was awful.' The crash happened just above the waterworks at Chessell and the supply to Brook and local houses was poisoned for two years by the kerosene that had seeped into the ground. The cause of the crash was later found to be engine failure thought to be due to a faulty fuel cut-off switch.

SIX BODIES LIE COVERED ON STRETCHERS. BEHIND, SEARCHERS PICK THROUGH THE BURNT-OUT WRECKAGE IN WHICH 43 PEOPLE DIED

# The Seely family

## at Brook and Mottistone

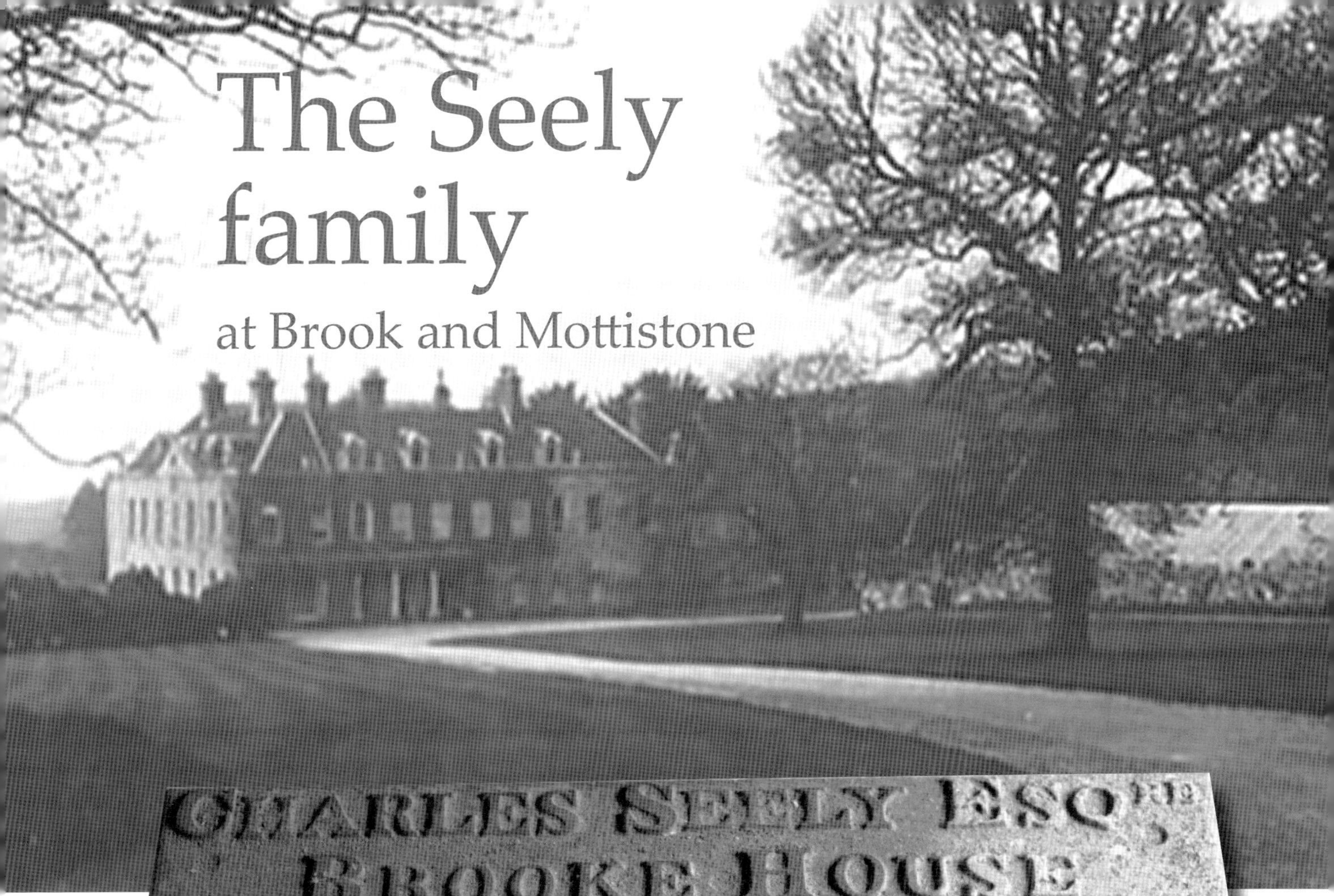

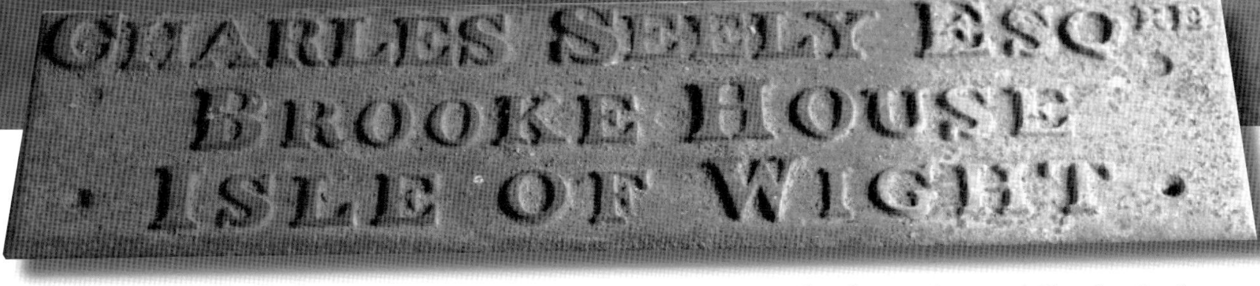


*From the time that they came to Brook in 1857, it is impossible to separate the history of the village from that of the Seely family.*

Born in 1803 of respectable but modest Lincolnshire millers, by the time of his death, in 1887, **Charles Seely** was one of the largest landowners in the country. He owned Sherwood Lodge with coalfields in Nottinghamshire, 1 Carlton House Terrace in London and a substantial part of the West Wight. It was said that he could walk from Brook to Newport, Freshwater or Yarmouth without stepping off his own land. Charles suffered from TB when young and was sent to convalesce with an aunt on the Isle of Wight. The story has it that while walking on the downs above Mottistone, he made a mental note that once, (interestingly, not 'if') he'd made his fortune, he would buy all the land he could see from the downs to the sea. He never forgot his vow and in 1857, by the time he had bought Brooke House and a number of other properties in the area, he was 53 years old and the Liberal MP for Lincoln (he defended the aspirations of the Chartists in the House of Commons). The descendants of Charles Seely continue to have strong connections with Brook and Mottistone today, with ten of his great, great grandchildren having homes on what was once his land.

Charles Seely was described by his grandson, Jack Seely, as: *an austere and benevolent man, very small of stature with aquiline features and though he looked frail, had, in fact an iron constitution.*

At the age of 81 he would still ride around the Brooke estate on his pony for four or five hours at a stretch. Less complimentary was a political opponent, who in 1856 said of Charles Seely: *This eccentric little politician wearing the wonderful jack boots and inimitable hat, a cross between a brigand and an Italian organ-grinder.*

In 1831 Charles married Mary Hilton, the youngest daughter of Jonathan Hilton of Newcastle-upon-Tyne. When they bought Brooke House in 1857 (the initial auction was in 1855), they enlarged the house and quickly became part of Island life and society. It is interesting to note that, despite being based in and coming from Nottingham, and with all their business and political interests on the mainland, the family developed a strong affection for the Isle of Wight with each of their three daughters marrying and settling in the West Wight. In 1860 Mary Seely married Reverend Thomas Renwick, Rector of Mottistone and Vicar of Shorwell. In 1861 Frances Seely married Benjamin Cotton, gentleman farmer of Afton Manor who was a patron of the painter George Moreland and is mentioned in Emily Tennyson's diary as 'a country squire of the old stamp.' Charles and Mary Seely's third daughter, Jane Anne (Annie), married Lt. Colonel Harry Gore Browne who received a V.C. for conspicuous bravery during the seige of Lucknow in 1857 and they settled at Pitt Place, Mottistone.

In many ways the history of the Seely family mirrors that of the country as a whole in the late 18th and early 19th centuries when scientific and technological developments were changing the face of the social and political landscape. It is said that in the 1840s Charles Seely's mother bought him a field to grow more wheat and that the field was soon found to be over a rich seam of coal on the edge of the Nottinghamshire coal fields. This may belie, however, the astute businessman that Charles Seely had become. His fortune was substantially made by his contract with the Royal Navy for pig iron, which was used in the 19th century as ballast for ships. It was a contract he famously held the government to long after the introduction of iron-clad ships which did not need such ballast. He was put up for Parliament as MP for Lincoln in 1847 and elected but later accused by his rivals of vote-rigging and lost his seat. His defence was that 'treating' was the custom in Lincoln. He was finally elected MP for Lincoln in 1861 and

*It was said of Charles Seely that he could walk from Brook to Newport, Freshwater or Yarmouth without stepping off his own land.*

Mary and Charles Seely. In *Adventure* (1930) Jack Seely wrote of his grandmother: *The people of Brooke loved her and talk of her to this day. She christened the first lifeboat on our coast.*

The other Seely residences, left: Sherwood Lodge, Nottinghamshire; below: Carlton House Terrace, on the Mall, London.

remained an MP until 1885, becoming 'father of the House.' His most significant work in the Commons was while Chair of the Committee on Admiralty Reform in 1868. His speeches show him as a thorn in the side of the Admiralty pointing out inefficiencies and mis-management with a businessman's attention to detail. In 1877, during a House of Commons debate on farmers' duty to give notice of diseased cattle, he says in an understatement, 'I happen to be the owner of a few cows.' As a Liberal M.P. Charles Seely supported the unification of Italy and invited General Giuseppe Garibaldi to stay at Brooke House in 1864 when it was thought he was in danger of being mobbed by adoring crowds in London. Both Charles and Mary Seely were entranced by General Garibaldi and wrote very affectionate letters to him (see *A King, a Queen,* etc.). The impact Garibaldi had on the populace worried Queen Victoria greatly and she was most displeased that Charles Seely did not urge Garibaldi to leave the country when she requested it.

The Seelys brought employment and the outside world to Brook and Mottistone. We see from the census that Harriet Marriott, for example, who

The staff of Brooke House in the late nineteenth century. Polly (Merry) Hookey of Downton Farm, Brook, is seated second from left, her husband to be, Arthur Cole from Lincolnshire, is standing to the left of her. The famous Mr Tribbick, gardener, must be here as well as the Linggards, the butler and cook.

Charles Seely in old age looking as upright as when he was young. Above: a cartoon in Vanity Fair 1878, captioned simply, 'Pigs' in reference to the Seely contract to sell pig iron to the government as ballast.

married the blacksmith, James Hookey, was born in Lincolshire.
Charles Seely was particularly committed to the education of the working man and used some of his wealth to establish the Isle of Wight Library Service, until recently The County Seely Library, and the Technical Institute. He also converted a barn into the village school at Hulverstone and funded its teacher. Perhaps he is best remembered for the part he played in setting up the first lifeboat station in Brooke and contributing to those at Brighstone and Atherfield. Charles Seely's son, who later became **Sir Charles Seely (1833-1915)**, was also a Liberal MP and continued his father's commitment to improving the lives of working people. Jack Seely's description of his father perhaps says more about himself: *My father was a Liberal Member of the House of Commons for 25 years. He was an enthusiastic volunteer, for twenty years he commanded the Robin Hoods of Nottingham. Almost my earliest recollection is seeing him ride away in uniform on an extremely good-looking bay thoroughbred.*
In 1857, about the time his parents came to Brook, Charles married Emily Evans, sister to Sir Francis Evans, MP for Southampton. Her youngest son, Jack Seely, recalled: *From her I inherited my love of music and the sea.* It was Sir Charles who designed and built the Reading Rooms for the men of Brook and Brighstone. He also funded the first 'free library' on the Isle of Wight, now Nodehill School. A plaque commemorates the laying of the foundation stone by his eldest daughter, Florence Seely,

*Charles Seely wanted, 'a library service... serving the whole Island, particularly those remote villages cut off in winter.'*

**WORKMEN'S SUPPER AT BROOKE HOUSE, 1888** IOW County Press

The extensive alterations at Brooke House, carried out by Mr James Denham, the well-known builder and contractor, of Freshwater, from the designs of Mr W T Stratton, architect, of Newport, are now completed, and Mr Seely, having personally inspected the work, has expressed himself entirely satisfied with the very efficient manner in which the improvements have been effected. On Friday evening, Mr Seely generously provided supper for all the workmen who have been engaged here, Mr and Mrs Linggard, the butler and cook of the mansion, carried out the arrangements in a way that left nothing to be desired. A bountiful repast was placed on the tables, to which ample justice was done by all present. About 70 sat down to supper, including the gardeners and other servants and friends. In addition to Mr Denham's employees, there was also present several from the firm of Messrs. Wood and Horspool, of Newport, who have had charge of the heating and sanitary arrangements. After supper pipes and tobacco were placed on the tables, with numerous bowls of punch and other beverages. Mr J Denham proposed the health of Mr Seely, the founder of the feast, and said it gave him great pleasure to be employed under so true and liberal a gentlemen. Mr Denham concluded by paying a tribute of respect to the memory of the late Mr Seely. The healths of Mrs Seely and family were next proposed and heartily responded to. Several capital songs were sung during the evening. Mr Linggard proposed the health of Mr W White, the foreman of the work. Mr White, in responding, spoke of the general good behaviour of all the men under him, and of their hearty co-operation, without which he could not possibly have completed the work in the time specified. The healths of Messrs. H and C Brown, of Dunsbury and Mottistone Farms were next proposed by Mr Linggard, who said how highly esteemed they were by the late Mr Seely. The healths of Mr Keely, coachman, and Mr Tribbick, gardener were also honoured, and the pleasant proceedings were continued till midnight, when the happy party separated with the singing of "God save the Queen," all being loud in their praises of the hospitable gentleman under whose roof they had spent so enjoyable an evening.

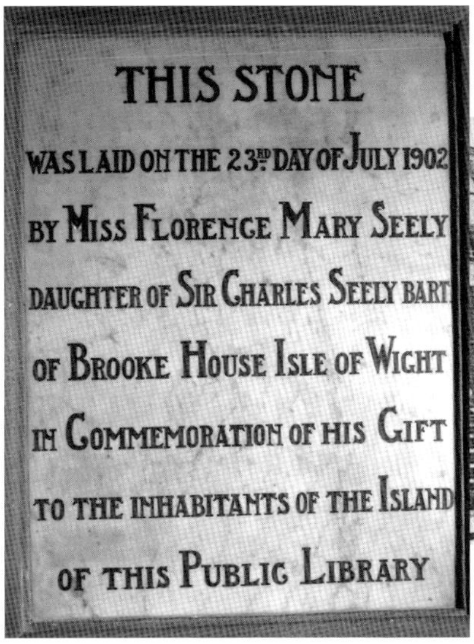


in 1902. Sir Charles funded the building and the books and designed lockable oak bookcases, some of which are still in use in village libraries today. In spite of his busy public life, Sir Charles was involved at every level of village life as chairman of the Seely Hall, the Lifeboat Committee, the Shipwrecked Sailors Fund and the Parish Council, to name a few. The village children will have been very aware of their benefactors as they provided the books and prizes for the school and in 1910 and 1911 the County Press records how at Christmas Miss Seely presented each child in the school and each member of the church choir with a white wool scarf. The Seely family had a tradition of hosting village events and providing harvest and lifeboat suppers as well as teas and games for the children of the village.

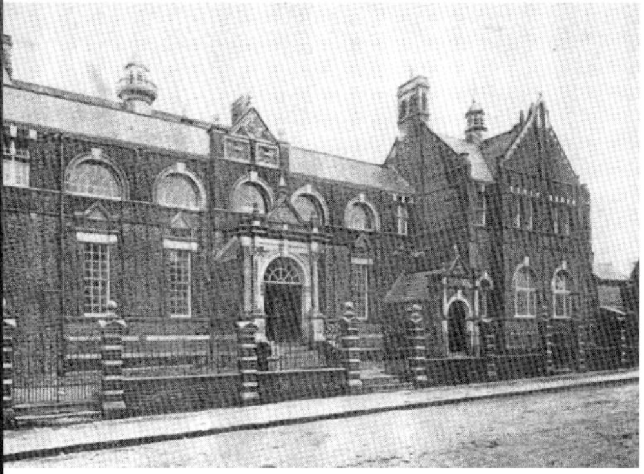

The first free Seely Library in Newport was built alongside the Technical Institute, now Nodehill School, and opened by Florence Seely in 1902.

**School treat**

About 90 children from Brook and Mottistone enjoyed an out of doors treat on Tuesday 30th August, in the beautiful gardens of Brooke House. The first part of the entertainment consisted of a sumptuous tea provided by the kindness of Miss Seely in Hulverstone School after which a march down to the park was followed by a long series of various sports. A special exhibition of the phonograph with songs and recitations caused much wonder and delight and a plentiful distribution of toys and buns completed the happiness of the young people.

Courtesy of *Isle of Wight County Press*

Sir Charles Seely (1833-1915).

The distinctively designed 'Seely cottages' which can be seen from West Wight to the centre of the Island, were built for the Estate workers. Sir Charles had running water put into all the labourers' cottages, a generous gesture in those days. He took the precaution, however, of putting the sink in a different place to the tap in case the villagers left the tap running. Sir Charles was a familiar figure to all in the area, striding over the Downs, followed by his groom, Henry Punch, who led a pony for Sir Charles to ride on up the steeper hills and carried a camp stool for him to sit on when he wished to enjoy the views. Widowed in 1894, Sir Charles spent an increasing amount of time at Brook supported by his elder daughter Florence (Florrie). In his later years he conceived the idea of building Brook Hill House both for the magnificent views and because he had bronchial trouble and was advised by the doctor to live higher up. The house was begun in 1910, from original drawings by architect Sir Aston Webb and follows many of the features of Dartmouth College. Sir Charles Seely died in April 1915, aged 84, just after Brook Hill was completed. When he died he left estate of £1,052,070 (equivalent to £493 million in 2007), making him one of the richest men in the country. Sir Charles had nine children, and, at the time of his death, over fifty grandchildren. The enormous fortune and estates dwindled over the next 40 years. The reasons for this are many: it was divided up among numerous children and grandchildren, some of whom were better at spending than

Pastel drawing of Daisy and Nancy, daughters of Charles and Emily Seely.

The audience at the Coronation festivities in the grounds of Brooke House in 1911.

The first motor car in Brook was owned by the Seely family. The chauffeur in the background looks like Essen (Sher'n) Downer. Above right: Anne (Nancy), one of the six daughters and three sons of Sir Charles Seely, in order of age: Charles, Florence, Daisy, Frank, Anne, Lillian, Jack, Sylvia and Mary.

The following story about Sir Charles appeared in the *Isle of Wight County Press* in 1889:

Portrait believed to be of Sir Charles Seely. It hung in the Hookeys' sitting room at Downton Farm and shows little evidence of the extremely wealthy man he had become.

Many years ago, a dear old friend, an artist, was making sketches of the coast of the Isle of Wight.Wishing to find his way to the shore at Brooke, he accosted a man whom he chanced to see before him closing a gate. The man was wearing a long and much-used mackintosh and slouched hat, and had a long hoe in his hand. Addressing him, the artist enquired the way to the shore at Brooke. The man replied 'I be going that way.' So they walked together, and coming to a field of fine wheat, the man stopped to look at it over the gate. My friend asked whose it was, and the man answered 'Oh, that belongs to the lord of the manor.' On asking whether there was a short cut across the fields to the seashore, the artist received the reply 'Why yes, only it would be trespassing, and the lord of the manor is sure to see us.' Not being a law breaker, my friend trudged along the road, stopping only to admire the sheep and the crops, all of which his companion informed him belonged to the lord of the manor. On arriving at a narrow road which turned to the left of the highway, the large old elm trees over-shadowing it with their branches, my friend's guide said it led to Brooke. Presently a fine old house became visible, standing in its park-like grounds, and the artist's question 'Who lives there?' and the reply came 'Oh, the lord of the manor.' 'But who is this lord of the manor?' inquired my friend, and his companion, turning and facing him, with body erect, left arm outstretched, and hoe in hand, said 'Why, I be the lord of the manor,' at the same time giving the artist a kindly grip of the hand and a hearty welcome to the hospitality of his home.

making money; external factors such as two world wars, increasing death duties, changes in energy needs and the nationalisation of the coal industry also took their toll. Sir Charles left the Brook estate to his youngest son, **General Jack Seely MP**, who was created Lord Mottistone in 1933. In 1895 Jack married Emily Crighton. They had seven children but sadly Emily (Nim) died in 1913, aged 42. As well as being a Liberal Member of Parliament from 1900 to 1922, Jack Seely was Secretary of State for War from 1912 to 1914. In 1917 he married widowed Evelyn Nicholson who had one son, John (later Sir John Nicholson, Lord Lieutenant of the Isle of Wight). During this time, Brooke House welcomed a number of politicians, including Winston Churchill and Lloyd George. The Astors and the Prince of Wales, later Edward VII, were regular visitors. In Cowes Week Queen Mary frequently visited the Seelys at Brooke House and later at Mottistone Manor while King George V was sailing (see *A King,*

Lloyd George visits the Seelys at Brooke. .House in October 1924.

Jack Seely, Lord Mottistone, as cox-swain in Brooke Lifeboat jersey. Jack walks out of the sea at at Brook during a lifeboat launch.

*a Queen,* etc.). Jack Seely's knowledge of Brook and Mottistone and those that lived there are threaded through the books he wrote to keep his family afloat. It is said that his proudest moment was the day he became a rowing member of the Brooke lifeboat crew. His descriptions of local events, people and places have been a rich resource for this local history. In *Galloper Jack,* Brough Scott describes an early memory of his grandfather and the tales he was told as a child:

He was just an old man in a dressing gown, one of those red and blue silk paisley things as I remember. He had a hook nose, a rheumy kindly eye and was sitting on a chair taking sips from an oxygen cylinder. He pointed to a black box on the wall and said 'that is called a Division Bell. When it rings we have to get up and rush across to the Houses of Parliament to vote.' It was 1947. Jack Seely was 79. I was only four. My grandfather didn't look like running very far.

He died later that year and, hard though I have tried, I cannot conjure up any other memories of the most flamboyantly heroic figure this country, let alone this family, ever housed. So on my mother's knee I was told tales beyond the wildest storybook imaginings. How her father had swum a rope out to a stricken ship on the Isle of Wight's stormy west coast when his local Brooke lifeboat could not be launched. How he sailed down to New Zealand a year later, and met a naked Maori princess out swimming with rather pleasant consequences. How he and my grandmother (not the aforementioned Princess) dined with Queen Victoria two days before he left for the Boer War with his white horse Maharajah now dyed brown for camouflage. How, after many amazing, bullet-ducking sagas, he came back two years later to discover he had been elected MP for the Isle of Wight by his wife going round in a horse and trap with a sign up saying 'Vote For Jack.' How his political career was locked onto that of his friend Winston Churchill who came down to Brooke to bully and inspire my mother and her sisters into building the biggest sandcastle ever. How Seely rose to Cabinet alongside Churchill but then, in the so-called Curragh Mutiny of 1914 became not the first, nor the last, Minister to crash over Ulster. How later that same year he and his famous horse Warrior were first off the boat to France and then survived the most astonishing front line adventures before both celebrated Christmas back at Brooke in 1918.

He may not have been a Prime Minister or Commander in Chief, but Seely was a hands-on witness to major moments in our history. He was also symbolic, not just of another age but of another set of values. *Galloper Jack,* Brough Scott, 2002.

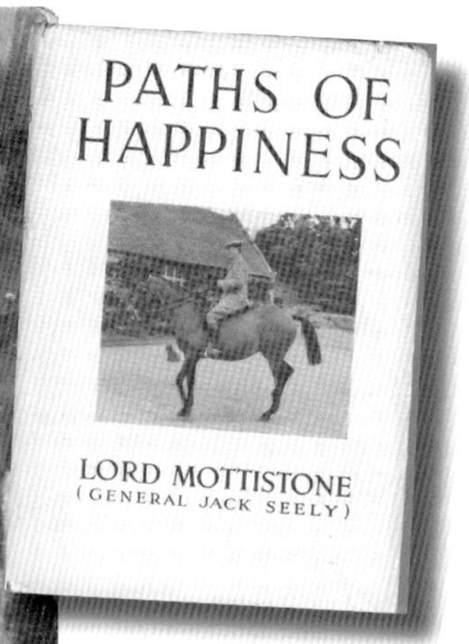


General Jack Seely and his daughter Kitty meet with the hunt outside Brooke House in the 1920s.

Nanny Williams with David and Louisa Seely in the donkey cart at Brooke in 1922.

Hon. David Seely's christening at Brook Church in 1922.

Louisa, Emily and David Seely with Nanny Williams outside Brooke House in 1922.

The staff of Brooke House in the early 1920s. Standing second left: Mrs Smith (cook); seated middle: Dorothy Smith; right: Doris Saunders.

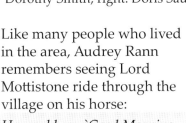

Irene Seely marries Mason Scott in Brook in June 1924. The bride and groom's path from the church was strewn with rose petals by children.

Like many people who lived in the area, Audrey Rann remembers seeing Lord Mottistone ride through the village on his horse:

*He would say `Good Morning Mrs. Barnes,' and bend down and shake hands with mother and others, and the old horse's head would come over the hedge of Bank Cottage. If Ken and I were out walking on Sundays, possibly having been to see Aunty Rose* (Ballard) *on Brook Green, we would see the Seely Family in their Rolls Royce going home from church and they often offered us a lift. There were seats which could be pulled down, facing those sitting on the back seats. We often had a lift in the car with them and when we got out they would give us 6d.*

Jack Seely and family on a ride above the cliffs at Brook in the 1920s.
Painted by Gilbert Halliday.

Evelyn, Lady Mottistone, JP, lived at Mottistone Manor until her death in 1976 and touched the lives of many who lived in Brook and Mottistone, especially the children. When Jack Seely moved with his family to Mottistone Manor in 1926, he sold Brooke House and Estate to his brother the second **Sir Charles Seely (1859-1926)**. In the same year Charles died unexpectedly and the Brooke Estate was inherited by his son **Hugh Seely (1898 - 1970)**. Hugh was the Joint Under-Secretary of State for Air for a substantial part of the Second World War (1941–45) and was created Baron Sherwood in 1941 (see picture in *Village trades and occupations*). Hughie (as he was called by his family) was a colourful character, who lived variously at Brook Hill House, The Red House and Gardener's Cottage (which he renamed Sherwood Lodge). He is remembered today mostly for his eccentricities and social life. David Hollis remembers tales of Edward, Prince of Wales, partying at Brook Hill during Cowes Week; although he tells us that the village girls who worked at the house would never speak about it. Hugh divided his time between London, Brook and his yacht in the south of France and is remembered arriving on the Yarmouth ferry in his Rolls Royce with his partner, or, as she was called in those days, his 'mistress', Kate Ranger. They wore matching red-lined cloaks and striped jerseys with *Lottie,* the name of his yacht, embroidered on them.

General Jack Seely and family at Mottistone Manor in about 1930. From left: Emily, Louisa, Kitty, Jack, John, Mason Scott, David, Irene, Evelyn Lady Mottistone, John Nicholson.

In 1965, in celebration of Nanny Williamson's 80th birthday, the Seely and Inglefield families gather at Mottistone Manor. Standing from left: Paul Paget; Brough Scott; Mabel Emmett; Charles Nicholson; May Newling; Janet Scott; Roddy Gow; Michael Gow; John Seely (2nd Lord Mottistone); Jenny Scott; xxx Inglefield; Kitty Haydon; xxx Inglefield; Irene Scott; Mason Scott (the younger); David Seely (4th Lord Mottistone); Patrick Seely (3rd Lord Mottistone); Emily Kindersley; Mason Scott (the elder); xxxx; xxxx; Maxwell Haydon. Seated from left: xxxx; Jane Gow; Belinda Inglefield; Mrs Inglefield; Katie Gow; Nanny Williams; Caroline Fletcher; Evelyn, Lady Mottistone; Jill Phillimore; Susanna Fletcher; Louisa Fletcher.

Shooting was his passion (in 1946 he bought James Purdey, the famous London gunmaker) and the rhodedendrons on Brook Hill were planted to provide good ground cover. Among those who came to Brook to shoot in the 1950s was Lord Boothby. Jane Cotton, who lived on the Estate, remembers being kept indoors when there were shooting parties, especially after the guests had had a generous liquid lunch. A poem *Heritage*, written by Elizabeth Bowyer, wife of the rector of Brook and Mottistone, mentions this 'eccentric peer' (see below). During World War II Brooke House was occupied by Canadian soldiers. The story has it that the house was later ruined when the top storey burned and collapsed. After the war it was converted into flats for the families of Estate workers and in 1957, exactly 100 years since Charles Seely first bought the house, the flats were sold by auction along with much of the Brooke Estate.

David Seely, 4th Lord Mottistone, (Lord Lieutenant of the Isle of Wight, 1985 - 1995). Here opening a Brook history exhibition in 1999.

The Hon Emily Kindersley (Seely), eldest daughter of General Jack Seely, who lived at Rose Cottage, Mottistone until she died in 1992. In 1918 she served as a VAD (Voluntary Aided Detachment) in Netley Hospital and throughout the Second World War. After the war she worked for the Red Cross and was awarded a special medal for devoted service. During the 1920s she worked as a secretary to her father, Jack Seely and under her helm, *Francesca,* the Seelys' Yarmouth One Design yacht, won a number of prizes. In 1937 she married her father's friend Lt. Col Kindersley and lived at Hamstead undertaking fund-raising for the roof of Shalfleet Church and Church Hall. She was elected as a County Councillor from 1956 to 1972, serving on both the Planning and Education Committees.

For a brief outline of the work of architect, John Seely, 2nd Lord Mottistone, see *A King, a Queen,* etc.

**HERITAGE**

Our village's elegant ruin
Was once owned by an eccentric Peer.
Navigating between four ladies
He would sometimes drop anchor here.

He attended church in his sneakers
And wrapped himself up in a shawl.
His rooms were all hot as a furnace
Although he could ride out a squall.

The War put a curb on his movements
But his place was let to the forces,
Who recovered their need for action
On finding Downs good for horses.

But alas, things became too festive:
Something set a chimney on fire.
It fell through the roof, but they all thought
It was safer not to enquire.

The War Office acknowledged the blame.
The Peer viewed the windfall with glee:
While battling head-on against fortune
Four ports proved too many by three.

But, while casting off moorings, the house
Had suffered from total neglect.
He found top floors ravaged by wood-worm
And damp when he came to inspect.

(A workman while testing the rafters
Fell down through the worm-eaten floor.
He fetched up, dazed, in the basement –
But otherwise much as before).

So he scooped out the middle but left
The south wing and fine north façade:
Cars now drive through the vanished front doors
To geranium tubs in the yard.

For the planned flats for workers misfired
(Their wives would not rise to the bait)
He auctioned them off to the public
Who set up a private estate.

Now, National Heritage while seeking
More 'listings' eyes us with favour –
But handed us all strict instructions
To follow their rules of behaviour.

Elizabeth Bowyer

# Brooke House

The key to Brooke House and the house in the early 1900s after extensive renovations were completed in 1888.

At the time of the Domesday Survey, Brooke was held in demesne by King William, having been forfeited by Roger, second Earl of Hereford, Lord of the Isle of Wight. During the reigns of Edward I, II and III, Brooke House was owned by the Glamorgan family. In the twelfth and thirteenth centuries it was held with Carisbrooke Castle by the Mackerel family then passing by the marriage of an heiress to the Glamorgans. John de Glamorgan was granted free warren in Brooke and Mottistone in 1326.

Hulverstone was held as a manor at the end of the thirteenth century by Robert de Glamorgan and John Paslew and by 1346 belonged entirely to William Paslew. John Roucle, Lord of Brooke, has acquired it before 1428, from which time it appears to have been merged in the manor of Brooke. On the death of Nicholas de Glamorgan without issue in 1362 the manor appears to have been divided among his sisters. The husband of one of these, Geoffrey Roucle, later called 'de la Broke', acquired, in addition to his wife's share, the shares of three of the other sisters and left this part of the estate to his son John, who was succeeded in 1450 by his son-in-law Thomas Bowerman.

In 1499 Henry VII was entertained by Thomas Bowerman and Joan his wife at Brooke House (see *Early History*). A descendant, William Bowerman, reunited the moieties of the manor by purchasing the share of the remaining Glamorgan heiress from her successors in 1566. Writing in the latter half of the eighteenth century Sir Richard Worsley observes, "the late William Bowerman rebuilt the manor house, which is pleasantly situated in the rich vale." At the beginning of the 18th century the manor house was rebuilt and continued in the direct line of this family until sold by William Bowerman to Henry Howe in 1792. In 1856 it was purchased from John and William Howe by Charles Seely, Esquire. When his son, later Sir Charles, inherited the house in 1887, he added a third storey for the children, with a sewing room, linen room, etc. At the top of the stairs on the landing there was a fine organ and the family and servants used to gather in the hallway below for a daily service. A travel guide of the early 20th century describes: *In this house ...the mantelpieces are particularly handsome, some being in inlaid marble. In the dining room is a beautiful black marble fireplace and a most decorative ceiling.* When Sir Charles died in 1915, Brooke House was unexpectedly bequeathed to his younger son, John Bernard Seely (Jack). Jack sold it to his brother Charles when he moved with his family to Mottistone Manor and in 1926 Brooke House was inherited by Charles' son, Hugh. During World War II the house was requisitioned by the War Office to house Canadian soldiers. After the war the house was converted into flats but today is again under one owner.

The lodge house at the top of Brooke House drive where Mr and Mrs Isaac Morey kept the gate for 35 years. The couple in this photograph are believed to be the Moreys. The writer of Isaac Morey's obituary in 1926 noted: *the somewhat pathetic coincidence that the esteemed lodge keeper at Brooke House, who had attained the great age of 93, should have passed away within an hour or two of the funeral of Sir Charles Seely.*

Mottistone Manor soon after it was renovated in the 1920s.

The present Mottistone Manor was built over a Saxon manor house. The east wing (on the right of the picture) dates from the 15th century and the great west wing, known as Magna, was built in the mid 16th century. In 1703, after a tremendous storm, one of the most severe storms known up to that time, the back of the house was buried by a huge landslip. The earth was left to lie almost up to the eaves making the west wing very dark and damp. For the next 223 years the house stood with the whole of the back buried in earth. As a farmhouse, the sunken garden became a farmyard and the various rooms became store rooms and dairies.

In 1861 the chain of events which eventually lead to the restoration of the house began when Charles Seely purchased the estate. The manor was lived in by tenant farmers until 1926. It was then that Jack Seely, persuaded by his friend the architect Edwin Lutyens, sold Brooke House to his older brother Charles and worked on bringing the Manor back to its former glory. The Manor stands at the foot of a wooded valley which in spring becomes a sea of bluebells. Today the manor is owned by the National Trust which opens the gardens to the public. Once a year part of the house is also open.

**Mottistone village**

The people of Mottistone mainly worked on the farms, at the Manor or at the Mill. In 1841 the population was 158 with occupations listed as farmers, agricultural labourers or servants. By 1861 the population had dropped to 141 inhabitants and we see carpenters and fishermen added to the occupations. In 1881 the population was 99 and in 1911, 100. Maps show 16 wells in Mottistone, most of which would have been sunk by hand with the bottom bricked in. The farm horse teams would have drunk morning and evening at the 15 horse ponds. In dry weather the wooden farm wagons would have stood in these ponds to soak and swell up the felloes of iron bound wheels, shrunken in the heat. Names that come up time and again on the census are similar to those in Brook and include Bull, Whitewood, Cotton, Brown, Jacobs, Woodford, Cassell and Cook and more recently the two unrelated Emmett families who were known as 'the Emmetts' and 'the other Emmetts.' The village green with its walnut trees is where people remember the Rev. Bowyer holding an annual Sunday service for the animals of the parish. Thanks to John Seely, 2nd Lord Mottistone, who passed the Mottistone Estate to the National Trust, Mottistone has changed little over recent

With thanks to Chris Bull for his extensive research.

Evelyn, Lady Mottistone, outside the wing of the Manor that she lived in until she died. This snapshot was taken by her brother, Lord Elibank, in July 1956

# High days and holidays

Daisy and Ethel Pragnell from Hanover with a friend eating strawberries in the walled garden of Brooke House. Behind them on the left is the 'muscat house' and on the right 'the vinery'. Daisy was gardener for the Seelys.

In 1901 the population of Brook and Hulverstone was about 221, and Mottistone about 90, but even so, social life was astonishingly rich for so small a community and relatives and friends from Brighstone and elsewhere joined in many social events.

Apart from marking national celebrations such as Queen Victoria's Diamond Jubilee and the coronation of George V at Brooke House, there were annual gatherings such as the Lifeboat and Harvest Home suppers. Village life included a vigorous cricket club, tennis parties, musical evenings at the school and whist drives at which 90 people might sit down together.

*social life was astonishingly rich for so small a community*

Familiar family names appear and re-appear among the organisers, singers, entertainers, actors, sportsmen and competitors from one generation to the next. Everyone seems to have taken part in everything; the men who competed in the regattas and played cricket also obliged with a song, dressed up for the pageant and took part in *A Midsummer Night's Dream*. While country dancing took place in the Rectory garden and maypole dancing at the school, most social events were held in the Seely Hall. During the Second World War there were dances for the troops stationed in Brook and a Valentine's Dance took place every year. When the Reverend and Mrs Bowyer came to the parish in the 1950s, the villages were brought 'up to date' and much changed. The Reverend Bowyer started a youth club in what had been the school at Hulverstone and organised ballroom dancing lessons which were very popular, with many a match made. One couple is still happily married 50 years on. One year Mrs Bowyer put on a Passion Play which she had written herself. It took place in the grounds of Mottistone Manor with almost everyone in Brook and Mottistone involved. She was very persuasive! Carol singing at Christmas around the village involved calling in at various houses for refreshments. The annual children's parties were held in the Seely Hall and these continued well into the 1990s.

*Everyone seems to have taken part in everything; the men who competed in the regattas and played cricket also obliged with a song and dressed up for the pageant...*

BROOK REGATTA,

July 17, 1896, weather permitting.

PARISHES OF BROOK, MOTTISTON, & BRIGHSTONE.

Entrance 6d. each event unless otherwise stated. Four to start or no third prize.

Brook Regatta on the beach in 1889.

## Brook Regattas

'A very welcome and pleasant relief to the monotony which generally marks the life of this district,' so the County Press condescended to report the first Brook Regatta, held on the 21st June 1889.

*The coastguards always challenged the fisherman in the boat tug-of-war, and always lost.*

No doubt Brook and its neighbours could not compete with the sparkling nightlife of Newport in the 1880s; but only a strongly social community could have organised an event which 'attracted a large crowd of spectators, the cliffs and beach being thronged.' Later, 'music and dancing took place in the evening, and altogether a most enjoyable holiday was spent.'

This ambitious event was repeated in 1896 on a grander scale, when the band of the Freshwater Volunteers, under Bandmaster A. Trollope, 'added greatly to the general enjoyment.' The only criticism of the County Press reporter was that he could not work out the outcome of one of the races since no less than three 'T. Hookeys' had entered it. The prizes will have been well-worth having; four shillings for first prize in the sack race would have had the spending power of £12 in today's money.

The regattas took place annually up to the First World War and were revived in August 1921 when 'the events, competed for in heavy fishing boats, provided capital sport.' That one was almost the last; but the regattas had helped bind together all parts of the local community. The local families that ran the Regatta Committees in 1889 and 1896, such as the Hayters, Jacobs, Castles, Hookeys, Cottons and Newberys were still doing so in the 1920s. The printed programmes show that the event was very well organised and must have been talked about and looked forward to for months. The rules are specific, for the Single-handed Punt Race boats were 'not to

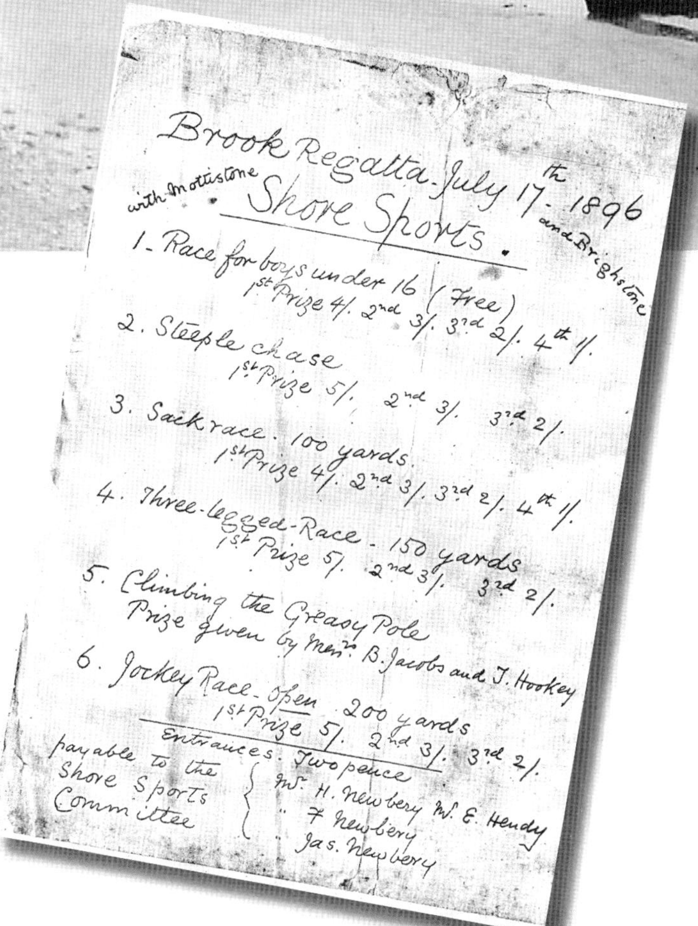

Brook Regatta. July 17th. 1896

with Mottistone and Brighstone

Shore Sports.

1. Race for boys under 16 (Free)
1st Prize 4/. 2nd 3/. 3rd 2/. 4th 1/.

2. Steeple chase
1st Prize 5/. 2nd 3/. 3rd 2/.

3. Sack race. 100 yards.
1st Prize 4/. 2nd 3/. 3rd 2/. 4th 1/.

4. Three-legged-Race. 150 yards
1st Prize 5/. 2nd 3/. 3rd 2/.

5. Climbing the Greasy Pole
Prize given by Messrs. B. Jacobs and J. Hookey

6. Jockey Race. Open 200 yards
1st Prize 5/. 2nd 3/. 3rd 2/.

Entrances. Twopence
payable to the Shore Sports Committee { Mr. H. Newbery, Mr. E. Hendy, " F. Newbery, " Jas. Newbery

*There was not sufficient breeze for the annual sailing match between the General's and the local fishermen's boats.*

Race 9—4.15.

**Pair-oar Race for Labourers**

(With Coxswain).

1st prize, 10/-; 2nd, 7/6; 3rd, 5/-; 4th, 3/6.
Five to start or no fourth prize.

F. Cassell ... **Black Duck**
R. Hayter ... **Meteor**
C. Harding ... **Bumble Bee**
G. Hawker ... **Bell**
B. Jacobs ... **Thistle**
J. Watson ... **Star**
E. Woodford ... **Johannis**

Race 10—4.45.

**Swimming Race.**

Lads under 18 years old. 100 yards.
1st prize, 5/-; 2nd, 2/6. Entries on the day.

Race 11—4.50.

**Swimming Race for Men**

Of the three Parishes. 200 yards.
1st prize, 7/6; 2nd, 5/-

W. Green A. Hunt
C. Holbrook W. Trust
J. Watson

Race 12—5.20.

**Tug of War** (Coastguards & Fishermen).

Best out of three pulls.
Prize, 10/-; Losers, 5/-

W. Harding ... **Nellie**
T. Hookey ... **Dulcie**

Race 13—5.40.

**Duck Hunt.**

Winner, 10/-; Loser, 5/-

**Duck** W. Trust **Hunter** A. Hunt

Race 14—6.0.

**Consolation 2-oar Race**

(With Coxswain).
1st prize, 10/-; 2nd, 7/6.

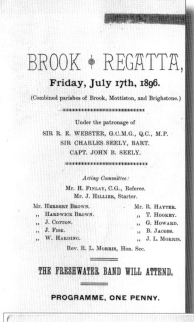

# BROOK ✦ REGATTA,

**Friday, July 17th, 1896.**

(Combined parishes of Brook, Mottiston, and Brighstone.)

Under the patronage of
SIR R. E. WEBSTER, G.C.M.G., Q.C., M.P.
SIR CHARLES SEELY, BART.
CAPT. JOHN B. SEELY.

*Acting Committee:*

Mr. H. Finlay, C.G., Referee.
Mr. J. Hillier, Starter.

Mr. Herbert Brown. Mr. R. Hayter.
" Hardwick Brown. " T. Hookey.
" J. Cotton. " G. Howard.
" J. Fisk. " B. Jacobs.
" W. Harding. " J. L. Morris.

Rev. R. L. Morris, Hon. Sec.

THE FRESHWATER BAND WILL ATTEND.

PROGRAMME, ONE PENNY.

*The County Press reporter could not work out the outcome of one of the races since no less than three 'T. Hookeys' had entered it.*

*Programme.*

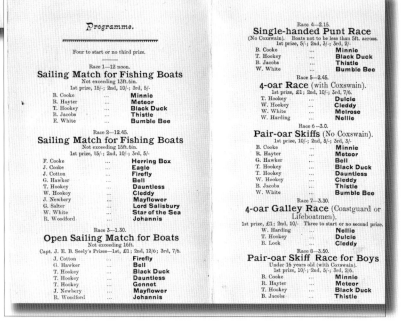

Four to start or no third prize.

Race 1—12 noon.

**Sailing Match for Fishing Boats**

Not exceeding 13ft. 6in.
1st prize, 15/-; 2nd, 10/-; 3rd, 5/-

B. Cooke ... **Minnie**
R. Hayter ... **Meteor**
T. Hookey ... **Black Duck**
B. Jacobs ... **Thistle**
E. White ... **Bumble Bee**

Race 2—12.45.

**Sailing Match for Fishing Boats**

Not exceeding 15ft. 6in.
1st prize, 15/-; 2nd, 10/-; 3rd, 5/-

F. Cooke ... **Herring Box**
J. Cooke ... **Eagle**
J. Cotton ... **Firefly**
G. Hawker ... **Bell**
T. Hookey ... **Dauntless**
W. Hookey ... **Cleddy**
J. Newbery ... **Mayflower**
G. Salter ... **Lord Salisbury**
W. White ... **Star of the Sea**
R. Woodford ... **Johannis**

Race 3—1.30.

**Open Sailing Match for Boats**

Not exceeding 16ft.
Capt. J. E. B. Seely's Prizes—1st, £1; 2nd, 12/6; 3rd, 7/6.

J. Cotton ... **Firefly**
G. Hawker ... **Bell**
T. Hookey ... **Black Duck**
T. Hookey ... **Dauntless**
T. Hookey ... **Gennet**
J. Newbery ... **Mayflower**
R. Woodford ... **Johannis**

Race 4—2.15.

**Single-handed Punt Race**

(No Coxswain). Boats not to be less than 5ft. across.
1st prize, 5/-; 2nd, 3/-; 3rd, 2/-

B. Cooke ... **Minnie**
T. Hookey ... **Black Duck**
B. Jacobs ... **Thistle**
W. White ... **Bumble Bee**

Race 5—2.45.

**4-oar Race** (with Coxswain).

1st prize, £1; 2nd, 10/-; 3rd, 7/6.

T. Hookey ... **Dulcie**
W. Hookey ... **Cleddy**
W. White ... **Melrose**
W. Harding ... **Nellie**

Race 6—3.0.

**Pair-oar Skiffs** (No Coxswain).

1st prize, 10/-; 2nd, 5/-; 3rd, 3/-

B. Cooke ... **Minnie**
R. Hayter ... **Meteor**
G. Hawker ... **Bell**
T. Hookey ... **Black Duck**
T. Hookey ... **Dauntless**
W. Hookey ... **Cleddy**
B. Jacobs ... **Thistle**
W. White ... **Bumble Bee**

Race 7—3.30.

**4-oar Galley Race** (Coastguard or Lifeboatmen).

1st prize, £1; 2nd, 10/- Three to start or no second prize.

W. Harding ... **Nellie**
T. Hookey ... **Dulcie**
B. Lock ... **Cleddy**

Race 8—3.50.

**Pair-oar Skiff Race for Boys**

Under 16 years old (with Coxswain).
1st prize, 10/-; 2nd, 5/-; 3rd, 2/6.

B. Cooke ... **Minnie**
R. Hayter ... **Meteor**
T. Hookey ... **Black Duck**
B. Jacobs ... **Thistle**

be less than five foot across.' The coastguards always challenged the fisherman in the boat tug-of-war, and always lost; the Rector was always the Hon. Sec., and 'the boat coxswained by General Seely had a special cheer on coming in last.' The Duck Hunt, which we believe was one man chasing another who ducked and dived in the water, was the cause of great hilarity and always came at the end of the day.

A Sunday morning bathing party in the 1920s includes Jim Hookey, Will Morris, Bert Morris and Jack Hayter.

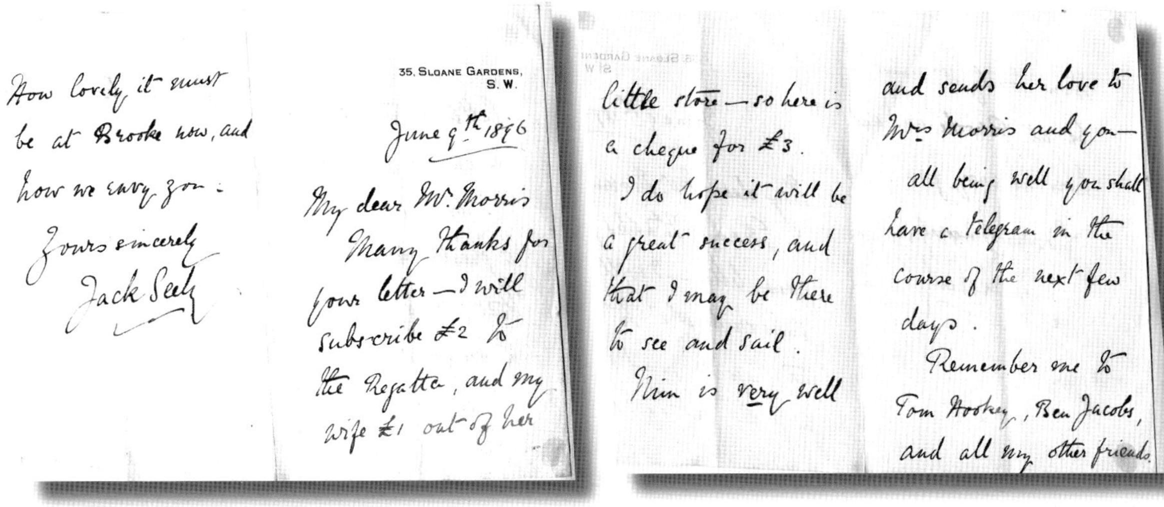
How lovely it must
be at Brooke now, and
how we envy you.
Yours sincerely
Jack Seely

35, Sloane Gardens,
S. W.
June 9th 1896
My dear Mr Morris
Many thanks for
your letter — I will
subscribe £2 to
the Regatta, and my
wife £1 out of her
little store — so here is
a cheque for £3.
I do hope it will be
a great success, and
that I may be there
to see and sail.
Nim is very well
and sends her love to
Mrs Morris and you —
all being well you shall
have a telegram in the
course of the next few
days.
Remember me to
Tom Hookey, Ben Jacobs,
and all my other friends.

Jack Seely writes to the Reverend Morris from London, he agrees to support the 1896 Regatta and says that he longs to be at Brook.

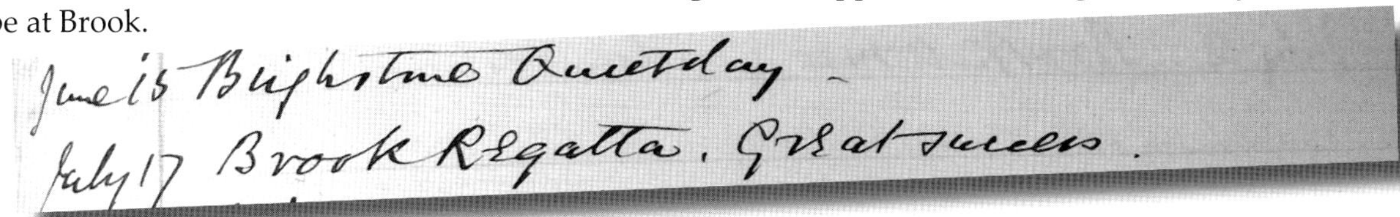
June 15 Brightstone Quiet day.
July 17 Brook Regatta. Great success.

The Rev. Morris' diary consists of a simple list of dates and events but there is justifiable pride and probably some relief in the entry for 17 July 1896.

On 27th August 1921 the IOW County Press reported:

The annual regatta took place in perfect weather at Brook on Saturday afternoon, and the events, competed for in heavy fishing boats, provided capital sport. Major-General Seely and the Hon. Mrs Seely were amongst those taking lively interest in the proceedings, the General acting as coxswain in the labourers' pair-oared race, whilst his children were prominent competitors and prize-winners. The lifeboat house, coastguard station and roads to the shore were gaily decorated with flags and quite a number of people attended. Mr T Hookey was hon secretary, the Rector (the Rev. C A Shaw) and Mr W Cogger were judges, Chief Officer of Coastguards Freeman was starter. Results and particulars of the events follow: Sailing race, 14ft boats – 1 A A H Wykeham, 2 R Hayter, 3 T Hookey, 4 H Cooke. Pair-oared (owners and two men) – 1 J Morris and F Hayter (C Newbery, cox), 2 W and F Cotton (Robert Hayter, cox), 3 John Seely and F Downer (Patrick Seely, cox). A splendid race, won by about three lengths. Pair-oared (boys under 16) – 1 W Morris and C Buckett (W Newbery, cox), 2 Sir John Nicholson and F Driver (F Downer, cox), was won easily. Pair-oared (labourers) – 1 C New and A Buckett (A Ballard, cox), 2 M Buckett and H Barnes (F Cotton, cox), 3 A Newbery and A Barnes (C Newbery, cox). A very close race, won by about three lengths. Single-handed – 1 W Cotton, 2 F Cotton. The winner had an advantage at the start and won comfortably. Ladies' pair-oared – 1 Misses Kitty and Sheila Seely (F Downer, cox), 2 Miss Irene Seely and Mrs Ward (J Seely, cox), 3 Mrs Morris and Miss Clifford (J Morris, cox). This was the most interesting event of the afternoon. The two young winners were given a start, but the result showed that they did not need it. They had a light dinghy, whilst the other ladies were in fishing boats, and the efforts of some of the dainty hands to control the unwieldy oars were amusing. Miss Irene Seely and her partner pulled splendidly, but could not overhaul their young rivals. Tug-of-war – Ben Jacobs, W Cotton, D Hookey, and A Woodford beat General Seely, F Hayter, F Cotton and J Morris. Four-oared – 1 F Downer, J Morris, R Marshall, and F Cotton (General Seely, cox), 2 A Woodford, D Hookey, W Cotton, and B Jacobs (Mr J Seely, cox). Greasy pole – 1 C Buckett. The pole was lashed to a boat, and the competition was as amusing as usual. Consolation race, four-oared – 1 J Hookey, A Downer, W Ballard, and A Newbery (A Ballard, cox), 2 Carpenter, W Higson, and C and L Barnes (F Newbery, cox). Children's tug-of-war on sands (prizes given by Mr A Peck, CC) – 1 Alice Cogger's team, 2 Nellie Leal's team.

General Seely expressed the great pleasure it had again given him and his family to take part in the regatta, and called for hearty cheers for the committee, and Mr Ben Jacobs, in response, led lusty cheers for the gallant General and his family.

Coronation festivities for King George V at Colonel Seely's residence, Brooke House, 1911.

**Scenes from the patriotic play *The Empire's Chain* presented by the children of Brook to mark the coronation of George V in 1911.**

A picture of Edwardian tranquillity at the Coronation festivities, Brooke House 1911. The Lebanon cedars that marked out the grounds in later years must have been saplings and Brook Hill House is starting to take shape up on the hillside.

Country dancing at the Coronation festivities at Brooke House in 1911.

Ladies' egg and spoon race at the Coronation festivities at Brooke House in 1911.

*They hauled a barrow-load of casks to the rollicking accompaniment of a song commencing, 'Ho! Ho! Let the wind blow.'*

The small figure on the ground at the left is schoolmistress Miss Clarence, who wrote and directed the pageants.

*A pageant descriptive of the history of the village in a manner which…may justly be described as brilliantly successful.*

## Brook pageants

The three village pageants of 1923, 1924 and 1925 perhaps marked the high point of the social life of Brook when it was still a farming and fishing village. They were produced by Miss Clarence, the headmistress of the school, and took place in Bush Rew, the field to the west of Brooke House.

The whole village must have taken part: the photograph of the 1923 cast shows at least 70 people, and many more must have been helpers. All three pageants included side shows, stalls, refreshments, competitions (villagers still competed for a live pig), maypole and folk dancing, and entertainment by the 'Black and Whites'. Only the band did not come from the village or the immediate neighbourhood.

*Cavemen, Ancient Britons, Jutes, Saxons, Romans, kings, queens, knights, soldiers, smugglers, and famous men of the various periods were all brought forth in their ancient glory of dress.*

Charlie New, Brooke lifeboatman, as the Bishop.

Dora Hookey, Kitty Hookey, Lance Barnes and Jim Hookey.

Brooke *Black and Whites* at the Pageant in 1923.

Hilda Newbery as Brittania, Ted Ecott, Jim Hookey and Barbara Hookey.

*The sea maidens performed a delightful dance clad in green muslin and sea-weed.*

**BROOKE AND ITS SUCCESSFUL PAGEANT** – The parishioners of beautiful Brooke have frequently shown their enthusiasm and ability in organising sports, regattas and homely little social functions, but on Thursday they demonstrated their possession of no mean historic ability by the production of a pageant descriptive of the history of their village in a manner which, all things considered, may justly be described as brilliantly successful. Miss Clarence, the popular and able headmistress of Hulverstone School was the leading spirit in the production.

Cave men, Ancient Britons, Jutes, Saxons, Romans, kings, queens, knights, soldiers, smugglers, and famous men of the various periods, who at some time or other have visited or had an interest in the village or the Island, were all brought forth in their ancient glory of dress, and each had something interesting and instructive to tell, and did it in a manner which showed very careful rehearsal by the author. Major-General and the Hon. Mrs J E B Seely, with their well-known geniality and helpfulness, enthusiastically supported the venture, and the committee responsible for the production, which was in aid of the County Hospital, was as follows: Messrs. W Heal, H Brown, J Hookey, J Morris, B Marshall, and A E Eccott (hon. Secretary), Mrs Brown and the Misses Clarence and Hollis. The event took place in the meadow west of Brooke House, which slopes upward to the wood, known as Bush Rew. It was an ideal setting, the trees forming an admirable shield for the players awaiting their call and a perfect background for the scenes enacted. General Seely, supported by Miss Clarence and Mr W Heal, declared the pageant open. The gallant General said he hoped that it would be the forerunner of many similar pleasing entertainments. He paid a tribute to Miss Clarence, who, he remarked, not content with educating and adding to the happiness of the children, was also determined to entertain middle-aged people like Mrs Brown, of Dunsbury, and old people like himself (laughter). The pageant opened with the appearance from out the wood of Father Time, who recited the Prologue, accompanied by an exceedingly handsome Britannia. The latter then called out presentations of her daughter nations and colonies and a company of pretty sea-maidens, who grouped themselves around the dais on which Britannia stood. The sea maidens performed a delightful dance clad in green muslin and sea-weed, after which the procession of the past began, each telling his or her story... Space will not admit of the description of each episode, but one or two must be mentioned. There was...the visit of Henry VII to Dame Bowerman, of Brook House... Sir John Cheke (tutor of the boy King, Edward VI) was impersonated by the smiling farmer of the same name, Mr Fred Cheke... Garibaldi, the last to appear, was also an interesting study, and spoke his lines with fine expressiveness. More fun was added to the piece by the entry of four bloodthirsty looking smugglers, in red and blue sailor dress. They hauled a barrow-load of casks to the rollicking accompaniment of a song commencing "Ho! Ho! Let the wind blow,"... Father Time, in his epilogue, concluded: 'And so our brief story closes on our beloved Island... The Island in the past has borne many onslaughts by foreign foes. Now the foreigner comes, not to pillage or destroy, but rather as a fellow worshipper with all true lovers of the Isle of Wight – the fairest spot in all the land.' Britannia recited a stirring poem, *Men of Wight*, and, after the players had marched in procession around the enclosure, they encircled her whilst, in a pure soprano voice, she impressively sang *Land of Hope and Glory,* all joining in the chorus. This made a fitting finale to a most creditable, pleasing and instructive masque, and the company again vanished into the wood after General Seely had led cheers for the King, the company, and the authoress. Mrs F Osborne's orchestra from Totland Bay played selections before the pageant and supplied music for dancing afterwards. *Isle of Wight County Press,* 9th June 1923

*Only the band did not come from the village or the immediate neighbourhood.*

# A Midsummer Night's Dream

25th June 1925

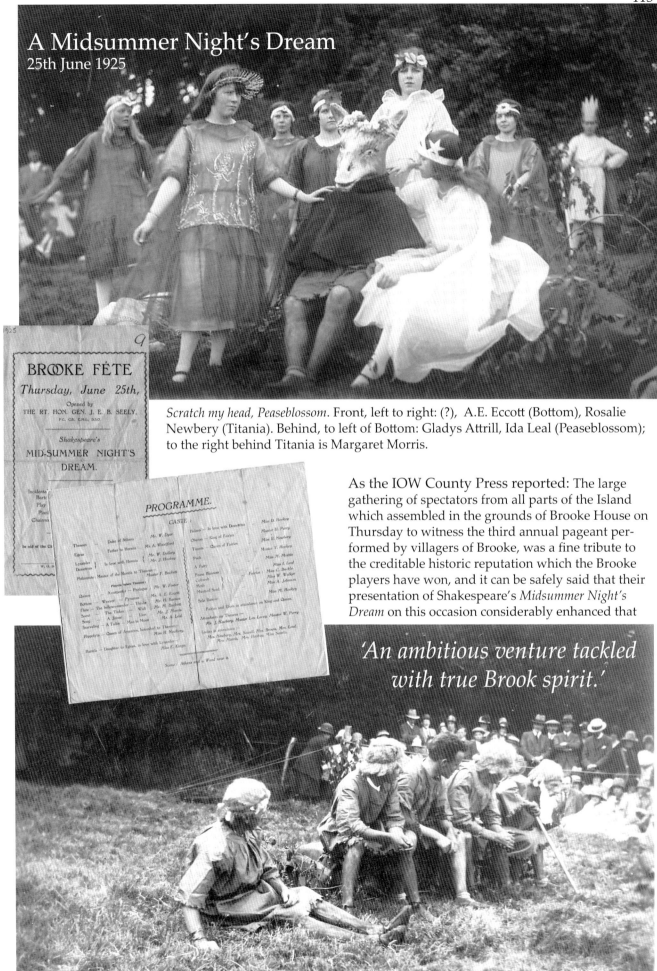

*Scratch my head, Peaseblossom*. Front, left to right: (?), A.E. Eccott (Bottom), Rosalie Newbery (Titania). Behind, to left of Bottom: Gladys Attrill, Ida Leal (Peaseblossom); to the right behind Titania is Margaret Morris.

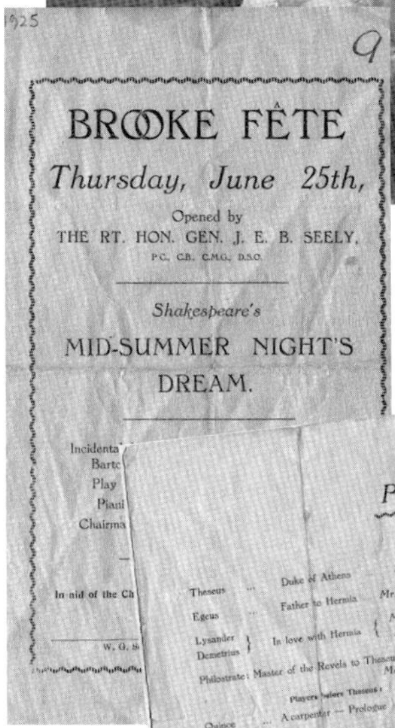

1925

9

BROOKE FÊTE

*Thursday, June 25th,*

Opened by

THE RT. HON. GEN. J. E. B. SEELY,

P.C., C.B., C.M.G., D.S.O.

*Shakespeare's*

MID-SUMMER NIGHT'S DREAM.

Incidenta

Bartc

Play

Piani

Chairma

In aid of the Ch

W. G. S

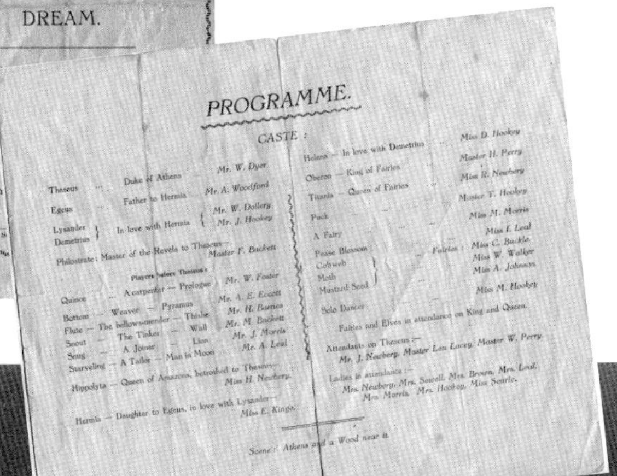

*PROGRAMME.*

CASTE :

Theseus ... Duke of Athens ... *Mr. W. Dyer*

Egeus ... Father to Hermia ... *Mr. A. Woodford*

Lysander, Demetrius } In love with Hermia { *Mr. W. Dollery*, *Mr. J. Hookey*

Philostrate: Master of the Revels to Theseus— *Master F. Buckett*

Players before Theseus :

Quince ... A carpenter — Prologue ... *Mr. W. Foster*

Bottom — Weaver — Pyramus ... *Mr. A. E. Eccott*

Flute — The bellows-mender — Thisbe ... *Mr. H. Barnes*

Snout — The Tinker — Wall ... *Mr. M. Buckett*

Snug — A Joiner — Lion ... *Mr. J. Morris*

Starveling — A Tailor — Man in Moon ... *Mr. A. Leal*

Hippolyta — Queen of Amazons, betrothed to Theseus— *Miss H. Newbery.*

Hermia — Daughter to Egeus, in love with Lysander— *Miss E. Kinge.*

Helena — In love with Demetrius ... *Miss D. Hookey*

Oberon — King of Fairies ... *Master H. Perry*

Titania — Queen of Fairies ... *Miss R. Newbery*

Puck ... *Master T. Hookey*

A Fairy ... *Miss M. Morris*

Pease Blossom, Cobweb, Moth, Mustard Seed } ... Fairies : *Miss I. Leal*, *Miss C. Buckle*, *Miss W. Walker*, *Miss A. Johnson*

Solo Dancer ... *Miss M. Hookey*

Fairies and Elves in attendance on King and Queen.

Attendants on Theseus :— *Mr. J. Newbery, Master Len Lacey, Master W. Perry.*

Ladies in attendance :— *Mrs. Newbery, Mrs. Sewell, Mrs. Brown, Mrs. Leal, Mrs. Morris, Mrs. Hookey, Miss Searle.*

*Scene : Athens and a Wood near it.*

As the IOW County Press reported: The large gathering of spectators from all parts of the Island which assembled in the grounds of Brooke House on Thursday to witness the third annual pageant performed by villagers of Brooke, was a fine tribute to the creditable historic reputation which the Brooke players have won, and it can be safely said that their presentation of Shakespeare's *Midsummer Night's Dream* on this occasion considerably enhanced that

*'An ambitious venture tackled with true Brook spirit.'*

Left to right: Joe Morris, H Barnes, Mark Buckett; others not known.

reputation. It was an ambitious venture tackled with true Brooke spirit, and Miss Clarence, the producer and every member of her company are to be heartily congratulated on showing what can be done in interpreting the works of the greatest of all playwrights even when the players have to be drawn from so small a community. It should serve as an example and incentive to the larger communities of the Island, for no more pleasurable and profitable entertainment can be imagined. The large audience thoroughly enjoyed the performances, which were productive of some really effective elocution and acting, and a series of beautiful pictures, staged in delightful sylvan surroundings

*The effect of the entrances was considerably enhanced by the sudden appearance of the performers from the dark recesses of the wood.*

on a perfect summer evening. The sloping meadow to the west of the Lord Lieutenant's residence (Bush Rew) was again utilised as the stage, with the fir coppice as a splendid background and serving as a convenient dressing room. The effect of the various entrances was considerably enhanced by the sudden appearance of the performers from the dark recesses of the wood. General Seely made a special journey from Town to witness the play and declare the fete open. He said that little Brooke, which had sent its sons to all parts of the world in peace and in war

Pyramus and Thisbe at the wall: *Mr Barnes' amusing stimulation of the female voice, in his character as Thisbe, was extremely funny.*

*It should serve as an example and incentive to the larger communities of the Island, for no more pleasurable and profitable entertainment can be imagined.*

to play worthy parts, had now gained quite a wide reputation for its pageants. He paid tribute to the splendid leadership of Miss Clarence, and hoped that as a result of the venture the church, the chapel and the children's treat funds would benefit substantially. The performance, which lasted over two hours, went through without the slightest hitch. There were very few lapses of memory in spite of the difficult dialogue entrusted to the principals, and both tragedy and comedy were admirably portrayed. The dancing of the fairies and elves in green, orange, violet and scarlet dresses was exceedingly pretty, whilst the final assembly of the whole company, during which Mr L Woodland finely sang *Land of Hope and Glory* was a brilliant spectacle. Miss R Newbery, with her beautiful dark tresses flowing free, made a strikingly handsome Titania and sang tastefully. Master H Parry did well as Oberon, Mr W Dyer acted with admirable feeling as Theseus, Miss H Newberry was a splendid Hippolyta, Mr H Woodford adequately played the part of Egeus, and Master T Hookey was a spritely Puck, but the chief honours are due to the four lovers, Lysander (Mr W Dollery), Demetrius (Mr J Hookey), Hermia (Miss E Kinge), and Helena (Miss D Hookey). On them fell the main weight of the dialogue and they all sustained it admirably, showing skilful versatility of expression, and excellent elocution. Miss Hookey declaimed her parts splendidly, and her persistent wooing of her scornful loved one, Demetrius, was perhaps, the best piece of acting during the evening. All four combined exceedingly well in interpreting the perplexing changes of passion consequent on the application of the potent love-flower by Puck. Special praise must also be bestowed on the graceful leader of the dancers (Miss M Hookey), the chief fairy (Miss M Morris), and on the company of players who appeared before Theseus, viz., Messrs. W Foster (Quince), A E Eccott (Bottom), H Barnes (Flute), M Buckett (Snout), J Morris (Snug), and A Leal (Starveling). They produced the fun splendidly. Mr Ecott's clever make-up in a realistic ass's head as Bottom and his stentorian voice and infectious leadership as Pyramus, were strong points in their displays. At the end of the performance Gen. Seely heartily complimented the company, and led three cheers for them, with an additional cheer for Miss Clarence, who, it should be mentioned, not only superintended the rehearsals, but, with members of her household, made the majority of the charming costumes. Gen. Seely added that he was sure the company were delighted to notice that neither Titania nor her attendants were bobbed or shingled (laughter). Before and after the play, visitors found plenty to amuse in the varied side shows of weight-judging and other competitions and in a dainty display of maypole and folk dancing in the afternoon by the scholars of Hulverstone School.

*General Seely added that he was sure the company were delighted to notice that neither Titania nor her attendants were bobbed or shingled (laughter).*

## Cricket

This cricketing song about the *Boys of Brooke and Mottistone* was written by Frank Fellowes in 1883, and in 65 lines ('It shall not be long...') celebrates the team of Renwick, Hilton, Watts, Read, Roberts, Frank Cook, Ben Jacobs, Wallis Lock, and John, Frank and James Newbery. Six years later, in 1889, the married members played the bachelors, so there were enough players for two teams at least. In 1910 Sir Charles Seely provided a ground – and aristocracy and clergy joined the team.

*The Boys of Brooke and Mottistone*
*– by that cricketing muff – the Knight of Saint John*

*I'll sing you a song, it shall not be long*
*Of the Boys of Brooke and Mottistone! Oh!*
*So trundle your bats, and put on your hats,*
*And it's off to the cricket field, let us all go!*
*And give a cheer Boys – stout and strong,*
*With the Bard who sings this cricketing song.*
*Hip! Hip! Hurrah!!! troll it along!*
*Hip! Hip! Hurrah!!! for the cricketer's song!*
*Hip! Hip! Hurrah!! – Hip! Hip! Hurrah!!*

*There's Renwick Charles, true to the death,*
*A better fellow, never drew breath,*
*An officer soon, in our army will be,*
*With warrant of pluck, and bravery.*
*He bats so steady, –he bats so strong,*
*He sends the ball, the field along,*
*And many a mile – trudge we may –,*
*Ere we shall see balls, put cleaner away.*

*There's Hilton too, a cricketer true,*
*The youngest of all, our cricketing crew,*
*And nobody knows at all, what he will do,*
*Be the ball a yorker, sneaker or screw,*
*For, come as it may, he sends it away,*
*In an easy, merry, frolicksome way;*
*And I think the youngster, as a bat,*
*Will lick the lot, for a' that, and a' that.*

*There's Watts, the captain, a bowler cute,*
*And Oh! By jingo! Don't his balls shoot!*
*As an underhand bowler, he has sway,*
*Though he's underhand, in no other way.*
*He oft, for our team, a wicket doth gain,*
*By sending the bails spinning over the plain.*
*There's Read, the sticker, though not a stick,*
*For keeping his wicket's a regular brick;*

*Whilst Roberts the slasher, slashes away,*
*Making runs fast, while Read doth stay.*
*And if you're bowling mind what you're at,*
*If Frank Cook faces as a bat.*
*One of the best, of our bowling men,*
*Is genial, jovial, Jacobs Ben;*
*His balls, as from cannon, come rushing along,*
*When hurled by his arm, so swift and strong.*

*There's Wallis Lock, who is good, all round;*
*And Newbery John, a slow bowler sound;*
*And Newbery Frank, and Newbery James,*
*The capital helps, in our cricketing games.*
*There's Fellows frank! Knight of St John!*
*A splendid fellow! – for looking on!*
*For – let but a swift ball, come his way,*
*And he's jolly sure....to bolt away!*
*So to make amends he pens this lay,*
*Of the jolly boys – who cricket play,*
*And hopes he may be with them long,*
*To celebrate their deeds in song.*

*Now will I sing of those who bring*
*Grace and beauty to our ring.*
*There's our kind hostess,... Renwick hight*
*Whom we love and respect, for her virtues bright,*
*For her goodness of soul, and her generous heart,*
*Oh! What should we do, were she to depart?*
*Our hostess fair, – is always there,*
*With her gracious smile and pleasant air:*
*Miss Mary, too, fair, frank and free*
*With her bright eyes beaming gloriously!*
*And then! Miss Frances! – gentle and dutiful!*
*Sweet as a rose, all blooming and beautiful,*
*Makes the Graces three.*
*I've sung you my song – It has not been long and ...*

**Saturday, 12th October 1889**
**Benedicts v Bachelors**

A cricket match was played on Saturday between the married and single members of the Brooke and Mottistone Cricket Clubs, and resulted in a win for the former by a narrow margin of three runs, Mr Sams Captained the Benedicts with great skill and judgement. Mr B Jacobs officiating for the Bachelors. The victory of the Benedicts was mainly due to the hard hitting of Mr F Newbery, who contributed 32 in fine style, his chief supporter being Mr F Cooke with 15. Messrs. F & J Newbery also bowled finely for their side. For the losers, Mr B Jacobs bowled splendidly for the Bachelors, his efforts being well seconded by Mr W Jacobs. After the match the combined teams with umpires and scorers sat down and did ample justice to a splendid supper provided by Host & Hostess Knellar of the Sun Inn, Hulverstone. After the cloth was removed, the order of the day was toast and song until closing time terminated the proceedings which all present fully enjoyed.
*Isle of Wight County Press*

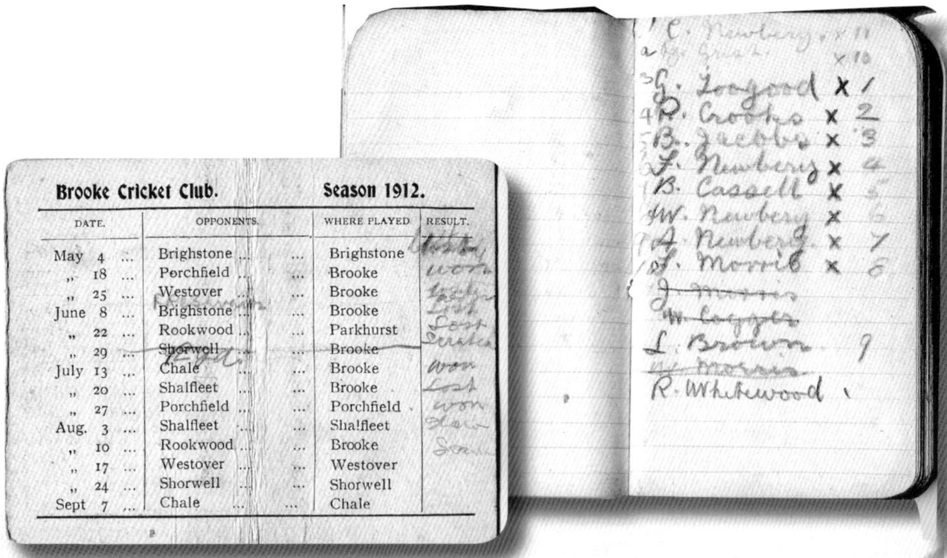

**Brooke Cricket Club. Season 1912.**

| DATE. | OPPONENTS. | WHERE PLAYED | RESULT. |
|---|---|---|---|
| May 4 | Brighstone | Brighstone | |
| „ 18 | Porchfield | Brooke | won |
| „ 25 | Westover | Brooke | |
| June 8 | Brighstone | Brooke | Lost |
| „ 22 | Rookwood | Parkhurst | Lost |
| „ 29 | ~~Shorwell~~ | ~~Brooke~~ | |
| July 13 | Chale | Brooke | won |
| „ 20 | Shalfleet | Brooke | Lost |
| „ 27 | Porchfield | Porchfield | won |
| Aug. 3 | Shalfleet | Shalfleet | |
| „ 10 | Rookwood | Brooke | |
| „ 17 | Westover | Westover | |
| „ 24 | Shorwell | Shorwell | |
| Sept 7 | Chale | Chale | |

The fixtures list and score card for the 1912 Brooke Cricket Club season

**Brook Cricket Club 1923**

Back row from left: G.Morris, R.Marshall, xxx ,Charlie Newbery, Alf Newbery, xxx , Alf Woodford, Dick Whitewood, B.Marshall, Harry Barnes, Walter Newbery, xxx , T. Eccott.

Front row from left: G.Foster, Jim Hookey, xxx, Jack Seely, Ben Jacobs, Arthur Buckett, Arthur Newbery, Lance Barnes, F.Buckett, H.Corden.

December, 15th 1900

**Brook Cricket Club Entertainment**

Given at Hulverstone School in aid of funds for the Brooke Cricket Club. The Rev. G E Evans presided over a crowded audience. An Australian lady who was visiting the neighbourhood at the time made notes of the event. Great credit is due to Miss Hollis, school mistress and her assistant, Miss Reid.

The cricket ground was at the bottom of Badger's Lane, behind Old Myrtle Cottage. Matches were played against other Island villages, and even Mainland teams. In the 1920s carpenter Walter Newbery, was Captain. Lance Barnes (seated at right in photo, with bat) was a star player who, in a match against Yarmouth in 1924, scored 49 runs and took 5 wickets for 10 runs. The vicars often seem to have been cricket enthusiasts. Ron Emmett remembers that when he was a boy in the 1930s: *Mr Winser, the rector, was keen on cricket and he tried to get us youngsters keen on cricket but without much success.That was the vicar's hobby - he seemed more interested in cricket than religion.*

There was a cricket team in Brook certainly up until the Second World War. Bert Morris stands in his cricket whites outside Hanover House in the 1930s.

## Tennis

The Rev Pellew Gaze's daughters were triumphant in the following tournament on October 5th 1889:

> **Return tennis match Brooke House**
> The return match in tennis tournament recently took place in the grounds of Brooke House, kindly placed at the disposal of the players by Mr Seely. The contest was between Miss Gaze's team and Mr Sydney Haigh's team. In the first match 160 games were played, of which Miss Gaze's team won 88 and Mr Haigh's 72, and in the return encounter 110 games were played, Miss Gaze's team winning 65, and Mr Haigh's 45.

Barbara Heal (Hookey) described how in 1925: *General Jack Seely gave a piece of land in front of Hanover House for a tennis court for village use. It was prepared and marked out by one of the gardeners of Brooke House and balls and racquets were provided free of charge. Tennis became very popular amongst the young people of the village, especially when holiday makers in the summer used to come and play as well.*

*The most difficult opponent was the wind*

Several old racquets and balls were kept in Hanover House for anyone who felt they would like a game and hadn't brought their racquets with them and young Barbara made the most of this: *I began playing when I was ten years old with one of the old racquets provided. However, the Rev. C. Shaw, thinking I had some skill, bought me a new racquet and I was able to improve my game. There was one big drawback – the wind. The tennis court was in a very exposed position and it was often too stormy to play. Unfortunately, in the early 1930s, the road which was gated at this point, was widened, and part of the tennis court had to go. We were then given a piece of lawn in front of Brook House. It was very sheltered there. The Seely family had already gone to Mottistone Manor to live. We spent many happy hours playing tennis in lovely surroundings until war came in 1939, and tennis had to end when troops were billeted in Brooke House.*

Tennis at Hanover, c.1930. Standing: Will and Bert Morris. In front: Barbara Hookey and her cousin, Jack Cook.

Compton Beach c.1930. The IOW Motorcycle Club held one or two races a year when there was a very low tide.

## Music

The newspaper accounts of concerts, pageants and Church festivals show that music featured regularly in festivals and holidays. The fact that the school had an orchestra must also have helped strengthen musical skills in the village.

During the 1920s, the village concert party, 'The Black and Whites', delighted a large audience at the school with an operetta, *The King of Sherwood*, and along with the school children they also put on *Jack and the Beanstalk*. They were continuing a tradition of entertainment by local people for their neighbours which was already lively in the 1880s, when Ethel and Helen Gaze, daughters of the Rector, produced 'a capital programme' of sketches, songs and piano and violin solos; and the school was 'literally packed with people of all ages'. We know, for example that the harvest festivals and Lifeboat Suppers occasioned a song or 'turn' from everyone present and that the road home from the Sun Inn rang with (often bawdy) songs.

Albert Whitewood's obituary photograph.

The pictures we have that show people with musical instruments (usually a violin) include the school orchestra, Albert Whitewood (Rita Whitewood's grandfather) and Phil Jacobs at a Toogood family wedding. Lilian D'Albiac, daughter of Sir Charles Seely, right, who lived at Little Brook, taught her nieces and Erica Newbery to play the piano in the 1940s. This was not a waste of effort as Erica continues as Brook church and choir organist today. Brook also had a highly successful ladies' choir throughout the 1950s and 60s (see *Seely Hall and WI)*.

Lilian D'Albiac

Brook School orchestra c.1911.

On the right a young Phil Jacobs stands with ready to play at a wedding party.

Brook Ladies' Choir in the Seely Hall.

# The School at Hulverstone

Hulverstone School in 1878. Annie Phillips and her sister Alice have been marked by a diagonal line in pen.

Some sort of schooling was provided in the mid-19th century at Elm House, Hulverstone and we know that Miss Hephzibah Hollis was teaching there from 1862. In 1872, Charles Seely MP, converted a barn opposite into a school house with two rooms – a third was added later for the infants – with a playground in front and a farmyard behind. There were about ninety pupils in the early days, from Brook, Mottistone, Compton, Chessel and Shalcombe. The school

School is out at Hulverstone in the early 1900s.

was 'cordially complimented on the number of attendance awards, especially as many children had to come long distances over very exposed roads.' The school records seem to give excessive prominence to scripture, drawing and needlework; but the church register shows the

*The church register shows the growth of literacy: in the 1870s about half the newly-weds signed with a mark; by the 1890s, all signed, often elegantly.*

growth of literacy. In the 1870s about half the newly-weds signed with a mark, by the 1890s, all signed their full names, often elegantly.

Hulverstone School c.1891. Charles Henry Newbery, later village carpenter and key member of Brooke Lifeboat, is fifth from left on bottom row.

David 'Daf' Hookey, later village blacksmith, on the left.

Writing in 1958, Ella Way Hookey describes how in the 1880s: *an infants' room was added and sanitation improved. Children walked to school – some a distance of two or three miles – bringing their dinner. They started school at three years of age and the number of children on the register was ninety to a hundred. The school mistress was Miss Hollis and she had two assistants. She stayed there until her retirement and lived on to a great age in Hulverstone. It seems sad now to see the school closed and falling into disrepair.* The description of special occasions and outings, such as blackberrying, sound idyllic from a distance but we know that many of the children had inadequate shoes to walk the long way to school.

Coastguard and boys with rifles, not identified except for Alf Woodford, front row 4th from left c. 1910.

Below: Miss Hephzibah Hollis 1844 – 1929, in a pageant costume. Miss Hollis became the first Headmistress and held the role for 47 years. She retired in 1909. Miss Hollis also played the organ in Mottistone Church and was a Sunday School teacher until a few days before her death.

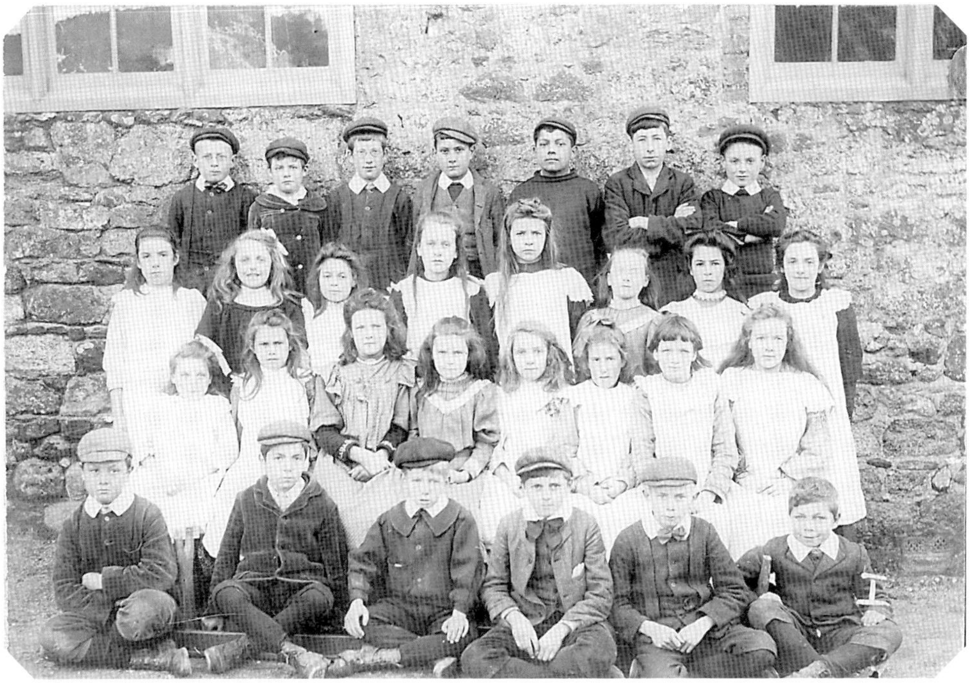

Hulverstone School pupils in the early 1900s

*Miss Hollis could exercise stern discipline if the necessity arose*

The following account of the funeral of Miss Hollis on 26th October 1929 shows what a key role she played in this small community:

**The late Miss Hollis of Brook -**
**Her Funeral Wish.**

The remains of the late Miss H. Hollis of Brook, for 47 years headmistress of the village school and 67 years a Sunday School teacher, who died on Friday week aged 85, were laid to rest in Brook Churchyard on Wednesday, amid many evidences of respect and regret at the passing of one who had spent a long and eminently useful life in the parish. Miss Hollis, who was a model of method in all she undertook, even carried her foresight to the extent of arranging for the bearers at her funeral. Amongst her effects was found a list of names of several of her earliest boy pupils, now men of about 60 and still residing in the district, from amongst whom she directed should be selected half a dozen to carry her body to its last resting place. Her wishes were respected and the following old boys, several of them lifeboatmen, performed the duty: Messers John and James Newbery, W. Jacobs, C. Cassell, D. Hookey, G. Morris. As they carried the coffin, nearly half a mile from the house to the church, the mourners and elder school children walked in procession behind it. The children were preceded by the Queen*, Marjorie Phillips, bearing a beautiful wreath from the scholars and teachers and her two immediate royal predecessors, representing recent scholars. The children also lined the pathway as the cortege passed from the church to the grave, which was made beautiful with flowers and bracken. Every seat in the church was occupied at the service which was conducted by the Rector (Rev.C.A.Shaw). As well as representatives from every family in the village, the Seely family was well represented. There was a lovely display of floral tributes including many little posies simply enscribed, 'from an old pupil' or 'from a friend'.

* May Queen

Courtesy of *Isle of Wight County Press*

*At the end of the 19th century there were about 90 children at the school – possibly more than 100 at times.*

Miss Clarence sitting beside the stage at one of the open air pageants she organised. She probably placed herself there in case a prompt was needed.

Emmy Kindersley (Seely) remembered being expected to save all her old shoes to give to the school children at Hulverstone in the early 1900s. The early school photographs, however, do not show the rather drawn, anxious faces so often seen in school photographs of the period. Sir Charles Seely, as Colonel of both the IOW Volunteer Force and the 1st Nottinghamshire (Robin Hood) Rifle Volunteers, attached importance to drill and rifle shooting, and gave some rifles (they could not be fired) to the boys for practice. They were trained by the coastguards but one day we are told that the boys used the guns to ambush Sir Charles from behind a hedge and he took the guns away again. At the end of the 19th century there were about 90 children at the school – possibly more than 100 at times. The trend towards smaller families may have been having some effect even before the First World War since the school numbers had dropped to 70 or 80 by 1914. During the 1920s there were still some 60 pupils at the school. Thereafter, the drift away from the land also took effect, and the drop in school numbers became more marked. When Miss Clarence became headmistress in 1921, she greatly expanded the social and creative part of the school's activities. She directed some ambitious pageants and a production of A Midsummer Night's Dream (see *High Days and Holidays*). An annual May Day celebration also became a highlight of the school year with the election of a May Queen, a procession and sports which also brought parents into the school.

In the winter there would be a social for adults with games, dancing 'and attractive musical entertainment.' On Boxing Night 1925: *A Christmas party was held, over 60 scholars*

*From its earliest years the school was a vital centre of social life for villagers of all ages.*

As an isolated, rural school, Hulverstone was perhaps unusual to have its own orchestra in 1911/12.

A Brook School group, 1919.
Not all identified, but 3rd from left is Lily Munt and the back row includes Fred Buckett, William Cassell, Charlie Buckett, Hedley Barnes, Bert Morris, Nell Leal, Dorothy Cassell, Lily Crabbe and Dorothy Smith. The middle row includes: Alice Death, Mary Hookey, Dorothy Barnes, Winnie Barnes, Vera Crabbe, Jesse Cook, Winnie Crabbe, Joyce Crabbe, Vera Barnes, Doris Lacey. The front row includes: Jack Hayter, Len Lacey, Dick Carpenter, Ben Lacey, Herb. Lacey, Robert Cassell, Ray White, Len Leal, Tom Hookey and Willie Dyer.

Left: May Day 1933, a group of children and their parents.

Below: Bert Morris' certificate for not missing even one day of school in 1917.

The first May Day ceremony, probably 1921. Back row left to right: Doris Attrill, Lily Munt, Winnie Walker, Eva Cheek (the May Queen), Mary Hookey, Alice Death. Front row: Winnie Barnes, Barbara Hookey, Ida Leal, xxx.

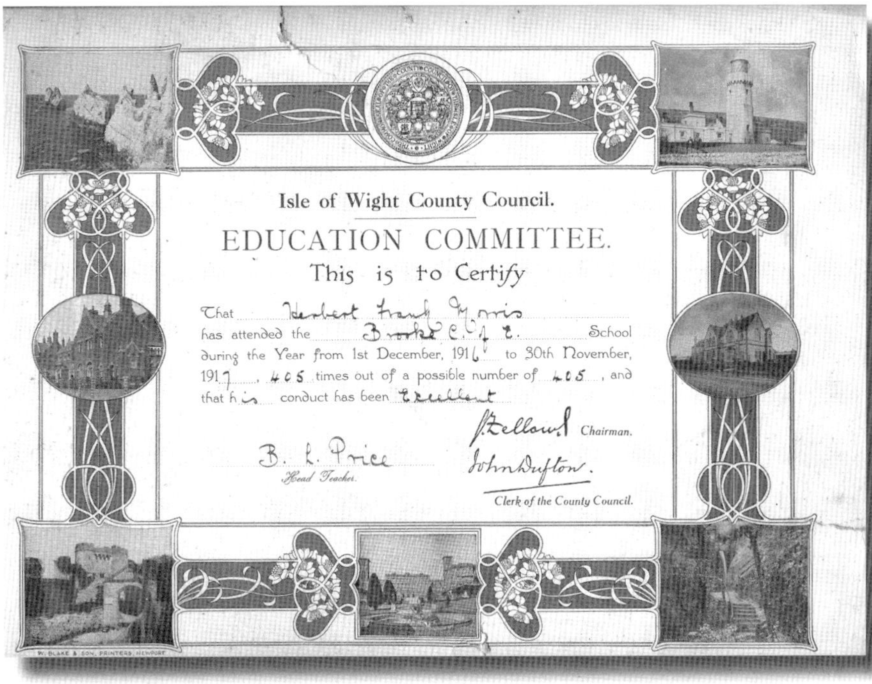

Isle of Wight County Council.

EDUCATION COMMITTEE.

This is to Certify

That Herbert Frank Morris
has attended the Brook C. of E. School
during the Year from 1st December, 1916 to 30th November,
1917, 405 times out of a possible number of 405, and
that his conduct has been Excellent

Chairman.

B. L. Price
Head Teacher.

John Dufton
Clerk of the County Council.

W. BLAKE & SON, PRINTERS, NEWPORT

Practising the maypole dance in the school playground about 1935. Teacher Barbara Hookey watches on. The children include Doris Emmett and Joan Woolbright. Ron Emmett remembers this was hard work, especially if your only shoes were hobnail or wellington boots.

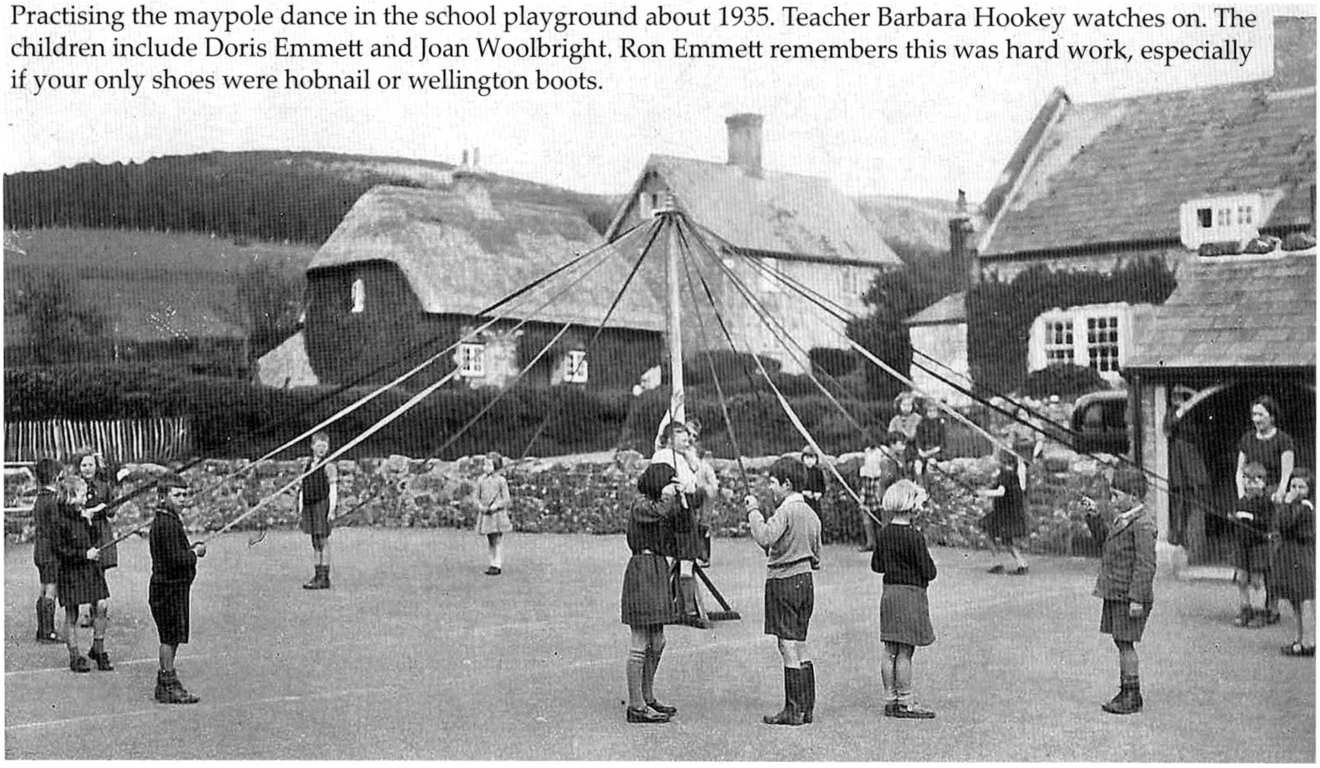

*attending…proceedings were enlivened by a jazz band, and with songs…and a long programme of games and dances.* After that, the school was the venue for the village pantomime, 'Jack and the Beanstalk', Miss Clarence producing. In 1928, at the age of three, Ron Emmett was keen to get to school: *my brothers used to go off to school, leaving me alone and Mother had to tie the gate to keep me in. One fine day I decided I'd change all this so I crawled under the gate and legged it off to Hulverstone School. I don't know how I knew the way, but anyway that's what I did. I got to the school, and was promptly returned home by one of the older boys in the school. After some discussion amongst the authorities and parents, it was decided that the best place for me was in school and there was no objection from the teachers, so off to school I went, at the age of three.* In the 1930s lunch hours were long and full of adventures as Ron Emmett remembers: *an hour and a half and during which time we could do whatever we wanted. Myself, Ken Barnes, Bert Attrill and Arthur Petitt, we'd leg it off sometimes to the beach at Brook or up Five Barrows or up round the mansion. We'd run all over the place and get up to all sorts of things and then at 1.30 we'd be back at school again ready for the afternoon lesson, all refreshed and tired out...*

Audrey Rann remembers starting school and how she was allowed to sit in the older class until she felt more confident: *School in Hulverstone does have fond memories. I was not the world`s best scholar but I was good at writing, reading and spelling, so I could get away with*

*I never, ever, heard Barbara or Dora Hookey raise their voices.*

A Brook School group (probably 1934).
Back row left to right: Dora Hookey (teacher), Evelyn Whitewood, Rita Whitewood, Minnie Phillips, Vic Dowland, Joan Pettit, Barbara Heal (teacher). 2nd row: Bill Barnes, Bill Crabbe, Bern Phillips, Roy Emmett, Ron Barron, Stan Wilson, Stan Emmett, Ken Barnes. 3rd row: Doris Crabbe, Evelyn Beckett, Gwen Davey, Ethel Salter, Helen Worthington, Mary New, Dorothy Keeping. 4th row: Mavis New, Doreen Keeping, Eileen Pettit, Joan Emmett, Alma Emmett, Pam Barnes. Front: Ray Keen, Ron Emmett, xx Smith, Ray Smith.

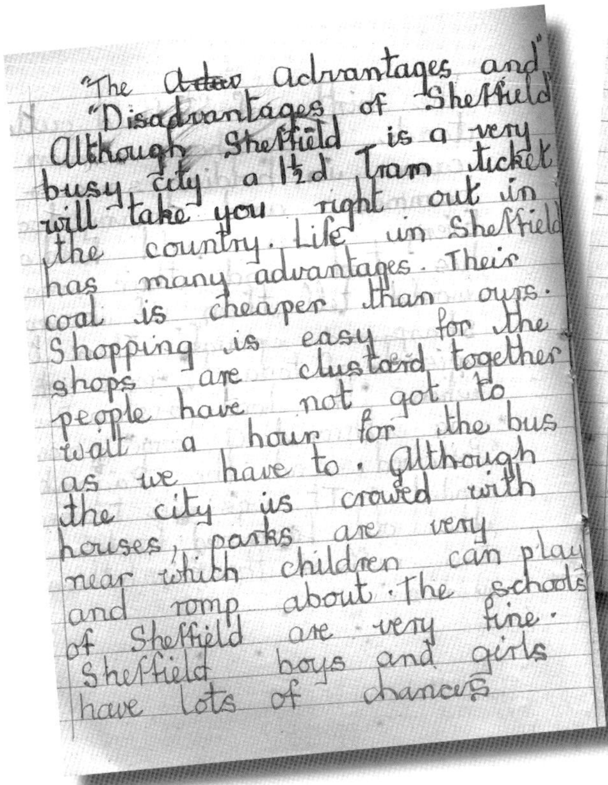

"The ~~Adva~~ advantages and
"Disadvantages of Sheffield"
Although Sheffield is a very busy city a $1\frac{1}{2}$d Tram ticket will take you right out in the country. Life in Sheffield has many advantages. Their coal is cheaper than ours. Shopping is easy for the shops are clusterd together people have not got to wait a hour for the bus as we have to. Although the city is crowed with houses, parks are very near which children can play and romp about. The schools of Sheffield are very fine. Sheffield boys and girls have lots of chances

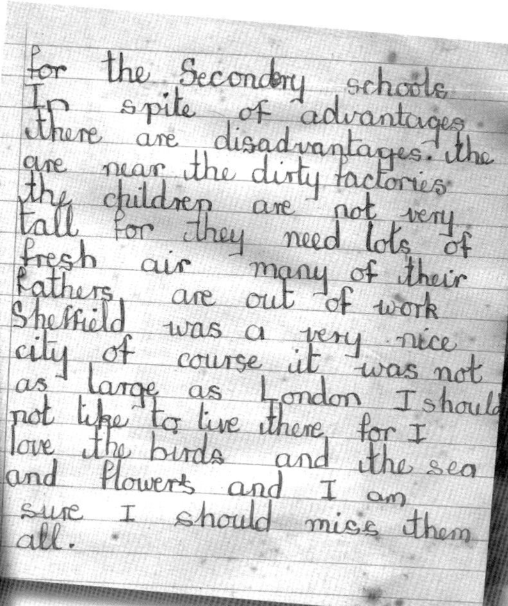

for the Secondry schools. In spite of advantages there are disadvantages. the are near the dirty factories the children are not very tall for they need lots of fresh air many of their fathers are out of work. Sheffield was a very nice city of course it was not as large as London I should not like to live there for I love the birds and the sea and flowers and I am sure I should miss them all.

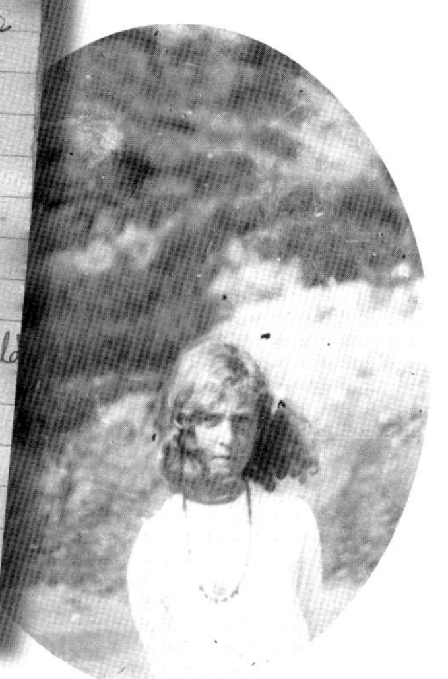

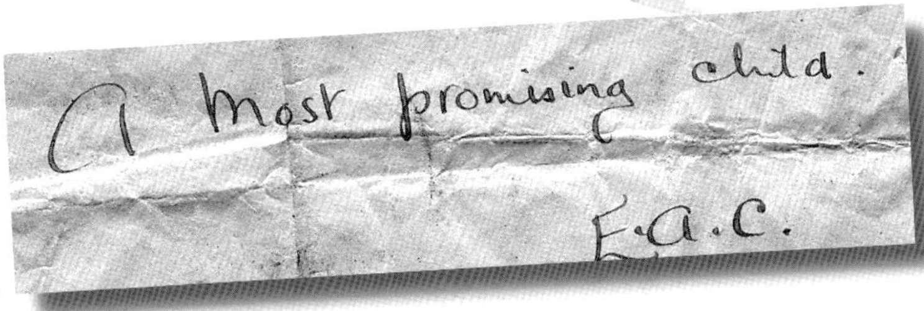

A most promising child.
E.A.C.

Rita Whitewood aged 10 and her thoughts on 'The advantages and disadvantages of Sheffield,' after a Hulverstone School visit to the city in 1933. It is perhaps no wonder that Miss Clarence signed her school report, 'A most promising child.'

*history and geography, but not maths. This didn`t make any sense to me at all, my brain would become scrambled. My favourite teachers were Barbara and Dora Hookey, sisters, from Brook. Barbara taught the infants. Both were nice and patient. We had a fire at each end of the big classroom. I can`t remember any heating in the small classroom but think there must have been. Later, Barbara Hookey got married and Dora Hookey moved onto Ventnor Infants` School, where she was Headmistress. There was some sort of a problem, I don`t know what it was, but one day something had been said or done and my brother had been accused. One morning, my mother took me by the hand, took Auntie Rose`s walking stick, as she was with us on this particular morning, and we marched across the road and into school. Mother opened the door, went straight up to Miss Clarence, who was Head, and shook the stick at her, then we left just as abruptly. I never knew what it was all about. If that happened today, there would be a right to do! Miss Cole was strict and would shout at you, but I did like her. I never, ever, heard Barbara or Dora raise their voices. I don`t know how or where they received their teacher training, but it must have been on the mainland. They were good teachers and taught us all the `3 Rs'.*

At 8 years old, Rita wrote over 35 pages about a memorable trip to London in 1929. It included visits to the House of Lords, London Zoo and the Daily Express offices. This extract describes the time the children had white hot type demonstrated to them in Fleet Street.

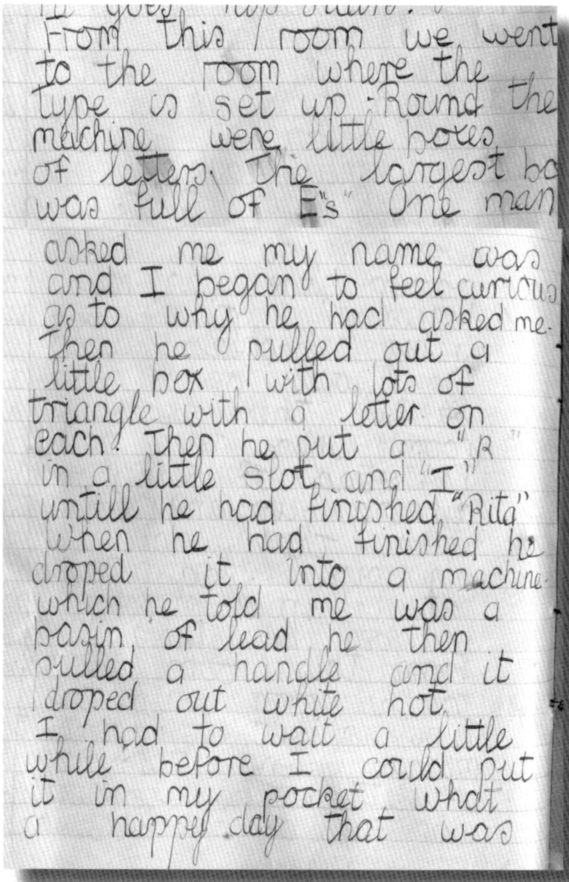

From this room we went
to the room where the
type is set up. Round the
machine were little boxes
of letters. The largest bo
was full of E's One man
asked me my name was
and I began to feel curious
as to why he had asked me.
Then he pulled out a
little box with lots of
triangle with a letter on
each. Then he put a "R"
in a little slot and "I"
untill he had finished "Rita"
When he had finished he
droped it into a machine
which he told me was a
basin of lead he then
pulled a handle and it
droped out white hot.
I had to wait a little
while before I could put
it in my pocket what
a happy day that was

From the 1940s, children went to Freshwater from the age of 11 (and the little school at Hulverstone gained its share of scholarships to Newport Grammar School). Audrey Rann (Barnes) remembers: *when the war began, the older children moved onto Freshwater School, the young ones went into the big classroom and the soldiers were billeted into the small classroom.* Children of all ages walked long distances to attend school, from Hoxall Lane in Mottistone, from the two cottages at Longstone (there was one thatched cottage, now long since gone), from Compton Farm, from Chessell, and even from the top of Broad Lane. Mary Pettit recalls: *the Kitsons and myself walked to Hulverstone School across the fields and the wood at the top end of Brook House grounds, and out through the main gate and along the road to Hulverstone. Miss Nichloson was our teacher, she was very strict, we often had a rap across the knuckles with a ruler or got the cane for some misdemeanour. I can remember being caned once for not obeying instructions on how to draw a table lamp to scale. My effort was about 2 inches high in the middle of the A4 size paper, and I received a stroke of the cane on each hand.*

Tony Pettitt who did the same walk when young, remembers when a Shotters' bus was provided: *Fred Driver who drove the bus, stopped to let us pick up conkers at Brook shute. We went to Compton Bay for swimming lessons, and on nature rambles to find wild flowers to press in books. We picked rose hips to send away for rosehip syrup.*

Although the school day finished at quarter to four, for Ron Emmett there was still much to be done: *In those days children never had time off as such, there was always plenty of work to do once you got home. My job after school was to go to the Sun Inn and help the landlord, Fred White. Fred was a bit of a cripple so I used to do all of the work like milking his two cows, sawing up firewood, digging the garden, swabbing out the stone floor in the bar. Fred's wages by the way were sixpence a week ~ a nice, shiny sixpence and sometimes I didn't get home 'til 9 or 9.30 in the evening, after leaving home at 8 in the morning and then, next morning of course, the cows still had to be milked, so before school it was down to the cowshed to milk the cows again and then off to school...*

Traditional rural influences remained strong to the end; the Rector took regular scripture lessons; the school closed for a week at potato harvest. But the modern world produced new problems – 'dinner now arrives by the 11.55am bus,' and no caretaker could be found. Margaret Pettit at age 16 was being employed to wash up. Soon there were no more than two dozen names on the roll. The School Log from 1940 to 1947 shows the decline in numbers and gives a brief insight into typical days at school. Nurse Rann regularly visited the school to inspect heads, and there was no outbreak of 'nits' at all in those seven years. The doctor was a regular visitor, as was the dentist. It is interesting to see how very little treatment was required in the early years. In October 1942 only three children needed dental treatment, but after the war, in January 1946 13 children needed treatment.

In December 1947 the school closed after 75 years, and the remaining pupils transferred to Freshwater and Brighstone. As the school roll declined, Anne Hookey at five remembers: *I don't have many happy memories of my early school days. I suppose coming from living on the farm I wasn't used to mixing with lots of other children and looking back there was some bullying involved. Anyway, no matter, when Brook School closed I moved on to All Saints Junior School at Freshwater and settled happily.*

It was a sad end to what had been a thriving and

Brook School 1939. Standing from left: Audrey Smith, Ray Compton, Dennis Phillips, Ray Keen, xx Compton, Alan Hughes, Erica Newbery. Middle row: Kitty Smith, Joan Woolbright, Margaret Pettitt, Audrey Barnes, Iris Emmett, Doris Emmett. Front row: Charlie Cassell, xxx, John Pettitt, Ray Smith, Ray Ryall.

successful rural school which had given a very good education to the children of agricultural workers. The generation that included George Humber, Rita Whitewood and Robert Cassell, for example, were rightly proud of their education and notable for their interest in nature as well as history and current affairs.

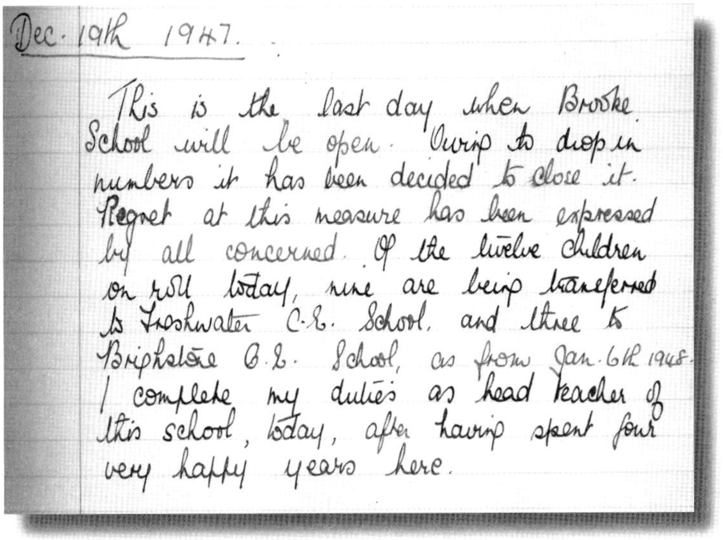

Dec. 19th 1947.

This is the last day when Brooke School will be open. Owing to drop in numbers it has been decided to close it. Regret at this measure has been expressed by all concerned. Of the twelve children on roll today, nine are being transferred to Freshwater C.E. School, and three to Brighstone C.E. School, as from Jan. 6th 1948. I complete my duties as head teacher of this school, today, after having spent four very happy years here.

19th December 1947: the last entry in the school log.

# Wartime

The Thimble at Hanover Point was built out of cement and sand bags. While a useful marker to fishing and sailing boats, its original purpose was to provide shooting practice for the cannons at Fort Redoubt in Freshwater Bay. Over the years a number of cannon balls (below) have been found in Brook Bay.

Coastal defences remain along Brook beach at the end of the Second World War.

Brook and its surrounding villages had their fair share of highs and lows during the two world wars. A stained glass memorial window in Brook Church gives the names of those people from Brook and the neighbouring parishes who served and those who died. In both World Wars, Brook people of military age went into the services unless they were in reserved occupations. But the village remained for the most part a peaceful place.

February 8th 1913
Torpedo on the beach
A large torpedo weighing about 2 cwt was discovered on the shore on Sunday morning by two labourers employed at Brooke Farm. It is apparently a British weapon of the Whitehead type.

Occasionally areoplanes came very close and one or two actually came down. Living on a coast which was a potential invasion site, there were worrying times for all.

The Brook, Brighstone and Shorwell Detachment of the Isle of Wight Volunteer Regiment, 1917.

This reserve force was made up of men above military age. The detachment above includes in the back row: Phil Jacobs (in bowler hat and suit, probably because no uniform was big enough), F. Linnington (to his left). Second row from back: David Hookey and Walter Brown (9th and 10th from L) and Henry Brown (far R). Third row from back: George Morris, Joe Morris, Bert Dyer, Tom Millmore and Arthur Buckett (the 5 men on the right). Front row: Jim Woodrow (2nd from L) and Walter Heal (4th from R) with Aubrey Wykeham (6th from R).

To the Glory of God and in loving memory of those who lost their lives in the Great War 1914-18. Pro Deo Pro Patria

**C.G.Seely**, Capt, Hampshire Regt.
k in action, Gaza 16 Apr 1917
**F.R.Seely**, Lieut. Hampshire Regt.
k in action, Arras 13 Apr 1917
**A C G Brown**, Lieut. RAF,
d of wounds received nr Perowne 3 May 1918
**J E G Brown**, Lieut, Royal West Kent Regt,
k in action Zillebeeke 22 Feb 1915
**C E Cassell**, Royal Fusiliers, d of wounds, Norwich Hospital, 31 Oct 1919
**W Cooke**, R F A, d a prisoner of war 1916
**L F Downer**, R F A, d of wounds
nr Entille Sept 1916
**P Downer**, Hampshire Regt,
k in action Ypres, 8 Nov 1914
**E F Newbery**, Lincolnshire Regt,
k in action Arras, 11 April 1917
**S White**, Somerset LI, d of wounds Linbury.

Left: The names of the men from Brook and neighbourhood killed in WWI and included in the Church memorial window. Below: A handwritten letter from Princess Beatrice to Sir Charles Seely, Lord Lieutenant, in 1919. In this note she offers her personal appreciation for the 'very valuable services which have been rendered' by the IOW Volunteer Force .

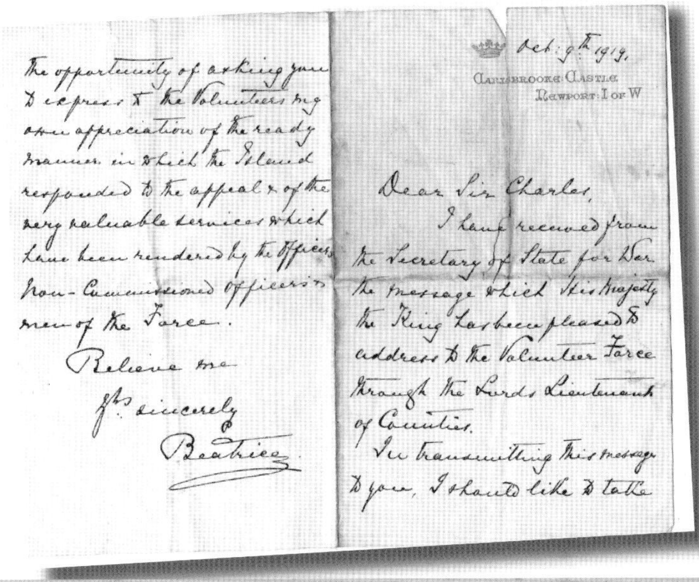
Oct. 9th 1919.
Carisbrooke Castle
Newport I of W

Dear Sir Charles,
I have received from the Secretary of State for War the message which His Majesty the King has been pleased to address to the Volunteer Force through the Lords Lieutenant of Counties.
In transmitting this message to you, I should like to take the opportunity of asking you to express to the Volunteers my own appreciation of the ready manner in which the Island responded to the appeal & of the very valuable services which have been rendered by the Officers, Non-Commissioned Officers & men of the Force.
Believe me
Yrs sincerely
Beatrice

Officers and men from Brooke and neighbourhood who served in the First World War. Back row from left: Alf Woodford; xxxx Westmore; Charlie Newbery; Alf Dollery; Lance Barnes; Alf Newbery; Charlie New; George Sewell; a land worker. Middle row: Bert Cook; Arthur Newbery; Frank Downer; a land worker; Chief Coastguard; J E B (Jack) Seely; Sir Charles Seely; Jack Seely's Batman; Essen (Sher'n) Downer (Mr Wykeham's chauffeur); Harry Smith (Jack Seely's valet). Front row: Fred Hayter; Toddy Dyer; Dick Whitewood, Frank Seely; Joe Thompson (Jack Seely's horseman); Harry Corden (Seely family chauffeur).

The first incident of the Second World War to affect Brook was announced by The County Press in 1939, when one of the new RAF fighters tested its guns before it was quite over the sea, 'more care should be exercised,' the IOW County Press calmly suggested.

## BROOK BOMBARDED

The people of Brook had an alarming experience on Wednesday morning at about 10-30, when for a few moments they thought the village was being machine gunned from the air. An R.A.F. fighter swooped over Mottistone Down, heading out to sea, and as it passed over the village there was a sudden roar of machine gun fire, smoke emerged from the plane, and then came a shower of brass cartridge cases and black metal clips, which played a tattoo on roofs and thudded into gardens. A few people who were about at the time, hearing the metal falling around them and fearing that they were bullets, dashed for cover, while others indoors came out to see what was happening, alarmed by the noise of the firing and the rattling of the falling objects on the roofs. Luckily no one was hit, but the occurrence caused considerable alarm. It was afterwards discovered that hundreds of the empty cartridges cases and metal clips had fallen in the village; children filled their pockets with them as they picked them up from the roads, fields, and gardens. About a dozen were found embedded to the depth of an inch or more in the Rectory lawn, showing that they would have caused serious injury, if anyone had been unlucky enough to have been struck by them. Mrs Winser, wife of the Rector (the Rev. A.A.P. Winser) told a 'County Press"'representative that she was indoors at the time, but heard what she thought was an explosion in the plane as it passed overhead, and the shower of metal striking the roof. Those who saw the plane said that a cloud of smoke trailed out after the firing, but the machine was apparently undamaged as it flew away towards Freshwater Bay. The probable explanation of the occurrence is that those in the plane were sending a burst of machine gun bullets from several guns into the sea as the plane dived, but started firing too soon. Whatever the cause, more care should be exercised as such objects falling from a height endanger life and property.

A few months later came the real war, and then the Battle of Britain. No bombs fell on Brook (two fell harmlessly between Compton Farm and Compton Grange). In fact, Erica Browitt (Newbery) remembers: *everyone saying Brook would not be bombed as the reflection of moonlight on Brook Hill House and the Orchard House in the walled garden of Brook House were too useful to the bombers as a guide out to the Channel. I do remember people saying there were a couple of spies in the village who were monitored very closely by the army...* On August 18th 1940, Oberleutnant Muller Freidrich was captured on Brook Down after bailing out of his Messerschmidt. A week later a Heinkel III Bomber crashed into the sea off Hanover Point. The crew were picked up by a German Air Sea Rescue Launch (see photograph below).

Throughout World War II troops were billeted all around the village, in the barns, the larger houses, in the school and, in summer, they camped in the fields. Soldiers were on armed guard at the top of Brook House drive and in Brook Chine. This meant that the people living there were under military control and had to show their identity cards to prove who they were before getting home. The soldiers used the old Lifeboat House as a guard house. Every time Maisie Minot (Bull) arrived home on her bike or got off the bus, she was challenged by the words, 'Friend or foe?' even though they knew who she was. She remembers how: *Mother made a pitcher of tea and I would take it along to the old lifeboat house for the men who were on guard duty.* Brook House was full of Canadian soldiers, Compton car park was full of huts housing soldiers from Jersey. Along the top of the cliff, a number of brick dugouts looking out to sea were manned for two hours at a time.

As well as their base in the lifeboat house, the army had a number of concrete and brick look-

A German photograph taken on August 26th 1940. Lieutenant von der Hagen (seated L) and Lieut. Karl Brutnning (standing R) are talking to members of the German launch which had picked them up off Hanover Point. (Andy Saunders from *The Isle of Wight at War,* Adrian Searle).

In joyful remembrance of the fate of the
MESSERSCHMITT 109
one of
HITLER'S NAZI CIRCUS
which finished its aerial career
at Bathingbourne Farm, on Friday, August 16th, 1940.

May its end be followed by many others.

Rita Whitewood of Rose Cottage kept this ironic and morbid 'in memoriam card' from 1940.

outs and dug-outs in woods such as Bush Rew and along the cliffs at Brook and Compton. Maisie Minot says that as far as she remembers the first troops to occupy Brook House were the Somerset Light Infantry, after that came the Devonshire Light Infantry. Mrs Myrtle Lewis (Newbery) has vivid memories of growing up in Brook in wartime: *The soldiers were stationed at Brook House. I was only little and it was towards the end of the war, we used to see the troops cross the field behind Little Brook and go into Bush Rew where they had dug outs. Rosemary and I would go and play in the tunnels - until they became unsafe. There were tanks parked under three elm trees opposite the engine house (at the side of the walled garden). One, a Churchill tank, was 'given' to me for my birthday. I remember a soldier lifting me up onto the tank while my father looked on. On duty at the Lodge gates was a sentry officer who was billeted at the Red House. On our return home from Newport one day, the sentry asked my father for his pass, he did not have it, the sentry was a new one and did not know my father, so he put him in the guard room until my mother returned with the pass.* Erica recalls the time when Brook House and its grounds were commandeered by the Government: *Soldiers lived in the house and the wooded land was used for the storage of fuel, ammunition, guns, tanks and other vehicles.*

After the evacuation of British troops from Dunkirk, the soldiers were dispersed across

*A searchlight to spot in-coming enemy planes and a Beaufort anti-aircraft gun were placed facing out to sea in the triangular field by the Military Road.*

southern England. The remnants of the Royal Northumberland Fusiliers were stationed in Brook and Hulverstone and some were billeted in one of the classrooms at Hulverstone School. Audrey Rann (Barnes) was a young girl at the school and remembers sharing the wash basins and toilets with the soldiers: *there were about 15 soldiers and they were responsible for the ack-ack gun behind our house (Bank Cottage). We all knew it was there of course, and it was fired when the planes were going over. All the soldiers were nice and friendly. Mr. Young was the officer who commanded the unit and he would go to the post office, next door, and buy bars of chocolate and give them to us school children. We didn`t eat them in school, we knew better than that, but would take them home. Sometimes at weekends a lorry would take the soldiers to Newport to the pictures or the pub.*

There were a number of defences established around the area as this was one of the more likely coasts to be invaded. After the war began, villagers had remembered a German holidaymaker cycling and taking photographs a year previously and think that this may have

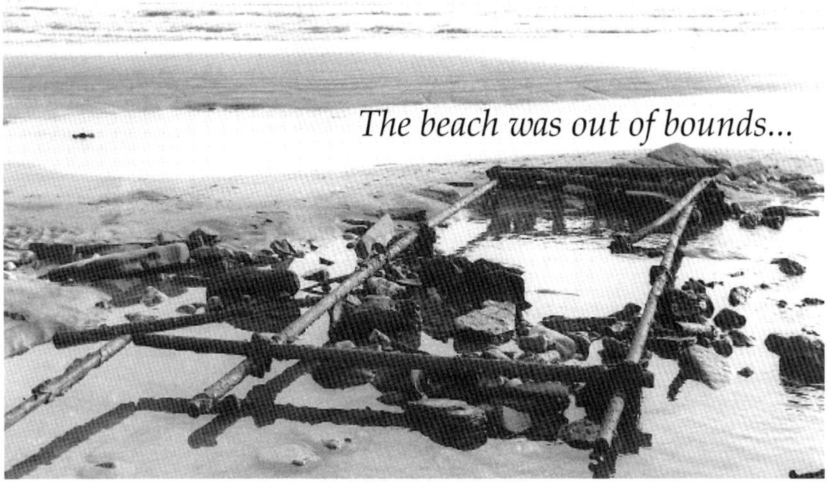


Remains of the coastal defences on Compton Beach in the 1960s. Those who were children in the 1950s and 60s remember having to avoid the rusty old scaffold poles and being told not to touch anything unusual in case it was a washed up mine.

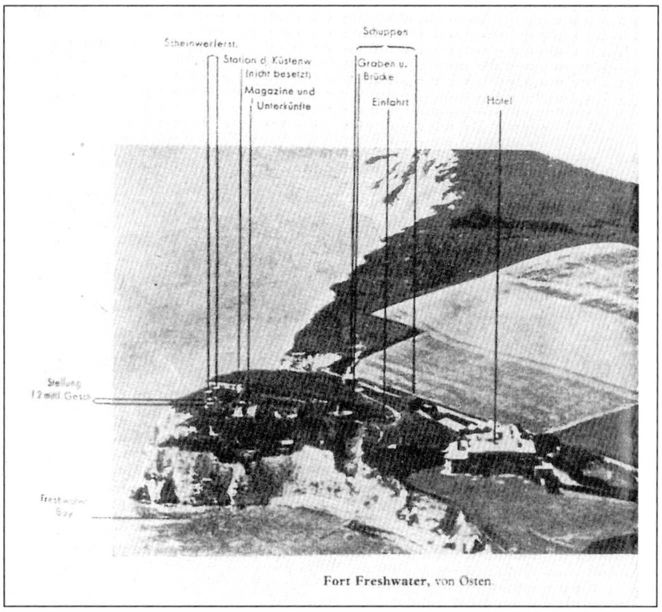

Fort Freshwater, von Osten.

Extract from a briefing book issued to German troops for the planned invasion of England in 1940.
*The Isle of Wight at War,* Adrian Searle.

informed the briefing book for German troops (see illustration). The beach was out of bounds and large tubular steel scafolding was erected along the sand to hinder any invading force. The present path down to the sea at Brook was mined. The mines were all exploded at the end of the war on a day when everyone was told to keep their doors and windows open to avoid damage from the explosion. Inevitably, perhaps, we are told it was a windy day...

A searchlight to spot in-coming enemy planes and a Beaufort anti-aircraft gun were placed facing out to sea in the triangular field by the Military Road. At first the searchlight was situated under the washing line at Hanover (next to the barn). This meant Hanover was at greater risk of being bombed so the Reverend Kirkbride ordered it to be moved aross the road into Mr Hookey's field. There were concrete pillboxes along the top of the cliffs at Compton and also at Chilton, opposite what is now Isle of Wight Pearl. Ken Barnes remembers: *In Brook village a road block was constructed near the gate of the Rectory to deter enemy vehicles. I think it did more to hinder local people. I was in the Home Guard for a short while. I remember that at the top of Brook Shute two combustible 45 gallon drums of a napalm-type substance was set into the bank on the right hand side of the road at the crest of the hill. This was supposed to be set off by an explosive charge in the event of enemy vehicles coming up the hill. We saw this demonstrated at a quarry on St George's*

**Brook and Brighstone Home Guard**
**1940 to 1944**

Back row: W.Sheaf, J.Higgins, A.Sivier, B.Westmore, H. Cassell, F.Hollis, G.Mariner, L.Attrill, C.Newbery, R.Cassell, C.Sivier. Second row: A.Emmett, C.Bullock, B.Phillips, J.Emmett, H.Cooper, H.Bullock, G.Phillips, B.Caven, A.Kitson, L.Hookey. Third row: R.Buckett, M.Cotton, C.Bennett, G.Humber, C.Linington, S.Mew, J.Whitewood, D.Carpenter, H.Brown, S.Hendy. Fourth row (front): S.Isaac, F.Driver, F.Taylor, S.Orchard, W.Emmett, R.Downer. N.B. There were others who are not in this photograph.

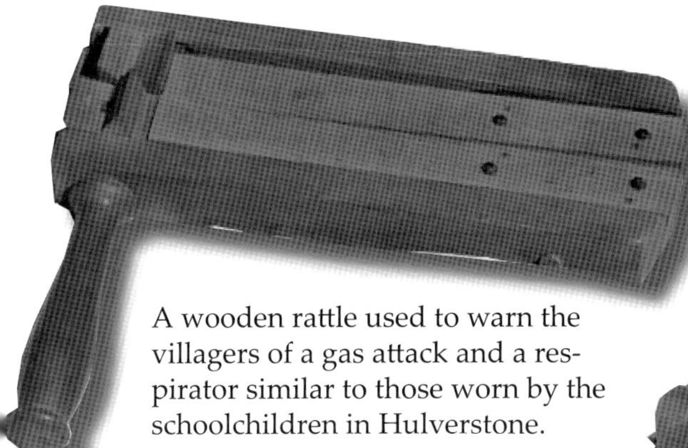

A wooden rattle used to warn the villagers of a gas attack and a respirator similar to those worn by the schoolchildren in Hulverstone.

*Down, it was a frightening sight. A great mass of sticky liquid blazing. I often wonder if the drums were ever removed from the site on Brook Shute!* Air raid wardens patrolled the village to make sure that no buildings were showing any lights. Anyone found carrying a camera was arrested and so it is perhaps not surprising that this chapter has so few local photographs. Between 1940 and 1944 those too young or too old to join up, or in the reserved occupations, formed the Home Guard. Including men who had fought in the First World War, they paraded at Hulverstone School, trained together on Sunday mornings, did guard duty one night in six on Brighstone Down and took part in exercises with troops guarding the coast. Robert (Bob) Cassell who worked at Hulverstone Farm, recalled one particular night when: *Another bloke and I had to go and man a machine gun post... It was right on the edge of the cliff and to get to it we had to go through a mine field. A regular soldier took us there and showed us the path to take. It was a bit scary, like. We stopped there until gone daylight.* Such duties were on top of a day's work: *After our nights on duty I had to be back at work at the farm at five o'clock in the morning*. In case of an invasion, there was also a 'secret army' of local men who were selected and trained in resistance tactics. Known as the Auxiliary Units, their aim was to wreak havoc behind enemy lines as a German invasion progressed. Russian commandos were brought to the Island to train these specially recruited men. Veterans of the First World War were preferred as were men who knew every inch of the countryside. They would hide in special underground chambers and the plan was that they would emerge at night and sabotage enemy supply lines and equipment.

Myrtle remembers that there were a fair number of false alarms as people adapted to the need to be on alert: *Mr Jasper Morris and my father were air raid wardens. On one of the Engine House posts (attached to the walled garden of Brooke House), there was a square piece of tin painted – I think yellow – and it was to be changed to another colour if there were any gases about. Mr Morris would come out and shout to Dad 'Yeller, Alf, yeller!' so Dad had to hurry to Dunsbury to warn them. When he returned he frequently met Jasper hurrying out with 'Air raid warning Red'. Only to run out again and meet Jasper coming back with 'Air raid warning Green' (all clear). They soon got fed up with that…* Similarly Babs Barton (Jackman) remembers her father was made head warden for the Mottistone area and had a whistle on which he needed to blow a specific number of blasts to let people know whether there was a high, medium or low level of risk. She remembers that after a number of false

*Anyone found carrying a camera was arrested.*

alarms, she was the one who was sent around the villages to blow the whistle. Life went on as best it could, children still went to school armed with their gas masks. Mary Petitt moved to Dunsbury in 1944 aged 6 and remembers: *Miss Nicholson had a Scottie dog, which she brought to school. If there was an air raid warning in school time, we all had to go into the Morrison shelter that was erected in the smaller of the two school rooms in Hulverstone. The dog came too. We all had gas masks*

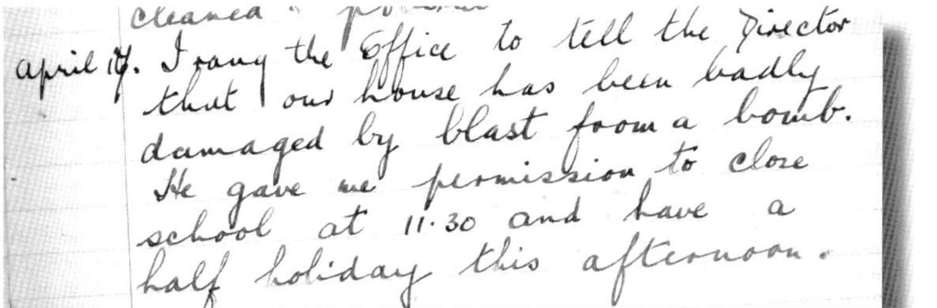
april 17. I rang the Office to tell the Director that our house has been badly damaged by blast from a bomb. He gave me permission to close school at 11.30 and have a half holiday this afternoon.

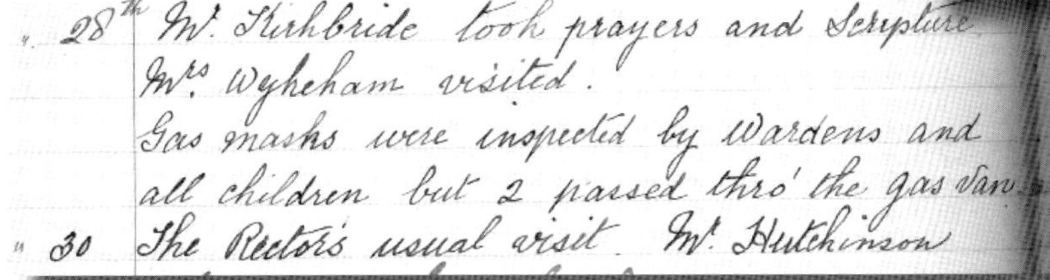
" 28th Mr Kirkbride took prayers and Scripture
Mrs Wykeham visited.
Gas masks were inspected by Wardens and all children but 2 passed thro' the gas van.
" 30 The Rector's usual visit. Mr Hutchinson

Two extracts from the Hulverstone School Log for 1942 describe the children's gas masks being tested and the results of the bomb that killed a number of army officers at Brighstone Grange.

Brook land girls and some of the farm workers they worked alongside. The photo was taken in 1945 when their work together must have been ending. Back row left to right: Fred Beaumont, Fred Morris, Alf Summerfield, Jim Davis, Percy Cotton, Deb Barnes, Snakey Abbott, Jim Harris, Steve Thompson, Moses Morris. Middle row: Gladys Baxter, Mrs Keen, Margery Phillips, Doris Kent, Sylvia Strickley, Muriel Kent, Phil Thompson, E.Beaucamp, K.Smith, Phyllis King. Front row: Unknown, Zoe Cotton, Charlie Thompson, Sadie Isaacs, Phyllis Bellman.

*during the war and they had to be tested every now and then. We had to go into a large grey van parked in the road wearing our masks to make sure that they were working.*

Myrtle recalls: *later in the War we moved to the thatched cottage on Brook Green. When the wind blew hard we could sit on our bicycles, hold out our coats and sail up to the village. On one occasion, my sister Rosemary and I were on the little bridge over the stream that runs down to Brook Chine when there was an almighty bang, my mother ran from the house and got us indoors, later we found out two soldiers had tried to cross the mined chine.*

The most serious loss was on April 17th 1942, when several army officers were killed by a direct hit on a hotel at Brighstone Grange and this tragedy is recorded in the Hulverstone School Log.

Audrey Rann (Barnes) lived at Bank Cottage, Hulverstone and remembers her father's inventiveness when it came to protecting his family: *When the war came, my father had a bright idea. If he emptied the logs from the shed, he could make the shed into an air raid shelter! He asked Mrs Heal, who had the farm at Hulverstone, if he could cut through the hedge and bank and dig out an area in the field behind our house, big enough to accommodate the shed. My father dug it out by himself with perhaps some help from my brother. He dismantled the shed, placed it into the hole, put it together again, filled in the sides and roof with soil, then put the turves onto the roof. From the sky it looked just like an ordinary field. The door was where father dug through the bank. We spent many nights in there when there was a warning and felt safe. Of course, we weren`t safe; if we had had a direct hit, it would have gone right through. However, it was a good idea as we were away from the house and the rest of the village.*

George Thompson remembers that in the war farmers got an extra £5 an acre ploughing up grassland to grow potatoes and cabbages, for example: *Dunsbury was more a vegetable farm and horticultural rather than agricultural. I started there with old Fred Barnes with a horse. When you dug early potatoes the land girls would pick up the potatoes, then you would go along with the horse and big hay dray and if any potatoes came up from underneath the ground they had to pick up twice.*

As George describes, the Land Army girls were an invaluable help. There were about twenty-two young women working at Dunsbury Farm who were tireless in back-breaking jobs such as picking up potatoes behind a tractor. At the start, many of them were unused to such hard physical work as Dorothy Higgins, who worked at Dunsbury, later recalled: *Cutting cabbage, sometimes in pouring rain, and picking frosty brussel*

*During snowy conditions, soldiers working on the coastal defences waited with frozen fingers for Hanover to open...*

*sprouts were some of the less comfortable jobs. We went to many other farms to gather their crops. We were taken on tractor-drawn trailers, causing quite a stir as we went through villages as some of the girls were very lively.* As a child Myrtle Newbery made friends with the land girls who worked on the Brook Estate: *At 'nammit time' we used to go round to the harness room where Margaret (Taylor) and Joyce (Phillips) would light the fire and have a drink and something to eat, then they would sing songs to us, like 'The White Cliffs of Dover' and 'Wide, Wide is the Ocean…'*

A number of voluntary groups were active in Brook and Mottistone during the Second World War. Members of the Red Cross were on alert in case of casualties and the Brook Women's Institute members met together in the Seely Hall and worked to can fruit, collect rose-hips and herbs and of course, knit for servicemen. They also collected clothes for people left destitute in bombed areas such as Portsmouth.

Mr Bill Emmett in Home Guard uniform with his daughters Joan and Doris in Mottistone in 1944.

Generally village people came off better than those who lived in the towns. Although food was rationed, families in the Brook and Mottistone area rarely went hungry. The farms provided milk and eggs, rabbits were in abundance, a lot of people kept a couple of pigs and most people kept chickens for their eggs. If you wanted beef or lamb, which was rationed, you used your coupons at the butchers. Everyone was encouraged to grow their own vegetables and 'DIG FOR VICTORY'. At Hanover they did a swap with Lithgows of Freshwater, icing sugar for castor sugar, so they could still provide cakes. If you had a good meal inside you, all was well. Everyone helped each other out and food 'swapping' or bartering was common.

With many soldiers billeted around Brook and the Royal Fusiliers camped in the barn next to Hanover, Mrs Joe Morris, her daughter Margaret and her daughter-in-law-to-be Gladys Winser, started to serve midday meals as well as teas. This later extended to breakfasts as well and they opened at 8.30 each morning serving sausage, egg and chips. The chips being cooked in out-of-date suet – with no complaint! During snowy conditions, soldiers working on the coastal defence waited with frozen fingers for Hanover to open, to get hot food and drinks. Also, Canadian soldiers from Brook House were known to have sat on the front path waiting for Hanover to open. The villagers were very sad when they later heard that most of the men who had become their good friends were later killed

*Roast rabbit featured regularly.*

at the battle of El Alamein.

There were no air raid shelters in Brook, so it was a case of 'hope for the best.' At Hanover they would crouch down under the telephone which was hung on an inside wall, but there was not much time to think about what might happen as they were kept busy providing hot food and drinks. Officers stationed at Arborfield (up Coastguard Lane) asked Margaret to hang up their uniforms at Hanover House so they would be smooth before they went on leave. On Christmas Day, Margaret and Gladys cooked sausage, egg and chips for the soldiers, before cooking their own Christmas dinner. There was no rationing on sausages in wartime. War time Teas consisted of a cup of tea (no pots of tea were sold), bread and butter and homemade queen or fairy cakes. Roast rabbit featured regularly for midday meals. A slate hung behind the kitchen door and every cup of tea and slice of bread and butter had to be accounted for. The village shop, which was part of Hanover House, supplied the tea room with

*Everyone helped each other out and food 'swapping' or bartering was common.*

stock using the necessary coupons and separate book-keeping.

When the war came in 1939, Joe Hulse joined the Army. He earned £2.19 shillings and was stationed on the Isle of Wight, manning the searchlight at the bottom of Hoxall Lane. A young Brook girl called Edie Morris, come rain (she often got wet through) or shine, came along to see the soldiers. She had no interest in any of the other soldiers but only had eyes for Joe. This was the start of a romance and then a long marrriage. In 1942 Bert Morris, a fitter and turner by trade, was working at Chevertons Garage in Newport. He installed new machinery in part of the garage given over to war work, producing component parts for Spitfires, landing craft, pumps for floating pontoons for bridges, etc, he worked from 8.00am to 8.00pm with a motorcycle journey to and from Newport on the top of it. Bert and his friend Sid Higgins described an eventful journey home to Brook one night: it started at Bowcombe when their motorbike got entangled with a cat: *we were alright, but sad to say the cat came off worse.* They slowly approached Shorwell where a road block was manned by soldiers of the Black Watch regiment. A soldier wanted to read some papers so he asked them for their headlamp, which consisted of a hood with thin strips of light. As they did this, one of the sentries discharged his rifle. Luckily no one was injured or killed. A court martial was later held about the incident and Mr Frank Cheverton said: *I am disturbed to*

Ron Emmett, lived in Church Cottage, Mottistone and will never forget the day in 1941 when, aged about 16, he was arrested as a spy:

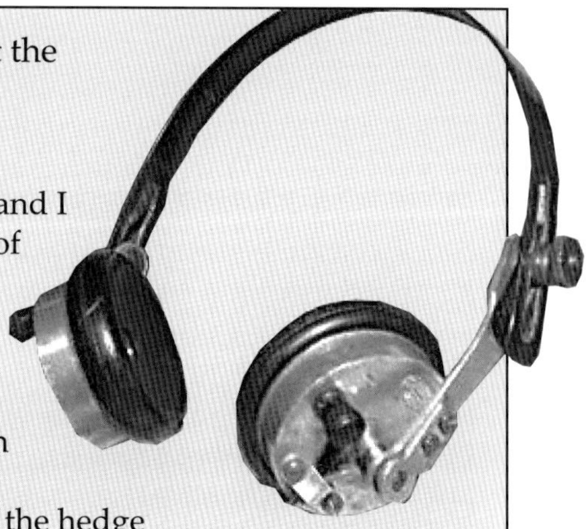

I had a keen interest in radio and all things associated with radio and was a member of the West Wight Air Training Corps. After experimenting, I found that you could put one terminal of a headphone to earth and the other terminal to a piece of wire and then do the same with another earpiece of a headphone. You could then speak into one 'phone, and hear the voice in the other - and you could do this over quite a distance. I had an old transformer which had probably a couple of miles of wire in the thing, so I thought, well I'll make a telephone wire and connect this up to my friend Ken Barnes' house – that's from Church Cottage, Mottistone to Bank Cottage, Hulverstone. So, one fine day, after many trials and tribulations, I set up one headphone in my bedroom and ran a very thin piece of wire over trees, bushes and fields, all the way to Hulverstone, and fortunately, without a break. The wire was enamelled so that it was insulated and, lo and behold, the ear piece worked, no power required. The coil in the earphones was sufficient to generate the energy needed to speak perfectly clearly with no interference over that long distance. And we'd have a little chat. First you would listen, then you'd speak, then listen and then speak. After a few days, slowly the wire began to have its weaknesses. Birds would break it or the wind or trees moving would snap it.

You must remember that at this time the Island was full of troops because we were expecting the worst. Anyway, one summer evening I was repairing a break in the wire by going along the hedges and putting one earpiece terminal on the wire and the other one to earth. If there was no hum you could locate roughly where the break was. I had got to the field opposite the Tollgate Keeper's Cottage and I had a whole pair of headphones on for some reason, I don't know why, and I decided to get on to the road, so I jumped through the hedge and landed at the feet of a patrol of a dozen or so soldiers who were out on exercise. They weren't too keen on seeing a civilian with headphones suddenly appear in front of them, so it was 'Right, what are you doing here, what are you up to?' and the next thing I knew was a Bren Gun carrier appeared and I was put in it, escorted by four or five soldiers. Off we went passing through Mottistone and my father (Mr Bill Emmett, head gardener at the Manor)happened to be walking across the road. I thought I had an ally in him, but I was wrong... he must have thought it was a game because he shouted: 'Shoot the b......, shoot him, he's a spy.' They took me up Strawberry Lane and through a gate into Grammars, or what I used to call Black Barrell, where they had their headquarters. They called the Adjutant and he came out to interrogate me. Strangely enough, I wasn't shaken or trembling like a leaf, you know. He asked me some detailed questions about the locality, like how far is it to places, and what's the name of this and that place. He wasn't very impressed that I was roaming about the countryside looking like a foreign agent but he sent me home on the same vehicle and all the troops came and had a cup of tea and everyone finished up quite happy.

*think the Army could shoot my men going home from work*. Bert and Sid then proceeded to the next checkpoint by the Crown Inn, Shorwell, only to be told there was a red alert and it would be best to put out what little light they had and carry on. They managed to get almost to Brighstone, but had to stop in the road because there were strings of flares coming down followed by bombs near to Grange Farm and what is now the holiday camp. Sadly on this occasion, many soldiers who were billeted there were killed. Bert and Sid were left struggling in the middle of the road pushing and pulling the motor cycle to get it under a hedge and out of sight. They eventually arrived home unscathed.
Edward Whitewood as a young child remembers staying at Hanover during the war and exploring the attic:

*One day I plucked up courage and ventured into the attic, it had always intrigued me. I couldn't believe my eyes - it was like an Aladdin's cave. There were unused painted buckets and spades with Mickey Mouse and Donald Duck on them, beach balls deflated in their packets and so perished I couldn't even blow them up, however hard I tried. There were sand castle flags and masses of other things I'd never seen the likes of before. What it was, of course, was the old shop stock. The beaches were out of bounds during the war and there were no holidaymakers, so such items were just put away and forgotten about. To me it was a treasure trove.*

Roll of honour
Those people from Brook and Mottistone who served in the Second World War

| | |
|---|---|
| + | Killed in action |
| * | Died on active service |
| ~ | Reported missing |

Brook churchyard also has three headstones commemorating unknown merchant seamen, buried on 8th July, 17th July and 21st October, 1940.

| | |
|---|---|
| Attrill, S J | Hookey, J B ~ |
| Bagg, G W | Horton, E |
| Barrow, H A | Henley, J C C |
| Barton, C | Jackman, D G |
| Barnes, W E A | Kiddie, C S + |
| Barnes , K A | Kenchington, W |
| Bull, H * | Keene, W H |
| Boon, H J R | Leal, L |
| Cassell, W | Lewin, G |
| Carpenter, H G | Morris, G H |
| Coward, G | Nicholson, Sir J |
| Crouch, J + | Paget, P |
| Campbell, F | Rann, F H |
| Charrington, J | Raymond, G H |
| D'Albiac, C H F | Sherwood, Lord |
| D'Albiac, R H | Seely, P |
| D'Albiac, P R S + | Seely, D P |
| D'Albiac, M P B | Seely, J H |
| Dunlop, W G * | Sivier, R T |
| Desdames, A | Sivier, L T |
| Emmett, F A | Wykeham, G C H + |
| Emmett, E G | Wykeham, J W |
| Emmett, S J | Whitewood, C F |
| Emmett, W R | Watson, S |
| Emmett, R G | Watson, K |
| Gallop, H J | Watson, C E |
| Hookey, T P | Davey, Gwendoline |

Some of those who went to war in 1939. Left: a passport photo Marjorie Clark (New) had made in London as ID so she could get home on leave to the Isle of Wight. Below left: Ben Hookey outside Myrtle Cottage. Top: Ron Emmett in West Wight ADC squadron in 1942. Centre: a young Ken Barnes. Right: David Seely, 4th Lord Mottistone. Below right: Frank Whitewood.

Compton Beach in the autumn of 1945. It can be used for the first time since 1940, but the barrier against landing craft is still in place, and in November the autumn gales washed mines onto the shore, two exploding at Chilton and two at Compton. Even into the early 1960s, children played on the rusting exploded torpedoes lodged firmly in the sand.

## Prisoners of war

Left: Willie, a German POW who worked on Peter Jackman's farm at Pitt Place, Mottistone from 1945 to 1948, and below left when he returned with his wife in 1981. Above: Jim Hookey, George Humber, Irene ..., Richard Pietschacher (German POW) collecting hay in Brook in 1946/7. See also *Farms and Farming*.

Mary Pettit was about 8 years old at Dunsbury Farm in the war and remembers watching as: *the German prisoners of war who worked at the farm cooked their main meals in a huge container in one of the barns. I remember having a plateful of stew with them once.* Both the Hookey family at Downton Farm in Brook, and the Jackmans at Pitt Place, Mottistone, had a German prisoner of war who was a great help on the farm and who became part of the family. While it is perhaps surprising that both men were still working in Brook and Mottistone in 1946, the extract below, taken from a Parliamentary debate in 1947, sheds some light on the thinking at the time:

...the future employment of German prisoners of war in this country was that arrangements were being worked out whereby prisoners of war could be retained in agriculture as civilians, provided the farmers employing them could accommodate them and that their remaining here was not detrimental to British workers. *Hansard*, April 1947.

# The Military Road

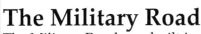

The Military Road was built in the 19th century to enable the rapid movement of troops along the coastline. Before that time the main local routes were from south to north across the Island. It was not until the County Council took over its upkeep in 1933 that the public were allowed to use the road. Before that there were gates across the road and children used to collect pennies by opening the gates for horses and vehicles. In the extract below, Jack Seely recounts how the history of the road reflects changes in England's friendship or hostility towards other nations. Sadly it is not the 'hereditary foe,' but nature, that is the greatest threat to the Military Road and as we write this book the battle to save this beautiful road is waged once more.

The old Military Road when it was just a farm track. Left: one of the decorative iron caps or 'helmets' placed on the top of the galvanised posts that skirted the Military Road when it was first built.

Sometimes the road has been in the possession of my family. Sometimes it has been maintained by the nation. Before the Crimean War it was just a series of farm tracks ten miles long. But then when the war came to an end and trouble began with France, it was decided that the Military Road must be taken over and rendered fit for the transport of troops and guns to repel any attempt at the French landing on the south-west coast of the Isle of Wight. My grandfather (Charles Seely, MP) duly handed over the road (in fact he sold it for £2883). The authorities repaired it and built fine bridges over the chines, strong enough to carry heavy guns. After a time, the Government decided that the French had ceased to be our hereditary foe and were not going to invade us, so my grandfather was told to take back the road, which he did. By degrees it relapsed into being a farm road again, as I first remember it when I was a little boy.

But then came further trouble with France over the Mekong River in south-east Asia…and my father, who has succeeded grandpa in the ownership of the Military Road, was ordered to hand it over to the War Office. This he duly did. The road was repaired and the bridges strengthened. All was made ready for the French Invasion, but war did not come and work on the Military Road was stopped.

Only a few years later came the Fashoda episode (a conflict in Africa between France and Britain), and work was resumed. Then came the South African War. The Boers were far away, but our European neighbours were none too friendly, so the War Office continued to control the Military Road. Then came the Entente Cordiale (friendship) with France. Papa was told that there would be no more wars and that he could take over the Military Road. Rapidly it became a farmer's track again.

After a time the German menace began to assume formidable proportions...Then came the World War and, of course, once more the War Office took over the Military Road. At the end of the War I was informed that there would be no more wars and that I must take over the road again. This I did.

But now, fortunately for myself, the road has passed into the control of the County Council and it is they, I suppose, who will have to face up to the problem of the ever-changing 'hereditary foe.'

*Paths of Happiness, J E B Seely* (1938)

Work underway on the cutting for the road at Compton in 1933 and the newly opened Military Road.

# Self-sufficiency and lucrative pastimes

A gardening group at the allotments up by the Coastguard Station. Included in this picture are Phil Jacobs, Joe Morris. Harry Barnes seen left by the horse, gardened with his peg leg which couldn't have been easy, but for someone who was also in the cricket team he didn't do too badly.

Even those who lived off the sea had quiet months and needed to turn their hand to other work in order to survive. The skills the locals acquired included boat building, thatching, brewing, bee-keeping and, especially vital before the NHS was established in 1948, creating herbal remedies. Vegetable and fruit growing was essential, alongside rabbiting and keeping chickens and a pig. The villagers had the right to cut gorse or furze ('fuzz', as it was called) on the Common, a slope of the Down, and this was used as fuel for cooking. Before container ships most cargo was carried in the holds, however the inshore current meant there was always something useful to be picked up by 'combing' along the beach in the early morning.

**Growing your own**

Living between the downs and the sea, with just one small village shop for most of their needs and little spare cash, everyone supplemented the weekly rations by living off the land and growing their own produce. The wise old gardeners knew how to get the best harvest and swore by planting in accordance with the stages of the moon. During the waning of the moon (full to new moon), they would plant the root vegetables, during the waxing of the moon (new to full moon), they would plant vegetables that produce crops above ground, such as runner beans and peas. They would never plant on a Sunday or on the day of the new or full moon. Spuds were planted on Good Friday. A toad was a welcome resident of the garden, keeping the slugs and snails at bay. The contents of chamber pots were beneficial if thrown on the compost heap, which was also handy if the gardener was 'caught short'; the tomatoes thrived on it!

Pat Tyrell remembers that fisherman, Alf Woodford on Brook Green: *was quite a good gardener but not a perfect one. He'd gut fish and bury the waste straight in the garden. It rotted down*

Joe Morris stands by his bee hives at Rectory Cottage (Badgers).

*and made beautiful manure! I suppose it's like this fishmeal you buy today, all quite natural with nothing added. He used to grow some good stuff there but I don't think it was one of his first interests. I can remember him having potatoes, rhubarb and all the stuff they grew in those days.* Robin Shepheard recalls how Meadow Cottage (opposite Hanover on Coastguard Lane): *had a large garden and my great grandfather, John Newbery, was a very good gardener. He grew all the old fashioned vegetables, he didn't use any purpose-bought sprays, just good old farmyard manure and lime. All digging was double trenched and I would follow behind with various buckets for collecting stones and weeds/roots.* Brook and Hulverstone gardeners had, as now, the prevailing south westerly winds to contend with. All sorts of windbreaks were invented and one story is of a canny gardener up Coastguard Lane who had his runner beans on a pulley system which he could let down in stormy weather and pull up again when the 'blow' was over. Ralph Cook remembers that people often specialised in one particular fruit or vegetable; in his father's case it was small cabbages as hard and compact as cannon balls. A good harvest of crops meant there would be enough for the family through the winter. Root vegetables

Joe Morris in his vegetable garden at Rectory Cottage in the 1930s.

Ben Jacobs and Harry (Stumpy) Barnes.

would be 'clamped down' for winter storage and other vegetables could be salted down, then bottled. Fruit was bottled in Kilner jars and various things were pickled, including eggs.

**Cooking and everyday life**

Most people kept a pig or two which would be reared, killed, then salted down and stored in a meat safe, ready to cook and eat over the coming weeks. Carole Worrall (Woolbright) recalls how, living at Briar Cottage in Carpenter's Lane, the large Barnes family: *kept a pig and used to kill it, cut it up and salt it down. There were no fridges, just a larder and meat safe on the outside wall.* In wartime, Myrtle Lewis remembers how: *Just before Christmas my father would go out with the bicycle and a large basket on the handle bars and come back when it was quite dark with a pig's head. Someone in the village had killed a pig and shared out the parts. My mother would make brawn, she would press the tongue and we even had the brains on toast!* Chickens were in most back yards, they provided fresh eggs and the occasional chicken dinner. Carole recalls: *Gran used to do the gleaning after the harvest. She'd pick all the straw up in the field and bring it all in for the chickens. I remember sitting in the back scullery listening to the clucking of the chickens all around us. After plucking a chicken they would burn off the remaining feather stumps with a candle.* Occasionally people kept goats which supplied them with milk. Eve O'Neil remembers vividly her childhood summers at Dunsbury spent with her grandparents, Fred and Emily Barnes: *Granny was a wonderful cook, lovely fruit cakes and pies. Grampy grew everything and his new potatoes were special. Granny would put all the small potatoes into a bucket and we would have them with cold meat and pickles at supper time. Mustard was made daily from powdered mustard. I*

Chickens kept in Brook in the 1930s. Thought to be behind the cottages on the main road and off Badger Lane.

*always remember her mustard pot, a silver dish with a blue glass interior. One of her lovely dishes was steak and kidney pudding; she would line a basin with suet pastry, fill it with the meat and gravy, then a suet lid would be placed on top covered with a pristine white cloth, tied with string and steamed all morning on the kitchen range. Granny used a tablecloth with a green border for breakfast and a blue bordered white cloth at dinner time. Grampy came home at dinner time and he would put a page from the Radio Times under his plate so he wouldn't spill any gravy on the cloth. Granny would cook a suet pudding in a cloth for Grampy. He would have half with his meat and vegetables and the other half with jam or golden syrup. Working on the land, he needed good meals to keep him going until he finished work.* In the 1950s domestic comforts for the villagers had not changed a great deal from before the First World War. As a child, Renella Phillips (Humber) lived with her parents at Compton Grange (opposite the car park): *An isolated house even now, we had no electricity or inside bathroom. Lighting was by oil lamp or candles. There was an old-fashioned range in the kitchen, but I think Mum cooked by calor gas. The 'bathroom' was outside the back door. It had a toilet, and a bath which, I think, had a waste outlet but no taps (no hot water), so had to be filled from the boiling copper, which was also there. There was a big garden, where Dad grew all the veg we needed, and an old apple tree, bent becauseof the winds. Before the public conveniences were built at Compton, we one day had a hiker knock on the door and ask if he could use our 'facilities.' We were highly amused to find, after he'd gone, a sixpence left on the seat in payment!*

Both a sign of the times and good use being made of the old pig sty at Briar Cottages, Carpenters' Lane.

*With no electricity, our main source of news and entertainment was a battery operated 'portable' radio, which seemed to weigh a ton! It had huge batteries which Dad would heat up in the oven when they began to run down to get a bit more life out of them. I remember listening to 'Children's Hour,' 'Listen with Mother' and 'Larry the Lamb'. At Christmas, we would put real candles on the tree, not fairy lights, and I never remember the tree catching fire! Mum would make the Christmas puddings early and store them in the attic to mature. She would put a flour-and-water paste on top of the pudding mixture to help preserve it, and a pudding cloth on top; one year mice nibbled through the cloth and the paste and ate the pudding. We were troubled by mice, but one became a friend – he would come and sit on the hearth in the evening and get fed crumbs!*

Eve O'Neil's memories give us a snapshot of village life: *On Saturday afternoon we would catch a Shotters bus to Newport... If the weather was wet Granny and I would wear our wellington boots to the bottom of the lane where we would go into a cottage and change into our shoes for our trip to Newport. When we got off the bus we would go back to the cottage and change our shoes to our wellington boots to walk home. The lady in the cottage used to give me a small jar of honey and a new laid egg for my tea.* When the weather was unusually severe, the villages would be completely cut off. Alice Morris remembered as a child: *One very exciting time was the deep snow of 1881. We had no bread for days, as even the men couldn't get on the roads*

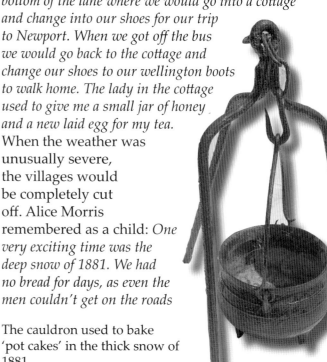

The cauldron used to bake 'pot cakes' in the thick snow of 1881.

*to get any. As we had plenty of flour and lard we did very well. The only drawback was we had nowhere to bake, only a brick oven which we couldn't heat. So we had to cook or bake in a gypsy cauldron. We made a kind of thick pancake which we called 'pot cakes'.* W.I. Scrapbook, 1958.

Audrey Rann describes the resourcefulness of her parents:

Mother used to make our clothes and the rag rugs for the floor. The latter would be put in front of the fire so you had something other than bare floor on which to put your feet. Mother used to knit our jumpers. She would unpick a jumper or cardigan, sometimes two to make one, given to her and make sweaters for us, often multi-colour. I didn`t like these but dare not complain as I was lucky to have something warm to wear. Father used to mend our shoes and mother also became quite good at repairs if he wasn`t around. Father always did the leather soles which had to be soaked to soften it. He used what was known as a Last which had three different sized feet, child, woman and man, which would stand on a table to allow you to use the size foot you wanted. There would be metal pieces put into the soles at the toes, shaped like the segments of an orange, and which were called Segs, so that the toes didn`t scuff too quickly. On the heel you had a stud shaped like a horseshoe. These used to make a noise when walking along the road and we used to enjoy trying to make sparks. Monday was Wash Day and took all day. It seemed to us that when we came home at lunchtime, mother was up to her elbows in soap suds, having started after we went to school. Lunch was always cold meat and potatoes, that was all. There was one tap in the corner, with a bucket underneath. As far as I can remember mother never had a mangle or a wringer, only hand wringing. We had a wooden clothes horse and a line across the kitchen. Otherwise it would be put outside and would freeze in winter. The loo was up the top of the garden, very basic. You didn`t want to go there in the night if you could help it! That stands you in good stead for later life! We did use a torch outside.

**Beekeeping**

The Reverend Morris is known to have kept bees in the Rectory garden in the late 1800s. This is probably how Joe Morris got his interest in bee keeping. When the Reverend Morris left the

Alice Morris 'Mrs Joe' at the back of Border Cottage inspecting her honeycombs. The veil on her hat covered her face and was her only protection from the bees.

Rectory at the turn of the century the bees stayed in Brook and Mr and Mrs Joe kept bees for much of their married life, producing some of the finest honey. Sue Mears (Stone) remembers how: *The wooden frames would be put into the hives and left for the bees to work. When the honeycomb was ready, it was collected, bulging with honey. The extra honey was scraped away to allow it to fit into the*

Bee puffer and skep used by local beekeeper Mary Case.

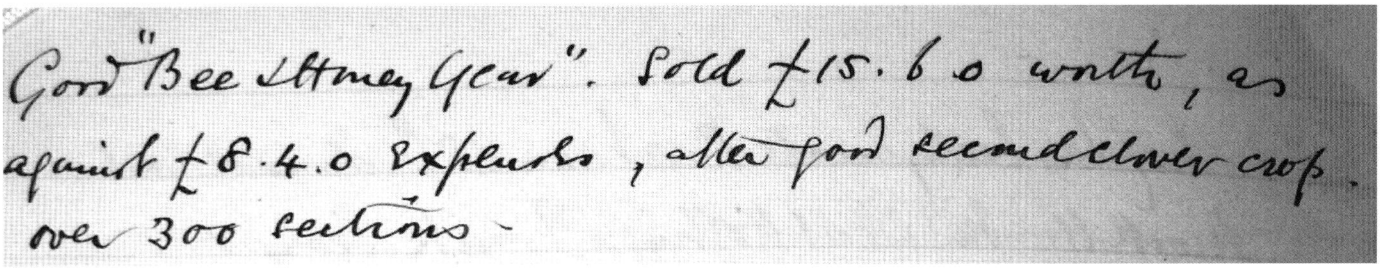

Good "Bee & Honey Year". Sold £15.6.0 worth, as against £8.4.0 expenses, after good second clover crop. over 300 sections -

In 1879 Rev.Morris uses capital letters to record in his diary a particularly good year for bees and honey production.

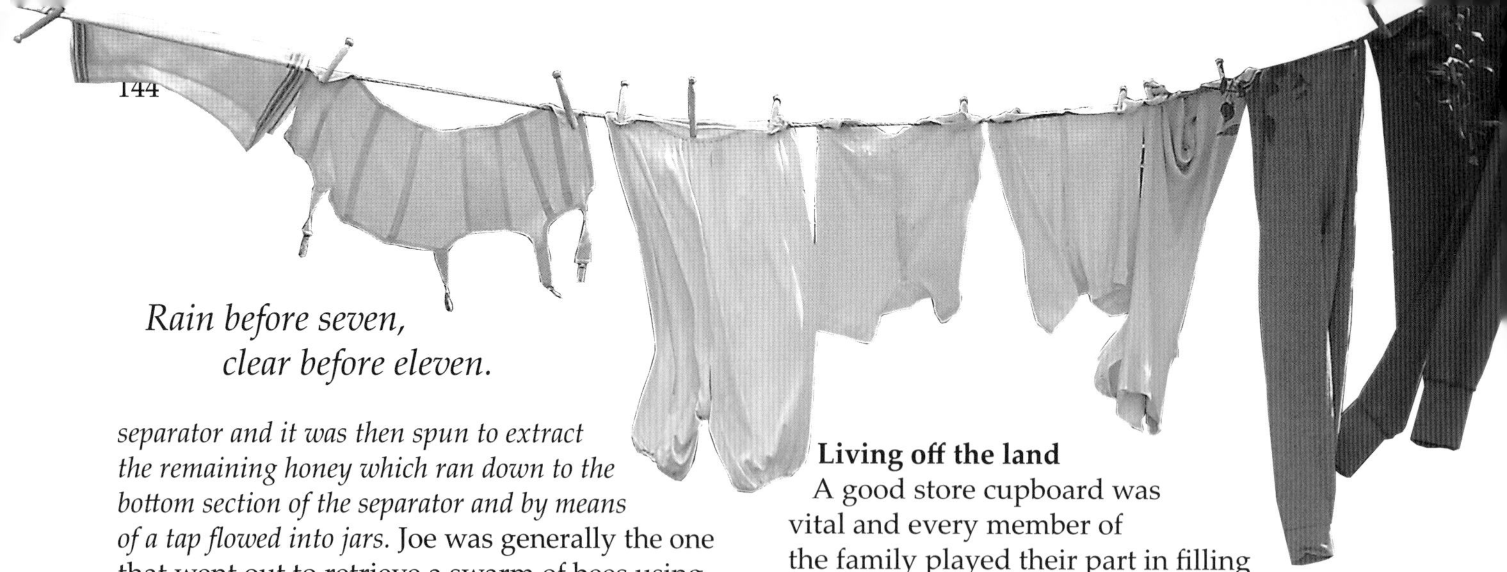

*Rain before seven,*
*clear before eleven.*

*separator and it was then spun to extract the remaining honey which ran down to the bottom section of the separator and by means of a tap flowed into jars.* Joe was generally the one that went out to retrieve a swarm of bees using his smoke puffer to make the bees drowsy; then collected the swarm in his skep to transport them back to an empty hive. The bees were fed on sugar water in winter and the hives covered in old carpet to protect them in the cold weather. Their son Bert took over the bee-keeping when Mr and Mrs Joe became too old. Bert said that in his opinion, nectar collected from clover was the one that tasted the best. It is commonly thought that bee venom is good for arthritis. Mr and Mrs Joe and Bert Morris were stung many times, but sadly they still all suffered from arthritis in later life. George Humber inherited the hives from Bert, taking them up to 'Flackstead' in the 1960s.

**Weather forecasting**

Knowing what the weather was going to do was as crucial to a good harvest as ensuring a successful washday. A wealth of observational knowledge and experience of local conditions was passed from generation to generation. An abundance of berries in autumn meant a hard winter, birds nesting high in trees in the spring meant a good summer. Seaweed hung outside cottage doorways told if it was going to be wet or fine. If cows were lying down it was a sign of rain. Those who worked the land every day noticed changes in visibility and the way sound carried in different conditions. Many locals said that if you can't see the Dorset coast from Brook it means good weather ahead. In an area with a predominantly south-westerly airstream the sayings included: *Wind in the east, three days at least; Rain before seven, clear before eleven; Mackerel sky, mackerel sky, never long wet, never long dry*. Observing birds and animals also helped forecast the weather as when seagulls fly inland to the foot of the downs it is likely that stormy weather is on its way.

**Living off the land**

A good store cupboard was vital and every member of the family played their part in filling it. The hedgerows were loaded with blackberries in the autumn and these could be bottled or made into jam. On September 10th 1941 the School Log records that: *The children were taken on a blackberrying expedition to the foot of the downs. Fourteen pounds of blackberries were gathered and taken home by the children.* Another ten pounds was collected by the children a week later. Sue Mears remembers going into Mr Hookey's fields at Downton Farm where the old goat roamed: *That's where the best blackberries were, you armed yourself with a walking stick to fend off the goat as well as to hook down and reach those big, juicy ones that were just too high to get hold of. We came home with arms scratched and purple fingers, but also a pudding basin full of delicious blackberries.* Home brewed concoctions of potent wines were made out of cowslip, dandelion, elderberry and stinging nettles and for the children on special occasions ginger beer, lemonade and various cordials were made.

**Beachcombing**

Brook, of course, had a good supply of fresh fish and flotsam and jetsam were other sources of 'free food.' An early morning walk along the beach after a stormy night often resulted in a good find, a tin of this or that, or a useful piece of timber. Alice Morris remembers how, in the 1890s : *We had great excitement if a ship came in loaded with coal, flour, wheat, sugar and many other things. Of course we helped ourselves when we had the chance. You might think it wasn't much good but the water only caked it on the outside. The inside was quite good. If the preventative men came again, there was great excitement running around to hide the goods. Only once or twice was anyone caught, then*

*If you came across a piece of timber propped up against the cliff you did not take it as you knew someone would be coming back for it.*

Rita Whitewood as a young girl with sacks of apples washed up on Brook beach.

*they had to go 'Up the steps' as they called it, which meant they had to go to the Town Hall and pay a fine.* WI Scrapbook, 1958.

In the 1940s Robin Shepheard looked forward to coming home from school in Freshwater: *There were so many things to do which were all free. Beachcombing was terrific fun. Over the years vast amounts of timber and deck cargo were washed up on the beach and some of it was carried from the beach back home. A great tradition when you were combing was that if you came across a piece of timber propped up against the cliff you did not take it as you knew someone would be coming back for it. Most of the decent stuff was washed up at Sudmore, a long walk from Brook. David Hookey came up with the great idea of positioning his father's tractor at the top of the cliff near the coastguard lookout hut (no longer there) and lowering me down the cliff on a rope. I would tie the timber or whatever to the rope and David would haul it up. At times you could get a bit greedy and end up with more timber than you knew what to do with. Once a whole cargo of pit props and bales of rubber that had been deck cargo lost in a storm were brought off the beach with most of the village involved. The bales of rubber were declared to Customs and Excise and a tax paid on it but there was still quite a lot of money made by the locals. Hard work, but worth it.*

**Poaching**

Most plentiful then, as now, was the rabbit. A good, wholesome rabbit stew was a weekly treat. No doubt the odd rook or blackbird made its way into a pie as well and poaching was commonplace. Carole Worrall remembers the kitchen at Briar Cottage: *That's where I learned to skin a rabbit by watching my grandfather do it. They used to catch rabbits by using ferrets to flush them out and they would put a net over the bolt hole to catch them as they escaped.* Ron Emmett describes himself in the 1930s as: *the number one poacher in the area.* He made his own bows and arrows and with his school friends used to go rabbiting regularly. Ron's first home-made bow is still in perfect condition (pictured below) and he remembers making it from a large tree at the entrance to Brook House drive. Because of his reputation, he couldn't go past the Keeper's house (Toll Bar Cottage) as a boy, so with Cyril Emmett, his next door neighbour (no relation), he used to go down across the fields to Fernfield (in the woods below Toll Bar), trying to knock rabbits out of their squats in the turf with a 'bunny bunker.' A 'bunny bunker' was any missile that could knock out and kill a rabbit. Ron tells us: *We would throw this thing and knock the rabbit over, just like that. We took the rabbits to Brighstone to sell to the village shop. We occasionally*

*A 'bunny bunker' was any missile that could knock out and kill a rabbit.*

Mrs Jasper Morris in the 1920s looking very at home with a shotgun and rabbit, perhaps surprisingly in what looks like her Sunday best. Inset: Ron Emmett's first home-made bow which he used to shoot rabbits.

*had the odd pheasant, but not very often.* Later, in the 1950s and 60s when food was more plentiful farmers and landlords were keen for people to catch rabbits. Robin Shepheard recalls how: *Mr French, the Estate gamekeeper, would lend us two ferrets, a pole cat and a bag of 50/60 nets. We would go off all day and catch an average 50/70 rabbits and sell them to a Newport butcher, Mr Stevens in Scarrotts Lane. The local farmers were pleased and we earned a few bob. Somehow seems cruel today.* Jane Phillips says Den (who farmed Compton) never had wages as such all his life. All he had was his 'rabbit money': *he went out on Sundays up the Downs to catch as many rabbits as he could, and woe betide any of the Tyrells who were up there poaching on his patch! He would take his catch of rabbits into Newport to sell to Mr Whapshot, the dealer.* Den was delighted when he reached the age of 65 and could draw his old age pension from Brook Post Office, he saved it in a tin which lived on the top of the corner cupboard.

### Home remedies

Some of the womenfolk were skilled herbalists, gathering all sorts from the hedgerows to cure every ill. Robin Shepheard remembers his grandparents, Walter and Daisy Newbery, making: *all kinds of potions and herbal remedies from rose hips, elderberries, blackberries, sloes, etc. which were all collected together with leaves from various plants. I swear there was not a plant or berry that could not be crushed to cure any ailment.* 'Mother Elder' was probably so named because every bit of the plant was useful - the berries, the flowers and even the bark can be used as an anti-histamine. Elder flowers infused with yarrow flowers and mint made a tea for curing colds and flu. The following ingredients for a 'Linament for Lumbago' were found among Rita Whitewood's possessions in Rose Cottage in 2007. This cure must have been much sought after for it to have been written down so carefully:

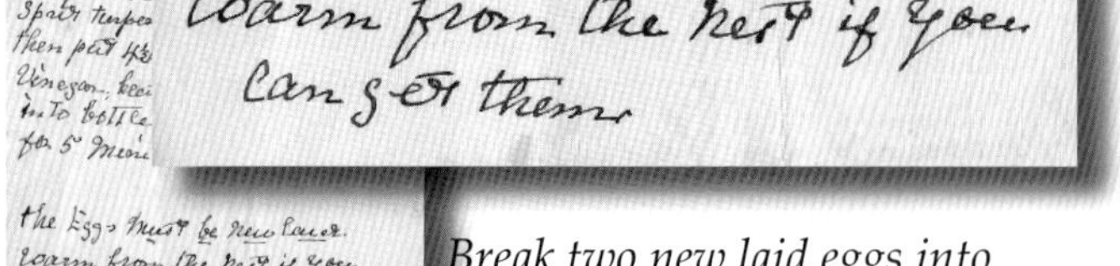

*Break two new laid eggs into a pint jug, beat up with a fork then put two eggcupfuls of spirit turpentine, beat up again then put four and a half eggcupfuls of best vinegar. Beat up once more, put into bottle and shake well for 5 minutes.* In a postscript to the recipe we are exhorted: *the eggs <u>must be new laid</u> warm from the nest if you can get them.* What it does not stipulate is whether you then drink it or rub it in... The cure for being stung by stinging neetles was to find a dock leaf, spit on it and rub it into the affected area. It would only work if accompanied by the rhyme, 'Dock go in, sting come out,' which had to be repeated all the time you were rubbing it in. It seemed to work! Syrup of figs would have been in everyone's medicine cupboard along with rose hip syrup for vitamin C. Joan Moss (Bull) remembers: *We picked hips from the hedgerows - there were plenty up Brook Shute above the Church and these were used to make rosehip syrup.*

A Ministry of Food recipe during the War:

**Rosehip Syrup (using 2lb of hips)**

Boil 3 pints of water. Mince hips in a course mincer and put immediately into the boiling water. Bring to boil and then place aside for 15 minutes. Pour into a flannel or linen bag and allow to drip until the bulk of the liquid has come through.

Return the residue to the saucepan, add one and a half pints of boiling water, stir and allow to stand for 10 minutes. Pour back into the bag and allow to drip. To make sure all the sharp hairs are removed put back the first half cupful of liquid and allow to drip through again.

Put the mixed juice into a clean saucepan and boil down until the juice measures about one and a half pints, then add one and a quarter lbs of sugar and boil for a further 5 minutes. Pour into hot sterile bottles and seal at once.

### Independent characters

Bill Ballard, his brother Alec and their close neighbour Alf Woodford, were good examples of self-sufficiency. Like the Jacobs' brothers from Cliff Cottage, they lived all their lives on Brook Green and never married. The Ballards lived in Chine Cottage and Alf behind in Therles. Like Alf Woodford, and Phil and Ben Jacobs, Bill held a long service certificate as a crew member of Brooke Lifeboat. He knew a great deal about the local countryside and coast and had been a farm labourer as well as a builder for Downers and Bucketts. Everyone who knew Bill knew what a strong-willed person he was. He planted all his own vegetables until two years before died aged 90 in 1989. He fetched water from his well (refusing the water board's suggestion that he boiled it), cooked for himself and refused to consider the need for an inside lavatory. Many people today remember Bill sitting on his bench outside the cottage, always with a pipe in his

A notice put outside Chine Cottage as a jokey response to the increasing number of holiday makers coming to Brook in the 1950s.

Bill Ballard on his bench outside Chine Cottage where he would talk to both locals and visitors about the lifeboats and days gone by. Inset: Bill as a young lifeboatman fifty years previously.

mouth. Alf was made of the same stuff and Pat Tyrell remembers: *Alf was always dressed the same; a very heavy jacket, a shirt with no collar and the sleeves rolled up, and a pair of overall trousers, always a bit short on him, and black boots. Alf never rode a bike but walked everywhere and never seemed far away. He'd walk up from his house to the shop, come up and get a drop of milk at the farm and never went far as I remember. I never went in Alf's house. I went to his door but never had any need to go in. Alec and Bill lived in front of him and they all got on well. They'd go in and out and look after one another.* It is interesting to consider the reasons why these men never married. They all lived with their mothers who they looked after until they died; all of them could live off the land and sea but may not have made enough money to support a family; they needed little and rarely left Brook to meet new people. While their sisters married and moved away, by the time their mothers died these batchelors were, perhaps, set in their ways and well able to look after themselves. Finally, the high casualty figures of the First World War did not lead to large numbers of unmarried women in the area since many men had stayed working on the land in reserved occupations. Anecdotes, often at each other's expense, were frequently told. The following refer to 'Safe' Edmunds, 'Lopper' Coleman and Buddy Edmunds:

I think it was an insurance man came to his house on Hoxall Lane. Safe was working away out in the garden there. This man said to Safe *'Does Mr Edmunds live here?'* 'Yes,' said Safe, *'he lives in there.* The man went and talked to the lady of the house then he came out and said *'You didn't tell me you was Mr Edmunds,' 'No, you never asked me.'*

It was a lovely day and a plane was flying up high and Jim (Hookey) says to Buddy: *'How would you like to be up there with he then Buddy?' 'Shouldn't care to be up there without him,'* he said.

'Lopper' met a friend at the bus top in Brook and they started chatting: *'Zetten off t'Nippert, bist thee?'* he asked. *'Oim off ter git t'Missus one o'they television sets,'* was the answer. *'Darn expensive bain't they?' 'Oi don't kees a cuss about expense.'* Not wishing to be outdone, Lopper retorted, *'Oim gittin' one o'they too.' 'Yew cain't do that, yew ain't got no electrics'* – *'Ah!'* he said, *' Oi be getting' one o' they Calor Gas ones!'*

Phil Jacobs with the newspaper outside Cliff Cottage, Brook Green in the 1930s.

# Village trades and occupations

Jasper Morris, Dick Whitewood and Phil Jacobs working the saw by the engine house on Brooke House Estate (it was attached to the west wall of the walled garden).

*Those old people, they knew a lot you know, we young chaps learnt a lot from them...we never forgot them and what they did for us. They weren't too proud to show us, or too secretive.* Fred Price, sheep shearer

As isolated villages between the downs and the high seas, Brook and Mottistone have always been small communities that thrived on hard work. Employment was mostly from the land and the sea and incomes depended on an intimate knowledge of the physical environment, the sea state and the weather. The inhabitants had to provide for themselves and it surprises us today just how many jobs were undertaken within the village. The 1841 to 1911 censuses tell us that every able-bodied man had a job, often more than one, and the same names crop up under different occupations.

The work of fishermen, coastguards, farm labourers, servants, school teachers and rectors is covered in separate chapters of this book.

In this section we piece together what we know about the local carriers, the blacksmiths, carpenters, shoemakers, gardeners, shop keepers, inn keepers, post mistresses and the much-needed district nurse. Most trades and professions outside the home were men's work and consequently there are few records of the contribution women made to the local economy by keeping the home clean and the family fed and healthy. When the men came back from a lifeboat rescue, not only were they aching so much they sometimes had to be carried home, but they also had difficulty sitting down for days as their backsides were chafed raw from the sea water, rough thwarts and their coarse trousers. Alice Morris recalled how she had to carefully apply vaseline to her husband's raw backside for days after a rescue.

In terms of women's work, in 1881 the census notes a 17 year old dressmaker, Mary Jane Morey, and in 1911 an Eliza Ward. Harriet Johnson is busy as a laundress from the 1880s and in 1911 is working alongside Jane Cassell and Mary Vinney. When the Seely family came to live in Brook they brought new kinds of employment and the census shows an increase in general servants, cooks, housemaids, nursemaids and parlour maids. Many young girls in Brook were employed at Brooke House, the Rectory and some of the larger farms. A number of workers came with the Seelys from Nottinghamshire and Lincolnshire and this provided welcome new blood in the village. We know, for example, that Polly Hookey married fellow servant Arthur Cole, from Lincolnshire, who will have come to Brook with the Seelys.

Work in Mottistone was mostly on the land or at the Manor Farmhouse and the very small hamlets of Compton and Chessell were entirely focused on agriculture.

| **BROOK CENSUS** | **1841** | **1851** | **1861** | **1871** | **1881** | **1891** | **1901** | **1911** |
|---|---|---|---|---|---|---|---|---|
| Coastguards | 4 | 5 | 6 | 6 | 5 | 5 | 5 | 5 |
| Blacksmiths | 4 | 3 | 3 | 2 | 2 | 3 | 4 | 4 |
| Agricultural labourers | 11 | 15 | 14 | 17 | 12 | 13 | 24 | 10 |
| Shoemakers/binder | 3 | 3 | 1 | 1 | – | – | – | – |
| Carriers | 3 | 1 | 2 | 2 | 2 | 1 | 3 | 3 |
| Carters | – | – | 1 | 2 | 4 | 2 | 5 | 3 |
| Carpenters + apprentices | 3 | 2 | 7 | 7 | 3+4 | 3 | 6 | 8 |
| Masons/builders | 1 | 3 | – | – | – | – | – | 1 |
| Female servants | 6 | 6 | 7 | 8 | 14 | 6 | 12 | 7 |
| Male servants | 3 | – | 1 | 1 | – | 3 | 6 | 1 |
| Gardeners | – | 2 | 2 | 6 | 6 | 6 | 7 | 8 |
| Clergyman | 1 | 1 | 1 | 1 | 1 | 1 | 1 | 1 |
| Inn keeper | 1 | 1 | 1 | 1 | 1 | 1 | 1 | 1 |
| Farmers | 2 | 2 | 2 | 3 | 3 | 3 | 2 | 3 |
| Fishermen | 1 | – | 2 | 2 | 8 | 5 | 6 | 4 |
| Sadler/harness man | – | – | 1 | 1 | – | – | – | – |
| Grocers/assistant | – | – | – | 1 | 1 | 1 | 3 | 1 |
| Decorators | – | – | – | 2 | – | – | – | – |
| Governess | – | – | – | 1 | – | – | – | – |
| Shepherds/cattlemen | – | – | – | 1 | 1 | 1 | – | 2 |
| Dairymen/women | – | – | – | 1 | 1 | 1 | – | 2 |
| Seamstress/dressmaker | – | – | – | – | – | – | – | 1 |
| Land agent/farm bailiff | – | – | – | – | – | – | 2 | 1 |
| Teacher | – | – | – | – | – | 1 | 3 | 2 |
| Clerk | – | – | – | – | – | – | 1 | – |
| Laundress | – | – | – | – | 1 | – | 1 | 3 |
| Postmistress | – | – | – | – | – | – | 1 | 1 |
| Basket maker | – | – | – | – | – | 1 | 1 | |
| 1 | | | | | | | | |
| No. OF HOUSEHOLDS | 31 | 28 | 32 | 37 | 33 | 41 | 54 | 57 |
| POPULATION | 150 | 141 | 161 | 171 | 209 | 214 | 221 | 220 |

## Occupations 1841 - 1911

The census records collated here give an idea of the variety of occupations in this small part of the Isle of Wight from 1841 to 1911. It is important to note that they are not always accurate as they were taken on one day of the year and the Seely family and their full compliment of servants, for example, may well have been in London or Nottinghamshire. The area covered by each enumerator also varied slightly year on year: while Hulverstone was consistently included in Brook, parts of Mottistone were at times included in Brighstone. People took on a variety of jobs to make ends meet but could only choose one for the purpose of the census. Mottistone in 1891 and 1901 are where we know the numbers printed here are unreliable.

**MOTTISTONE CENSUS** N.B.. the 1891 and 1901 Census is incomplete, likely numbers in brackets

| | **1841** | **1851** | **1861** | **1871** | **1881** | **1891** | **1901** | **1911** |
|---|---|---|---|---|---|---|---|---|
| Blacksmith | | | | 1 | | | | |
| Miller | 1 | | | | | | | |
| Agricultural labourers | 25 | 45 | 45 | 32 | 31 | 12 | 10 | 19 |
| Stone mason | | | 1 | 1 | | | | |
| Gamekeeper | 1 | | | | | 1 | | 4 |
| Chauffeur | | | | 1 | | | | |
| Carpenter | | | 1 | | | | | 1 |
| Assurance agent | | | | | | | 1 | |
| Gardener | | 2 | | | 2 | 3 | | 3 |
| Almsman | | | 1 | | | | | |
| Farmer son/daughter | | 4 | 6 | 5 | 6 | 3 | | 1 |
| Female servants | 3 | | | | | | | 10 |
| Male servant/groom | | 1 | 1 | 1 | 3 | 1 | | |
| Mariners | | | 1 | 1 | | 1 | | |
| Fishermen | | | 5 | 5 | 2 | | | |
| Tailor | 1 | 1 | | | | | | |
| Seamstress/dressmaker | | | 4 | | 1 | | 1 | |
| Nurse / midwife | 1 | 1 | | | 4 | | 1 | 4 |
| Shepherd | 1 | | 2 | | 4 | | 1 | 3 |
| Dairywoman | | | | | | 1 | | 1 |
| Land agent/ bailiff | | 1 | 1 | 1 | 1 | | | 1 |
| Fund holder | | | 1 | | | | | |
| Sexton | | | | | | | | 1 |
| Chelsea pensioner | | | 1 | | | | | |
| Maltster | 1 | | | | | | | |
| POPULATION | 151 | 156 | 160 | 170 | 143 | 59 (97) | 17 (89) | 100 |

# Blacksmiths

David 'Daf' Hookey outside the smithy at Downton Farm in the 1930s.

Barnabus Cooper bought the blacksmith's shop at Downton Farm in 1799 and was the first recorded blacksmith in Brook. John Hookey, who was the son of a Shorwell blacksmith, was apprenticed to Barnabus and later became his son-in-law when he married Barnabas' eldest daughter, Elizabeth. We are fairly sure that there were two blacksmiths' workshops in Brook in the 19th century, one at Brook Villa, run by the Hayter brothers and one at Downton Farm, run by the Coopers and later the Hookeys. In 1841 the census notes five blacksmiths in Brook: Barnabus Cooper, aged 65, John Hookey, Isaac Low (apprentice) and John and James Hayter. From 1841 to 1871 the Hookeys and Hayters were the smiths in Brook. In 1871 there was also 16 year old Tom Jackman, a blacksmith who was living and working at Mottistone Mill. In 1881 and 1891 the only blacksmiths in Brook were James and John Hookey with the addition of young Thomas Hookey. By the 1911 census we see that the brothers, James David (Daff) and Thomas Hookey had taken over as the village blacksmiths. Tom Hookey also became coxswain of the Brooke Lifeboat.

The Hookey family continued to run the blacksmith shop at Downton Farm well into the 1950s. In 1958 Ella Way Hookey, widow of Tom, recalls how at the turn of the century: *there was a great deal of work mending wheels so there was a prosperous blacksmith's shop in the village. The Hookey family ran this and had a pony cart in which they carried the shoes round to the various farms and shod the animals on the spot to save them having to travel far…* Tom died at the relatively young age of 55 (see *Ship Ashore!*) and his widow Ella and her children then exchanged Downton Farm with her brother-in-law David's family and went to live at Myrtle Cottage, next to the Methodist Chapel.

James Hookey and his three daughters at Downton Farm in the mid 1880s.

In *Forever England* (1932), General Jack Seely describes his friend the local blacksmith, David Hookey: *I have never known a human being with so much quiet energy… He is the oldest member of our lifeboat crew, and has never once missed either a practice launch or a wreck.*

A number of people today still remember David (Daff) Hookey, in later life, chewing and spitting out his twist tobacco. His niece Kitty remembered him as an unusual character, an irascible man who would, at times, stand in the road shouting at people. Apparently only his brother Tom could deal with him. David Hollis remembers: O*nce father used to hire out horses and carts for the Council. We went to Brook one day and the horse's shoe was loose. I went in to see Daff Hookey, as he was called, 'Yes, we can do that', he said, but he had to have his breakfast first. By the time he had had his breakfast and then gone out for a yarn with people, half the morning was gone before he got our horse out onto the road.* As a young boy, Robin Shepheard remembers in the 1950s: *I was a bit scared of 'Granfer, who was always telling David and me off for messing around in his blacksmith's shop, particularly when we started up the fire and played with the bellows. David became very clever with metal and iron work, all of which he picked up from his grandfather.* The Smithy was left untouched from the day the last tool was put down in the 1950s until 2010 when the farm was sold.

*I well remember the pleasant sound of the hammer and the sparks flying in the evening.*

Ella Hookey, 1958

Like all skilled tradesmen, Barnabus Cooper made his own tools. The initials 'BC' stamped into the chisel (below) are how the blacksmith used to identify his tools. The oldest identifying punch used at the Forge was that of two clay pipes crossed and this mark can still be seen today on the ironwork of the gates at Mottistone Church. Even nails had to be made from scratch, see the nail anvil, left. The giant bellows below were worked by two huge, roughly-hewn branches.

In Forever England (1932), General Jack Seely describes getting back to Brook after a busy week in Parliament and going to visit his friend the local blacksmith, David Hookey:

When I get back tired and cold on an autumn or a winter's evening, it is good to be allowed to go to the forge…those of us who are allowed to gather there mostly sit and watch, trying not to get in the way. Incredibly deft are the strokes of the hammer on the well-nigh molten metal, the result of forty years of experience and generations of inherited skill. So we sit there on a bench facing the glow, with the rain drying off our faces and our clothes, talking in whispers, until David Hookey has finished the job in hand. Then he must have a rest, for it is hard work swinging a great hammer for minutes on end without a moment's respite. When all is done for the moment, David addresses us, sometimes about the weather, the heavy ground-sea, the absence of shingle on the beach at Brooke and the accumulation of sand at Compton, the difficulty of getting the lifeboat out unless the shore changes for the better; but sometimes he sets us extraordinarily interesting puzzles. One delicious question, only the other day: 'Would this new Tariff policy help what his grandfather and mine called 'Free Trade'?' We all understood the question perfectly, including the senior next to me on the bench. David was not being mischievous; his skilful brain, released for five minutes from the strain of making the perfect horse-shoe, was playing round the problem. Nobody said a word in answer to the question, while one could hear the faint crackle of the cooling embers on the hearth of the forge. There was a pause; then, to the huge delight of the rest of us, the coastguard officer loudly cleared his throat and gave a cough. Not a word did we say. Then David remarked: 'I was reading a book, in which I read that eighty years ago the Isle of Wight produced more than twice as much of everything that was needed for the inhabitants. I remember my grandfather told me the same, but he said wages were low, and, but for one thing, I don't think folks could have been very happy. Well, I must make the next shoe.' Then, still blowing up the fire, he put the bar into the red-hot embers and continued to blow. In a pause he said, 'But my grandfather said folks were not so unhappy as you might think in those days; the smuggling was a real help to all classes.'

Downton Farm smithy was left largely untouched from the 1950s to 2010.

# Carriers

*Our red letter days were trips to Newport by carrier, which took a full day and were always an adventure in the horse-drawn covered van.*

George Shotter's carrier van transported people and parcels between, Brook, Brighstone, Shorwell and Newport c.1890. Here the van has stopped outside what is now the *Three Bishops* in Brighstone.

Mary Millmore (above and left with her children) continued to run the carrier business from Sudmore, Brook, after her husband died. *Put Out the Flag*, Derek Sprake.

Carriers were vital to village life as they provided the only transport from the villages to the market town of Newport. When she was 87 years old in 1958, Alice Morris remembered the excitement of going to Newport to shop in the carrier's cart when she was young: *Starting at nine in the morning and getting home any old time. Just depending how many times the driver stopped at the local. Often they were very gay before they reached home.* Carriers often ran their own small farm and as transport was needed to take their animals to market, they could earn a little more money by collecting and delivering goods for others as well as taking people into town. If you needed the carrier to call on you, you would 'put out the flag', which meant getting their attention by putting a flag on the end of a stick and putting it in the hedge or out of a bedroom window. We know that the Millmore family of Leigh Cottage at Sudmore, east of Brook Green, were operating a carrier business in the early 1800s. The Millmores were the longest running carriers in the locality. When James Millmore died, his widow Mary carried on the business until the early 1900s. She is documented on the 1911 census as a general carrier with her sons Ruben and Martin Millmore as her assistants. In 1841 three carriers operated from Brook, they were James Raynor, Richard Tickner and Richard Hayter. In 1852 Richard Hayter appears to be the only carrier, but by 1855 he is joined by Mrs Hannah Tomkins who operated from Brook to The Castle Inn, Newport on a Saturday and Henry Woodford who operated for many years from Brook to The Bee Hive in Newport on Mondays, Wednesdays and Saturdays. By 1861 and 1871 William Hayter was the carrier and Roland Hayter (who was also coxswain of Brooke Lifeboat) continued running the business until the early 1900s when horse and cart were replaced by motor transport. Edward Whitewood recalls when he was young in the 1940s: *Tuesday was a big day - it was market day in Newport so if anything was needed it was the day the carrier came. To get the carrier to call required a flag to be flown. This was a red and yellow diagonal cross and was poked out of the bedroom window. I felt very important to be allowed to go up and hang out the flag.* Until 1956 when Southern Vectis took over, Shotters ran the bus service. Audrey Rann remembers: *There were no bus stops in those days* (1940s). *If you wanted the bus, you stood in the road and put out your hand.*

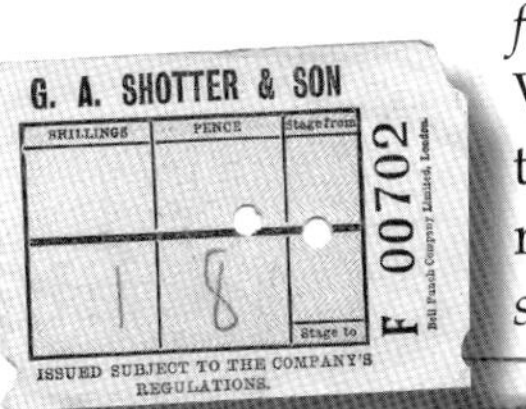

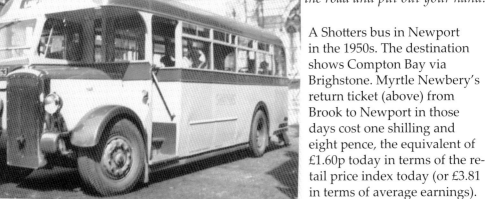

A Shotters bus in Newport in the 1950s. The destination shows Compton Bay via Brighstone. Myrtle Newbery's return ticket (above) from Brook to Newport in those days cost one shilling and eight pence, the equivalent of £1.60p today in terms of the retail price index today (or £3.81 in terms of average earnings).

Old Myrtle Cottage where the Hayters had a shop.

*Miss Hayter had a 'flexible' pricing system, depending on whether you were a 'regular' or a 'popper–inner'.*

Rita Whitewood with loaves of bread outside the beach cafe at Compton just before World War II.

In 1871, Thomas Mussell, a grocer, is recorded at the Sun Inn, Hulverstone. It wasn't until 1881 that there was a mention of any sort of shop in Brook, or Mottistone. The Hayters' shop was in the front room of No 1 Old Myrtle Cottage, above, run by John Hayter, a widower aged 76. By 1891 it was run by John's daughter Elizabeth. Many still remember her and that she had a 'flexible' pricing system depending whether you: *be a reglar or a popper–inner.* She was also known for putting a finger on the scales to make things weigh more. The Hayter family were still trading in the early 1930s. In *An Eventful Life,* Robert Cassell mentions a shop at Hulverstone situated behind The Elms in the 1860s and 70s and run by a Mrs Willington. In 1933 Bert and Margaret Morris saw an opportunity and opened a shop at Hanover (see *Hanover Stores and Tea Rooms).* Before the war there were also tea shops down on the cliff top at Brook, one was run by Harry Barnes and his wife and one by Charlie and Julia Bennett, supported mainly by visitors. When the war came, it came to an end as no one was allowed onto the beach at that time. Rita Whitewood also ran a small tea and beachware shop at Compton in one of the beach huts. Many people today will remember the Munts' shop in the 1960s at Compton car park, which sold beach equipment and ice creams and each winter moved a little nearer to the cliff edge.

# Gardeners

Gardeners Phil Jacobs and Dick Whitewood

By the turn of the 20th century there were seven full-time gardeners employed in Brook. Some worked for local folk who couldn't manage their own gardens, but mostly they were employed at Brooke House, Brook Hill House and Mottistone Manor. The first mention of a gardener in Brook is Henry Taylor on the 1851 census. By 1861 he was 64 and living at Brook Lodge, probably helped by his son, William Taylor who is listed as a garden labourer. By

Brooke House gardens at their most formal in the 1880s and 1890s when Mr William Tribbick was Head Gardener. The lawns were mown by a horse-drawn mower, the horse wearing rubber boots to protect the turf.

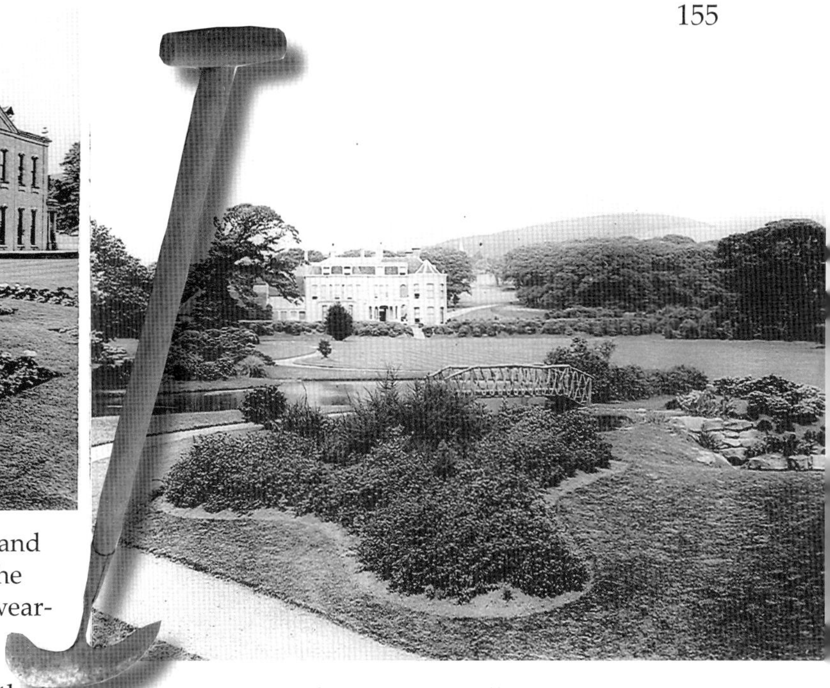

1871 the Seelys were focused on landscaping the grounds of Brooke House and there was plenty of gardening work to be had. The census shows George Hendy, Isaac Morey and William Hall as local gardeners, and Adam Gray and his son Albert, who had come from Aberdeen and Luton and whose family was living in Rose Cottage. In the 1891 census we see gardeners with now familiar local names: Frank Cassell, just 14, and James Jacobs. Isaac Morey was gardener at The Rectory. William Tribbick was head gardener at Brooke House for nearly half a century from approximately 1870 to 1920. He was a very knowledgeable and respected man, a member of the Royal Horticultural Society and author of several published papers on the growing of fruit and vegetables. Working as under-gardeners to him were Augustus Blake, Frank Newbery and James Ford. In William Tribbick's obituary on 3rd January 1927, The Isle of Wight County Press reported:

> William was a very skilful gardener especially at indoor cultivation, he was ever ready to impart his fruits of experience to others and sometimes he would do this in a novel way. His houses at Brook - gardens were pictures of orderliness and cleanliness.

By 1901 Brook lifeboatman William Jacobs (better known as Phil), Frank Newbery and labourer Percy Downer are listed as gardeners. In 1911, the year of George V's coronation and when there were great festivities in Brook, there must have been a great deal of gardening

Phil Jacobs and Dick Whitewood pose in the walled garden of Brooke House in the 1920s. The photograph was probably taken to record the huge cauliflower on the ground and the 10ft high rows of beans behind them (we know Phil was at least 6ft tall). Phil (left) tends the cold frames with Gardener's Cottage in the background.

*We used to enjoy going up into the muscat house where my mother would get up on the staging to thin out the grapes.*

Alf Newbery (1893-1955) and Tiger in front of the arch leading to the Coach House of Brooke House.

Daisy Newbery (Pragnell) who, from a young age, expertly tended the famous Brooke House vines.

work as we see eight men and boys working on gardens: John Hookey, Benjamin Cassell, William (Phil) Jacobs and William Tribbick, Frederick Morris, Henry George (Jasper) Morris and Alfred and Frederick Newbery.

Alf Newbery took over as the Brooke Estate's head gardener after Mr Tribbick died aged 70 in 1927. He was assisted by his wife Daisy and Jasper Morris. Daisy specialised in fruit-growing, especially the famous Brooke House vines. Daisy grew up at Hanover and remembered how she: *always loved to be in the open air so I suppose it was not surprising that when I grew up I became a gardener. For twenty to thirty years I worked in the garden and the greenhouses of the Seely family at Brooke House. My work was mostly with peach and nectarine trees and grapes grown in large glass houses. I managed to get my sweetheart (Alfred Newbery) a job as gardener on the Seely estate too and later we were married. When our three daughters were born we called them after much loved local plants which were in flower at the time of their births: Erica, Myrtle and Rosemary.*

Daisy and Alf's daughter, Myrtle, remembers as a child: *We used to enjoy going up into the muscat house where my mother would get up on the staging to thin out the grapes. It had a wonderful smell in there. They grew figs, white grapes as well as the black ones, peaches, nectarines and many other soft fruits as well as vegetables, flowers etc.*

Joe Morris was gardener at Brook Rectory for many years. He kept the walled garden neat and tidy and produced some fine fruit and vegetables for the Rectory table. Mr and Mrs Joe Morris lived in Rectory Cottage (now Badgers) which had a gate through into the walled garden. As children Janet and Susan Stone remember it as: *Our secret garden - full of succulent strawberries, raspberries and fruits of all kinds. We would seek out the toad that was always around somewhere, keeping the slugs and snails at bay. Grandad would give us a ride in the wooden wheelbarrow along the long grass pathways which were very neatly trimmed and went between the various plots of vegetables.*

Mr Bill Emmett, the much respected Head Gardener at Mottistone Manor for 40 years.

# Carpenters

The only known photograph showing the Newbery brothers' carpentry workshop (centre left at bottom of picture) in Carpenters' Lane in 1968.

There was always work for carpenters in Brook and the surrounding villages. In 1841 there were three carpenters, Benjamin Groves, 54, his son Barnaby, 28, and a William Leigh, 45. In 1851 the carpenters were Walter Jacobs, Barnabus Groves and a young William Newbery, aged 21. In 1861 something big was happening in Brook; there was an influx of carpenters and they were lodging in various houses in the village: James Rendell, George Childs, George Simmonds, William Hale and William Smith came from Kent, Bristol, Hastings, Lincolnshire and Middlesex and worked alongside William Newbery, now aged 31. The Seelys had recently bought Brooke Estate and extensive carpentry work must have been needed both in the House and in the outbuildings. In 1871 we see that William Newbery, now 41, has five local men and three apprentices in his employ, two of them being his own sons William, 18, and Henry, 16, with William Cook aged 20. By 1891 things had changed again and the carpenters must have needed to seek work further afield as we see John and James Newbery are now listed as 'carpenter journeymen.' In 1901, Henry Newbery is listed as a Master Carpenter, aged 46, alongside brothers John and James Newbery, now in their 40s. John's 16 year old son William, and Frederick Newbery, a nephew, were apprentices. The three Newbery brothers traded as carpenters, joiners and wheelwrights and were appointed as carpenters to the Seely Estate making, typically, farm gates, posts, fencing and farm carts and wheels. The brothers were also responsible for looking after the many private and Estate houses, making and mending doors and window frames and also making furniture for the Seely family at Brook and Mottistone. 1911 was another boom year for carpenters in Brook. The census lists eight carpenters and joiners: John Hookey, Walter Hookey, Ernest Tribbick, Robert Hayter, Frederick Hayter, Charles Newbery, James Newbery and William Newbery. This demand for work was probably driven by the construction of the monumental Brook Hill House for Sir Charles Seely up above the Church. As well as general carpentry, the Newbery brothers made coffins and organised funerals. Mr H Newbery, for example, made the arrangements for Ben Jacob's funeral in 1929. When John Newbery died, the business was taken over by Jim's son William (Walter) Newbery (1884 – 1971), who lived with his wife Daisy and daughter Joan in Meadow Cottage on the corner of Coastguard Lane. As a young man, Walter had worked for builders in Freshwater, Yarmouth and Lymington, and would ride his bike to and from wherever the work was each day. Under Walter, the business thrived and he was helped by William (Bill) Newbery and by

*If anything needed mending in the village there was something in the carpenters' shop to fix it, finding it was a little harder!*

Bill Humber from Mottistone. Carol Worrall (Barnes) remembers as a small girl the strong smell of fresh sawdust as you walked up the lane past the Newbery brothers' carpenter's shed and sawpit. Walter Newbery (1884-1971) is still remembered today by many people, and especially his grandson Robin Shepheard:

My grandfather, Walter Newbery, was the Seely Estate carpenter and had his workshop at the top of Carpenter's Lane. My grandfather was always on call for Lord Sherwood and his partner Mrs Ranger and would regularly be making and repairing furniture, especially I recall, sash windows. These were quite elaborate with weights, but if made correctly were very efficient. One project I remember he was called upon to make was four large four-seater oak seats with all the correct joints (mortise and tennon etc. 'NO nails'). These had to be placed at various sites around the Estate, located at an easy walk from the house. One was quite close, at the end of Bush Rew, one at Brook Church and another at the end of a long avenue of trees which ran from the road going into Brook towards Hulverstone. The most difficult site of all was the one on top of Five Barrows... it took most of the day to get there, walking and carrying the seat up Brook Shute, resting on the seat all the way. I think Bill Humber helped us. It must be remembered that in those days all joinery work. was completed by hand with hand-made planes and shaping tools, although saws and jigsaws were available. The workshop was a great place for me with the smell of timber being worked on and the smell of various wood glues was very strong –no need to sniff anything in those days! Most of the implements such as planes, awls, etc. were home made. If anything needed mending in the village there was something in the carpenters' shop to fix it, finding it was a little harder! I can remember using many of the tools in the shop in the years between 1947 and 1957. Although everything seemed to be in a mess with planed and un-planed wood everywhere, boxes of nails, screws, catches and just about everything one would require. Travellers would come from suppliers, typically Hursts and Plumbleys, with just about everything the business needed. Moreys would supply all the timber. Walter Newbery died in 1971 and the business ceased as no one was willing to carry it on and by then other larger builders were well established in the area

Walter Newbery, Kate Ranger and Sir Hugh Seely, Lord Sherwood, outside the Seely Hall in the late 1950s.

# The District Nurse

Nurse Rann stands by her gleaming car - the first in the district.

With no doctors in the countryside and no National Health Service, the district nurse played a vital role in village communities. The 1871 census lists a nurse, Mary Hendy, aged 55 and living in Brook. Until the NHS was established in 1948, Nurse Rann was funded by the Seely family for 27 years. Most people of 60 years and over, and who grew up in the area, remember Nurse Rann. She lived in one half of the cottage next to the school in Hulverstone (Garden Cottage). For many years she travelled to her patients' homes on a bicycle with a basket on the front to carry her black medicine bag. Later she had a Vespa scooter and then was the first person in the village to own a car, a Morris 8 bought for her by General Seely. Audrey Rann (no relation), who lived next to the Post Office in Hulverstone fell over one washday. Having dropped her big rag doll down some steps she hit her head on the ground and Nurse Rann came over the road and put iodine on the cut. It must have been a bad one because at 80 Audrey still has the scar to prove it.

Nurse Rann was also the school nurse, and regularly went into Hulverstone and Brighstone Schools to check for head lice and other common childhood ailments. Few babies were born within a 7 mile radius, between the early 1920s and the late 1940s, who were not delivered by her. No one knew her by any other name, and even her niece remembers calling her 'Nurse Rann' and cannot remember her having any other name. When the newspaper lists her presence at a funeral she is simply 'Nurse Rann.' She was still working at the birth of the National Health Service in July 1948 and Nurse Rann appears to have been needed, loved and respected by all who who knew her.

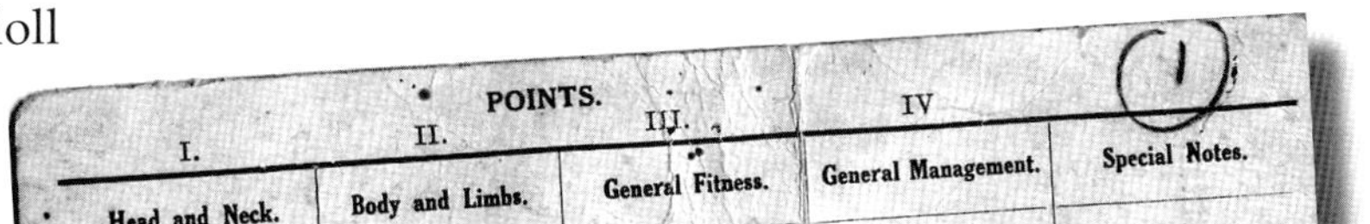

POINTS. (1)

| I. Head and Neck. | II. Body and Limbs. | III. General Fitness. | IV General Management. | Special Notes. |
|---|---|---|---|---|
| (a) Fontenalles | (a) Chest | (a) Development | (a) Feeding | |
| (b) Eyes | (b) Abdomen and Back | (b) Intelligence | (b) Clothing | |
| (c) Nose | (c) Bones & Joints | (c) Weight & Size | (c) Cleanliness | |
| (d) Mouth | (d) Glands | (d) Firmness | (d) Fresh Air and Exercise | |
| (e) Teeth | (e) Skin | (e) Deformities or Stigmata | (e) Clean and regular habits | |
| (f) Ears | (f) Buttocks | | | |
| (g) Glands | | | | |
| Marks 25. | Marks 25. | Marks 25. | Marks 25. | Full Marks 100. |
| Dr. 25 | Dr. 25 | Dr. 25 | Nurse 23 | 98. |

The scoring criteria for the All Island WI Baby Show, won in 1931 by Joyce Downer's 3 month old brother, Norman.

Nurse Rann in 1941 sitting in the armchair (a precious commodity in wartime) presented to her in appreciation of her 21 years service. She is surrounded here by some of the babies she had delivered.

# Gamekeepers

Mr French with his dogs on the Seely Estate.

A house given a wide berth by many young lads and poachers was the one known as Keeper's Cottage (Toll Bar Cottage) in Hulverstone. In 1841 a 30 year old game keeper, Henry Caws, lived there, as did the gamekeeper William Bartlett, from Kent who is also mentioned in the 1891 census. In 1911 Alfred Summerfield is the gamekeeper living at the Lodge of Brook Hill House. In the 1930s Ken and Audrey Barnes remember a Mr Becket and after him, a Mr Kiddie, living in the Toll House. The best remembered keeper was Mr Bob French who lived in Ivy Cottage, Brook from 1949 and worked as gamekeeper for 30 years. Mr French (as he was known by everyone) was appointed by Lord Sherwood who then owned the Brooke Estate and was himself a keen gunman and had regular shooting parties. He was always immaculately dressed in tweed plus fours, had a gun under his arm and was accompanied by two very obedient gundogs. Latterly Mr French also became a Special Constable, a role he enjoyed and which helped him in his work. He met many people, gamekeeping can be a solitary occupation, and gained their respect. Young people, in particular, learned a lot about the countryside from him as Nicolas Hawkes, son of Jacquetta and stepson of J B Priestley, remembers: *There was a big Forestry Commission plantation above Brook and deciduous woods too, owned by Lord Sherwood. Mr French told us not to go into them, for obvious reasons, but I was a SKULL-COLLECTOR, and interested in the array of dead jays, magpies, crows, squirrels, moles and stoats which Mr French hung up in his 'larder' on the edge of the woods. There was also an occasional weasel, which was rare, a sparrow-hawk and one Little Owl. Mr French was kind to me and advised me to clean skulls by burying them near wood ants and digging them up some time later.* Avice Mariner (French) remembers her father's work routine: *He rose early and went on his rounds to inspect his traps and snares, also in the early summer, to feed the pheasants and partridges. He would return for breakfast then go off again for the whole morning. His work would be varied; in the winter months it would include cutting out rides, rabbiting with nets and ferrets, and organising the several Shoots which took place between November and February. This entailed marking out where the Guns should stand; finding Beaters and Stops; organising transport for the Guns and food for the Beaters. At the end of the day, Beaters and Stops had to be paid and pheasants hung ready for collection by the local butcher, Mr Cooper from Brighstone. I remember my father getting very anxious before a Shoot in case there would not be a good supply of pheasants for shooting or the Guns would not be accurate shots, thereby not producing a `good bag` at the end of the day. I remember very few winter evenings when my father would be home. Usually he would be walking the woods looking for poachers who seemed abundant in those days. As a young girl, I was allowed to be a Stop. It was always very cold and boring but I did earn money! I wouldn`t do this nowadays as I prefer to see the birds strutting around rather than being killed. On*

An unknown gamekeeper from Rita Whitewood's collection.

*On the morning shoots the guns were very accurate, but after a good liquid lunch at Lord Sherwood's house, things went downhill...*

*some Saturdays in the winter I would accompany my father on his rounds. I enjoyed these days and from him I learned to walk quickly as he always had many miles to cover each day. I used to go rabbiting with him using the ferrets. Once I was bitten by Betty, a large female and I worried that it might turn septic, so I didn`t tell anyone. During the Summer holidays I would go in the harvest fields and help to run after the rabbits which waited until the last before running away from the combine harvester. I remember wearing shorts and wellingtons, the latter because of the sharp stubble. I think I looked a weird sight.*

Robin Shepheard lived in Meadow Cottage, Brook and remembers as a young lad being called on to help with the shoots: *Mr French organised very good pheasant shoots on the estate. I started off very early in the morning as a 'stopper.' This meant being in position, about 5am, usually up at High Crate, a wood under the Downs running down to Dunsbury Farm road. The idea was to make just enough noise with your stick to keep the pheasants in the wood but not frighten them, so that they were still there when the beaters started the first drive of the day. As I got older I became a beater and later I became a gun loader. The Guns I loaded for included Sir Robert Boothby, MP, complete with plus fours and bow tie, and Colonel Moulton Barratt of Westover Manor, Calbourne. On the morning shoots the guns were very accurate, but after a good liquid lunch at Lord Sherwood's house, things went downhill in the afternoon (anything that flew would be shot at). The beaters had a very good ploughman's lunch at the Sun Inn. The first drive after lunch was in the long copse running from Tollgate Cottage right to the Military Road. The guns would all be positioned in the marsh and Alf Woodford's withy bed at Sudmoor.*

Rabbits were a feature of life in Brook as they are today. Nicolas Hawkes noted in his diary that in 1954 there were hordes of rabbits because while myxomatosis had not yet reached the Island, no one would buy them as meat because of the scare... Once the distressing disease arrived it wiped out the rabbit population for a couple of years but in one of his eleven speeches in the House of Lords over the Rabbits (Prohibition of Spreading) Bill of 1956, Hugh Seely, Lord Sherwood, said:

Now I have just heard from my keeper that in the last four weeks he has killed over 200 rabbits. So it is clear that the rabbits are coming back. That figure of 200 represents only what my keeper has killed. I am afraid that only about twenty rabbits will have been accounted for by the farmers, for the simple reason that, as a result of the operation of the Agricultural Wages Act, wages are so high—nearly £7 a week—that there is no point in having a rabbiter on an estate. You cannot sell rabbits because no one will buy them. *Hansard, 1956.* Parliamentary copyright,

*In April 1954 Lord Sherwood offered £1 a bird for cock pheasants brought to him LIVE; there were huge numbers of them.*

Nicolas Hawkes remembers: *from my very first visit to Brook Hill in spring 1953 I was interested in learning how to shoot rabbits, and at first I was lucky. Mr French was generous with his time, and I killed a few. But it was beginner's luck. After a while I grew unreliable and over-keen on going out with him and Charlie Smith, the under-keeper; so Mr French grew impatient with me - understandably. On one occasion we went out to where the burrows were in the midst of brambles. He took a dog and a ferret in a sack, with a ferocious-looking home-made hacking tool to get through the brambles, to put the ferret down the hole.*

Mr French with his keeper's 'larder' behind him in the trees.

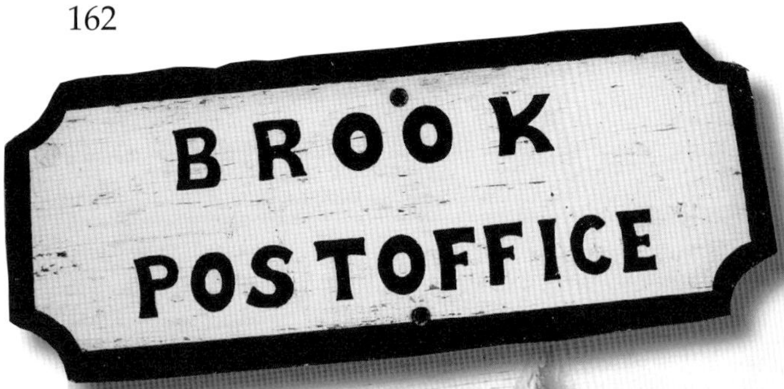

Miss Louisa Newbery outside the Post Office in Hulverstone in the 1940s. The sign (above) can be seen just below the roof.

Frank and Elizabeth Newbery outside Brook Post Office (Bank Cottage, Hulverstone) c.1885. The postcard above caught the 4 o'clock post in 1907 and is franked with a Brook postmark.

Hulverstone Post Office was run by the Newbery family. In living memory 'Old Mrs Newbery' (Elizabeth) and her daughter, Louisa, sold stamps, postal orders, sent telegrams and the usual post office requirements. The Post Office was in what is now Bank Cottage, Hulverstone and Carol Worrall who lived in Briar Cottage, Brook, remembers it as *a long way to go to get a stamp*. The Post Office also sold a limited amount of stationery and sweets to keep the children happy. No child minded going for a stamp if they could have a sweet as well. Joan and Doris Emmett couldn't wait to see Miss Newbery with: *our ha'penny pocket money to buy acid drops, bulls eyes, winter mixture and aniseed balls. We always kept two for Mum and Dad. At Miss Newbery's funeral they tolled the bell for the number of years she had lived.* The Post Office was a busy place and as well as local post it dealt with important parliamentary business for Sir Charles and later, General Jack Seely. In the late 1950s when the Seely Estate was sold, the Post Office was taken over by Mrs Margaret Stone at Hanover Stores, who ran it until 1969 when she retired. It was then taken over by Mrs Doris Barton who lived in The Laurels, Hulverstone and had previously worked at Freshwater Post Office. Doris ran the post office from a green caravan on the front lawn at Hanover House. After the great storm in 1987 it was re-housed alongside the main road in one of Mr Jim Hookey's fields. Since then, a new portakabin, this time complete with electricity, has been home to Brook Post Office. Doris

A happy snapshot taken of postmistress Elizabeth Newbery with her children, Louisa, Alf and Mabel outside Bank Cottage.

retired in 1994 after being Postmistress for 30 years. She had kept up the tradition of a being a 'sweetie haven' for the local children despite the protests of parents worried about their children's teeth. Mrs Kath Dobson took over as postmistress in 1994 and in 2010 still runs a flourishing post office where you will always meet someone you know and catch up on the latest news.

ISLE OF WIGHT COUNTY PRESS — FRIDAY, OCTOBER 6, 1995

ID COUNTY NOTES

**Gifts as Doris, 85, quits her caravan post office**

Mrs Doris Barton, 85, beside the caravan post office which serves villagers in and around Brook.

SPRIGHTLY Mrs Doris Barton, 85, retired last week as Brook sub-postmistress — but the caravan she established as a post office facility for the village will remain open.

Mr Colin Lovegrove, the Island's retail network manager for Post Office Counters Ltd, confirmed this week it would remain open on Mondays and Thursdays from 9 am to 3.30 pm under the supervision of Mrs Kathleen Dobson, of Brighstone.

Mrs Barton, of Hulverstone, said she was sorry to retire, recalling how she had fought hard to set up one of the country's most unusual post offices in 1977.

The village post office had previously been accommodated in Hanover House, but when that was no longer available Mrs Barton engaged the help of a postmaster to transform the caravan which she had bought at Bembridge.

She said, "I had to fight to have it in the village. I had to put it on the grass and had to make sure it was the right colour of green."

Mrs Barton, who had previously worked at Freshwater and Hulverstone in a career with the Post Office spanning 40 years, said Mondays and Thursday would never be the same again.

"I enjoyed my work over the years and met so many nice people. I don't know what I'm going to do now," she said.

At a party at Seely Hall, Brook, on Saturday, Mrs Barton was presented with a cheque for £500 from Brook, Hulverstone and Mottistone villages, a picture, bouquet and an autograph book signed by villagers.

She was also given a huge greetings card in the shape of a caravan, made by children, and a valedictory letter and portable colour television set as thanks from Post Office Counters Ltd.

Mrs Barton collects for Cancer Research, is a member of Brook Methodist Church and enjoys gardening.

Sub-postmistresses Doris Barton (above) and today Kath Dobson (right) who have kept the unique Brook Post Office caravan open and provided a vital local service for many villagers for the past 33 years.

# Shoemakers and cobblers

In 1841 there were two shoemakers in Brook, James and Robert Raynor, and a shoe binder called Elizabeth Collyer (the shoe binder added the upper to the sole). From then until the 1880s there was always at least one shoemaker in the village. It was in the 1930s that Mr Leal, or Alf, as he was better known, came to live in Brook. Short in stature with little round glasses, a peak cap and brown apron, Alf was a baker who had retired through ill health and was affectionately known as the 'bunman'. He and his wife, Louisa, raised their three children, Ellen, Ida and Leonard at Compton Grange, Brook. They later moved to No 1 Coastguard Station when Alf became a coastguard. Alf bought a plot of land half way up Coastguard Lane and built a wooden workshop which he covered in black tar and which became the village cobbler's shop. Alf could be seen standing in his 'shop window' looking down to the sea and taking in the air. A notice hung outside saying: 'Shoes soled free to any person over 80 bringing their mother and father with them.' The workshop has been described as 'organised chaos,' but Alf knew just where everything was. The tools of his trade hung on the wall and there was a sewing machine on the work bench. Alf charged tuppence for every job that was done. He played a game with the village kids dodging them to try to stop them coming into the shed, but the youngsters would dart in through his legs. It is said that he didn't like children much! We hear that the ladies too, were apprehensive of him and would throw their shoes in the door for repair, for fear of having their legs tickled! Alf was also very clever at watch and clock repairs and very good at playing the hand bells. 'Skinny Leal' was apparently his nickname when on the carrier's van. Stories told about Alf Leal include: *One night they were all up the Sun Inn and someone said, 'Who drew up the plans for your shed then Bunman?' 'Plans, I never had no plans. I made it all out of my own head,' 'Yes,' said someone, 'and had enough wood left over to make a fowl house as well.'* Bill Humber took his father's shoes to be mended and Alf started to complain about the workmanship of the previous repair: *Rough job this, who did them last time? and I said, 'You did, Mr Leal.'*

Mr Alf Leal

# The Sun Inn

The history of the Sun Inn at Hulverstone goes back many years. Its early history is unclear, but we know for sure that an ale house was on this site in 1816 owned by a William Cooke. It was sold that same year to Benjamin Mew, a brewer of Crocker Street, Newport. The 1841 and 1851 censuses mention an elderly man, John Moorman, as the innkeeper. By 1852 the Sun Inn was run by James Jacobs and by 1855 by Charles Wolfe, who was also a leather collar and harness maker. In 1860 it was sold by W B Mew to Charles Seely who promptly leased it back to W B Mew. According to David Seely, Lord Mottistone, his great grandfather approved of the pub being in Hulverstone as: *it meant the men would be sobered up by the time they got home, having walked in the fresh air back to Brook or Mottistone.* We hear that the walk was also an opportunity for a good singsong. At that time the Sun was run by Henry W Mussell. By 1871 it had been taken over by Henry's widow, Rhoda Mussell and her son Thomas, who was also a grocer. It is possible that they ran a small shop from the Inn. In 1881 Benjamin Denness, age 66, was the innkeeper and had the grand title of a Licenced Victualler. In 1895 and 1911 we see that Frederick White is the innkeeper. Frederick and Sophia White continued to trade at the Sun Inn for many years. Fred is remembered today by some locals. Ron Emmett describes how his job after school was to: *go to The Sun Inn and help the landlord, Fred White. Fred was a bit of a cripple so I used to do all the work that was required, like milking his two cows, and sawing up firewood, digging the garden, swabbing out the stone floor in the bar and the one I didn't like doing was emptying the spittoons. He had these big, iron spittoons there, full of sawdust and poor old Fred used to have to clear his throat a lot. I'd be about eleven then and this was after school. During the summer time, when things were a little busy, I used to stay on after I'd done those chores and help out in the bar that meant Fred would draw the pints in the cellar from the wooden barrels and put them on a tray, give them to me to take into the bar and serve up- it would only be locals then, there were no visitors, as such, and dish these out and take the money and I used to make more in tips than Fred used to give me in a week's wage. Fred's wages by the way were six pennies a week- sixpence - a nice, shiny sixpence and sometimes I didn't get home till 9.00-9.30 in the evening.*

David Hollis remembers: *Several of us was in the Hulverstone Sun one night. Shotters' bus pulled up, A chap came back on leave, there was a shortage of drink in wartime, Bob Cassell's brother Will, he was in the Navy. We stayed there till three in the morning and drunk the pub dry to celebrate his return from the Navy. Popular place it was.*

Robert (Bob) Cassell lived at The Elms opposite

Jan 1st 1938 **Cyclist collides with cow**

A cyclist collided with a cow whilst cycling down Hulverstone Shute on Tuesday evening. Mr George Raymond of Thorncross collided with a cow belonging to Mr F White of the Sun Inn, which was straying in the road. Mr Raymond was thrown from his machine and received injuries to his face. He was conveyed by car to Dr L Way of Limmerstone, and after attention was taken home.

the pub and in 1997 when he was 84 he recalled how different it was when he was young: *What is now one room was two very small rooms with a passage way between. The tap room had a stone floor covered with sawdust and there were spittoons with sawdust in them. It was furnished with scrubbed deal tables. There was also a kitchen range there which the old lady used to cook their meals on. No meals were cooked for the customers to the pub. There was no bar or nothing, like there is now. If you wanted a pint of beer or ale the landlord would go down to the cellar to get it from the barrel for you. Ale was five pence a pint (those are old pence which makes it about two of today's pence) and beer was four pence a pint. Old Fred White was the landlord, he suffered from gout a lot. Sometimes he was in bed for six months at a time.* Like Ron Emmett (see *The School at Hulverstone*), as a boy Robert worked for Fred at the Sun Inn before and after school.

The pub was a popular place throughout the 1950s and 60s and Ralph Cook remembers it being so full at New Year's Eve that the only way in was to climb through a window.

The IOW Hunt meets at the Sun Inn in the late 1960s.

George Thompson recalls how: *on a Saturday and Sunday you could nearly always say who was in the pub before you went in there, all locals.* There have been many landlords over the years and one who is remembered best is Alan Elliman who was landlord in the 1960s. Alan was also a member of the cliff rescue team.

Harry Barnes, Jill Simpson and Alan Elliman, the publican, behind the bar.

Albert Kitson, Alan Elliman, Jill Simpson and Chris Bridges.

Three photos taken in the Sun Inn public bar in the 1960s.

From left: Tony Benfield, Colin Emmett, Edie Hulse, Terry Stallard, Sue Gould, Joe Hulse snr, Chris Bridges, Joe Hulse, and sitting in foreground, Frank Zeeman.

*Comparing themselves to the cogs of a clock, the Rev. Morris said Mr Seely was the mainspring which set them all in harmonious motion.*

Opening of the new Reading Room in Brook, 1893

In November 1893 the IOW County Press announced: *The Parish Room which Mr Seely M.P. has generously presented for the free use of the parishioners of Brook and Mottistone is of stone and of solid and handsome appearance. It is divided internally by folding doors, so as to form one or two separate rooms as required. The front portion will be the general reading room well supplied with daily and weekly papers and with a library connected to the free Jubilee Club in Newport. The recreation room behind is fitted with a very perfect full sized billiard table and various other games are freely placed at the disposal of visitors.*

Charles Seely, like many enlightened industrialists and Liberal politicians of his day, believed strongly in the benefits of education for the working man. He understood that the people of Brook and Mottistone had no easy access to newspapers and books, nor did they have the leisure time or transport to get them to the developing 'free' library in Newport. When the Seely Hall was built it was 'the best there was.' The opening of the Reading Room coincided with the annual Lifeboat Supper in November 1893 and the newspaper reports: *The vice-chairman (Rev. Leslie Morris) spoke of their great indebtedness to Mr Seely and his family for unnumbered acts of generosity and kindness. Comparing themselves to the cogs of a clock, Rev. Morris said Mr Seely was the mainspring which set them all in harmonious motion. The toast was enthusiastically drunk with a specially added cheer for Mrs Seely.*

*When the Seely Hall was built it was 'the best there was.'*

A management committee was appointed with Mr Seely as president and chairman and the Rev. Morris, as secretary and librarian. The rooms were open each evening between 6pm and 10pm, except for Sundays. Daily newspapers remained available in the Hall for three days and weekly papers until the next week's papers arrived. The rules for members were clearly laid out and included:

*The Hall also served as a refuge for sailors whose boats were stranded or wrecked on the rocks at Brook*

- *No one will be admitted under sixteen years of age*
- *No intoxicating drinks, gambling, betting or bad language will be allowed*
- *No member shall keep a paper longer than 10 minutes after he has been requested to give it up.*
- *The Billiard table, and other games, are not to be used by the same persons for more than one game, if others are desirous of using them.*
- *That no idle play be allowed in the Billiard Room.*

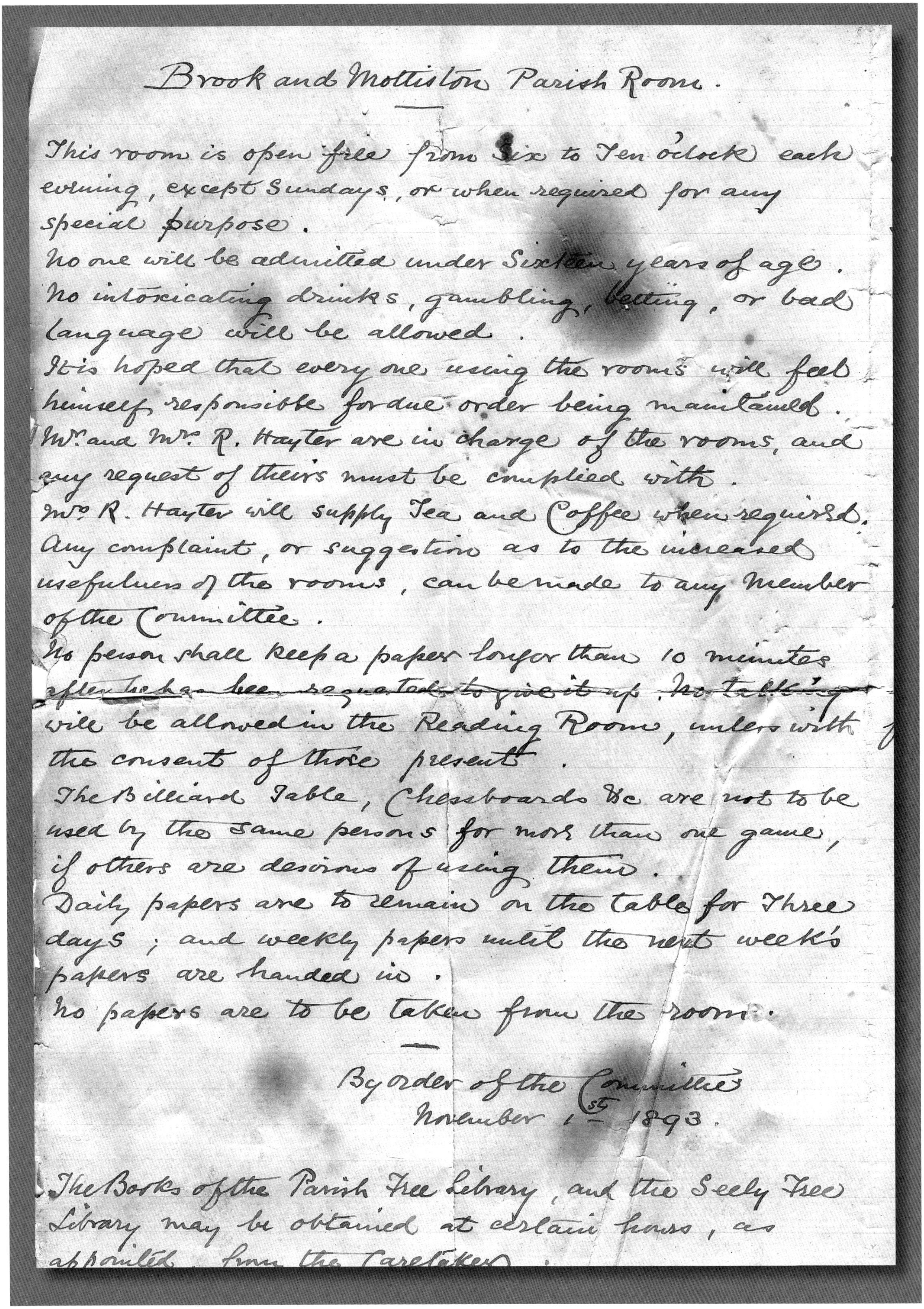

Brook and Mottiston Parish Room.

This room is open free from Six to Ten o'clock each evening, except Sundays, or when required for any special purpose.
No one will be admitted under Sixteen years of age.
No intoxicating drinks, gambling, betting, or bad language will be allowed.
It is hoped that every one using the rooms will feel himself responsible for due order being maintained.
Mr. and Mrs. R. Hayter are in charge of the rooms, and any request of theirs must be complied with.
Mrs. R. Hayter will supply Tea and Coffee when required.
Any complaint, or suggestion as to the increased usefulness of the rooms, can be made to any Member of the Committee.
No person shall keep a paper longer than 10 minutes ~~after he has been requested to give it up. No talking~~ will be allowed in the Reading Room, unless with the consent of those present.
The Billiard Table, Chessboards &c are not to be used by the same persons for more than one game, if others are desirous of using them.
Daily papers are to remain on the table for Three days; and weekly papers until the next week's papers are handed in.
No papers are to be taken from the room.

By order of the Committee
November 1st 1893.

The Books of the Parish Free Library, and the Seely Free Library may be obtained at certain hours, as appointed, from the Caretaker.

The rules of the new Parish Room, agreed with Sir Charles Seely and carefully written out in 1893 by the Hall secretary and librarian, Reverend Leslie Morris.

Seely Hall stalwarts, here acting as judges at the 'C' Club, Daisy Newbery, Margaret Stone, Alice Morris and Doris Barton.

In the early days kettles for tea were boiled in Brook Villa (next door) where the caretakers, Mr and Mrs Robert Hayter lived. They carried them through the connecting passageway (now the gents' loo) into the Hall to provide many cups of tea. The first public event recorded in the Seely Hall was suitably educational and extremely popular:

AN ASTRONOMICAL LECTURE
by Dr. A.H. Fison
A very interesting address at the Parish Rooms on THE MOON was given to a large and attentive audience. The lecture was illustrated by a series of very beautiful photographic views thrown on a sheet from a powerful oxy-hydrogen gas lantern.
*IOW County Press*, December 23rd 1893

In 1896 we hear of a more light-hearted use of the Hall for a free parish concert. Jack Valerie was a popular singer and a family friend of Rev. Morris:

A large and enthusiastic audience assembled and many items obtained encores. Mr Valerie's description of himself as 'Longshoreman Billy' and Miss Bartram's charming rendering of 'Dolly's Revenge' were all greatly appreciated. The resolute attitude and the refrain of the local police afforded much amusement… 'The Two Gendarmes' was sung by Mr J Valerie & Rev. R L Morris and 'The Verdict was...' by Miss Sylvia Seely.

In the thirty years between 1920 and 1950, three ladies: Mrs Joe Morris, Mrs Daisy Newbery and Mrs Ella Hookey kept an eye on the 'goings on' in the Hall. In those days the kettles were put to boil on the stoves in the Hall using kindling wood gathered from the Green opposite. Those two small fires would also have warmed and dried many cold, wet bodies since the Hall also served as a refuge for sailors whose boats were stranded or wrecked on the rocks at Brook; and for campers in the 1950s when the rains washed them out of their tents.

The Seely Hall has been the venue for many entertainments over the past 120 years and has been much appreciated by villagers past and

The village gathers in the Seely Hall for Anne Hookey's wedding in 1962. Sharp eyes will spot Margaret Stone, Janet Stone, Jim Hookey, Olive Hookey, Rita Whitewood, Gladys Morris, Rev Robert Bowyer, Elizabeth Bowyer, Alf Woodford, David Hookey, Joan Shepheard, Molly Humber.

*A decision was made that the girls should be allowed to play billiards.*

present. Brook Social Club minutes for 1950 and 1951 show that the club was open to people of 12 to 100 years. Membership was one shilling and Club nights which included billiards and table tennis were held on Wednesdays from 7-9pm. The money collected contributed to village social evenings such as the firework display on 5th November (held in the field behind the Seely Hall). In May 1951 an outing: *was arranged through the British Railways to the Festival of Britain exhibition on London's South Bank.* There are signs of a possible dispute between the younger members as we read in the Minutes that: *a decision was made that the girls should be allowed to play billiards; also that*

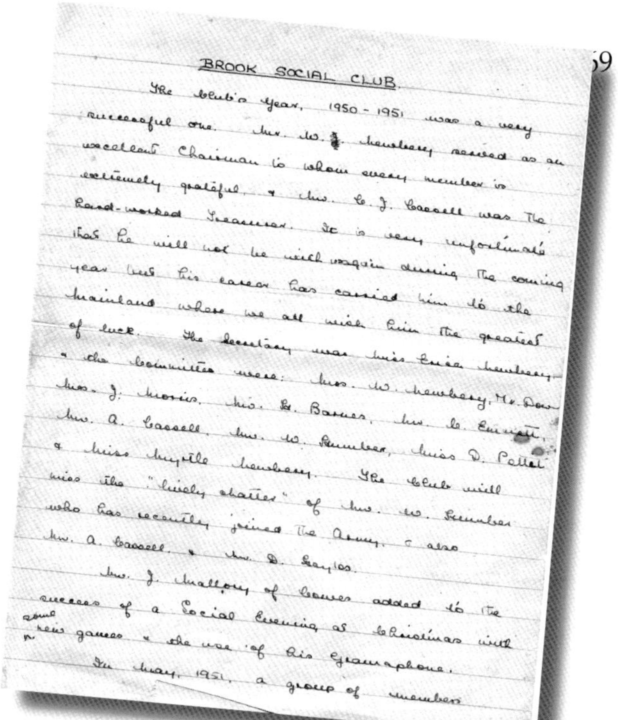

BROOK SOCIAL CLUB.

The club's year, 1950 - 1951 was a very successful one. Mr. W. J. Newbery served as an excellent Chairman to whom every member is extremely grateful, & Mr. C. J. Cassell was the hard-worked Treasurer. It is very unfortunate that he will not be with us again during the coming year but his career has carried him to the mainland where we all wish him the greatest of luck. The Secretary was Miss Erica Newbery & the Committee were: Mrs. W. Newbery, Mr. Dow [illegible] Mrs. J. Morris, Mrs. G. Barnes, Mr. C. Emmett, Mr. A. Cassell, Mr. W. Humber, Miss D. Pottel & Miss Myrtle Newbery. The club will miss the "lively chatter" of Mr. W. Humber who has recently joined the Army, & also Mr. A. Cassell & Mr. D. Gaylor.

Mr. J. Mallory of Cowes added to the success of a Social Evening at Christmas with some new games & the use of his Gramophone.

In May, 1951, a group of members

*the boys should have the table tennis for one hour and the girls one hour each evening.* Harvest and Lifeboat suppers were well-attended each year and a Valentine's Dance was a most popular annual event until the early 1960s. The Seely Hall has also been the venue for many wedding receptions and private gatherings. Events such as weekly whist drives, annual plant sales and jumble sales have been needed to meet the ever-increasing costs of running and maintaining the Hall. Activities have changed over the past 100 years from the Astronomical Lecture in 1893 to today's yoga and art classes. Most recently bingo evenings, coffee mornings, a village supper and the biennial Village and Church Fete, for example, have brought the community together at the same time as raising money for the Hall. Ensuring the Hall survives is a constant challenge, especially now that we have less contact with our immediate neighbours and when entertainment is more focused in our own homes.

# 100 years of Seely Hall celebrated by Brook residents

A COUNTY Press cutting sparked off the centenary celebration for Seely Hall, Brook, which was marked in style on Saturday when Island dignitaries and local residents joined together to mark the occasion.

The cutting was unearthed in September by Miss Rita Whitewood, who lives next door to the hall, and she showed it to her friend, Mr Dennis Whettingsteel, who felt a celebration should be organised.

They approached Mrs Kath Dobson, secretary of the hall, and frantic organising, with help from villagers, took place until the event.

The hall was built by Sir Charles Seely in 1893 as a reading room for the men of the village and since then has been used by the WI, children's clubs and for parties as well as for the Local Look exhibition, organised by the IW Natural History and Archaeological Society every August.

Lord Mottistone, the Island Governor and Lord Lieutenant, son of Sir J. E. B. Seely, whose family owned Brook House, was present at the evening with his wife and addressed the 75 guests, aged between seven and 80.

Other guest speakers included Lord Mottistone's sister, Mrs Lou Fletcher; the last surviving member of Brook Lifeboat crew, Mr Bob Cassell; the last teacher at Hulverstone School, Mrs Barbara Heal; farmer of Compton Farm, Mr Den Phillips; villager Mr George Humber; author of books on the history of West Wight, Mr Eric Toogood; and farmer of Downton Farm, Mr David Hookey.

Decorating the hall for the event were flags and displays of old photographs of the village, provided by residents.

In 1993 the Seely Hall marked its centenary. Particularly moving were the personal accounts of those who spoke at the gathering.

Courtesy of the *Isle of Wight County Press.*

Brook is awarded Best Kept Village for the first time in 1982.

**Children's entertainments**
Every Christmas money was collected for a children's party in the Seely Hall. This tradition continued for 60 years, well into the 1990s, and there are many adults today with happy memories of them.

The 1987 children's Christmas party (pictured top left) included: Ella and Rosie Dorley-Brown, James Cave, Lucy Hayward, Oliver and Freddy Scadgell, Ruth and Penny Gardener. In the centre Sue Cook with Becky and below: Ruth and Penny Gardner left, with John Cook and David Cave right.

## BROOK

**Pantomime.** — A cast of 19 children aged from two-and-a-half to ten performed the pantomime Snow White and the Seven Dwarfs at the Seely Hall, Brook. Victoria Carter was Snow White and the dwarfs were played by Timothy Carter (Doc), Oliver Scadgell (Grumpy), Freddy Scadgell (Dopey), James Cave (Happy), Abbie Taylor (Sneezy), Rosie Dorley-Brown (Sleepy) and Carla Lewis (Bashful). Other roles were: Queen, Holly Hogg; king, Ella Dorley-Brown; prince and huntsman, Philippa Simson; mirror, James Lewis; maid, Maisie Taylor; fairy, Lucy Haywood. Appearing as animals were Rachael Wright, David Cave, Martha Taylor, Maisie Taylor and George Dorley-Brown. The producer was Doris West and scenery was by Maisie Watson. Others connected with the production were Wally West, front of house; Yvonne Wright, wardrobe, and Brian Wright, stage manager. Of the £85 raised, £50 went to the Great Ormond Street Hospital Wishing Well Appeal and £35 to the Seely Hall Fund.

In the mid 1980s a pantomime of *Snow White* involved a cast of 19 Brook children and was produced in the Seely Hall by Doris West.

# COME TO BROOK FOR LOCAL LOOK!

Local Look made its home in the Seely Hall for the month of August in 1965 and returned every summer for 25 years. It was a very popular event with people coming from all over the Island to see it and is still talked about and remembered today. Local Look was initially set up by members of the Island's Natural History Society with the aim of having a permanent natural history museum. Oliver Frazer, President of the Society, and his wife Dorothy, became the driving force behind the exhibition which was first staged in 1961 in Newport. Oliver had been charged with putting together a display which was cheap, highly adaptable and mobile. In the beginning it consisted of static displays of the geology, fauna and flora of the Island but as time went by it became more ambitious and included living creatures. In 1981 it became illegal to have captive specimens, but many remember the adder who produced a family on 15th August 1967. As Oliver Fraser described the event: *Parturition was a lengthy process, lasting for most of the day and a ten year old visitor, much to the concern of his distraught parents, was determined to see the process through to the end. He corrrectly counted eleven youngsters and was eventually restored to his parents declaring that it had been the best day of his life.* There were also grass snakes, lizards, slow worms and toads on display, creatures that many visitors from the towns had never seen before. People brought various things to be identified and displayed. A different theme was chosen each year. In 1969 it was 'Woodland' in honour of the Jubilee of the Forestry Commission. Other themes included 'Shapes and Patterns' and 'At the Water's Edge'. The exhibition made a big impression on a young Renella Phillips (Humber): *Because Mum had a cleaning job at the Seely Hall, I was able to go with her in the school holidays and have a 'private viewing'. My favourite things were always the live exhibits – snakes, tadpoles, newts, butterflies and moth caterpillars and so on, kept in glass tanks. The hall was also full of information boards and photos, stuffed birds and animals. As a child, it seemed very impressive. One year, Mr Frazer came to thank my mother for her work at the Hall and gave me a book about natural history which I kept for many years.* Brook people were more than happy to have this event in their village and it put Brook well and truly on the map.

*Eleven baby adders were born that day in the Seely Hall*

The last Local Look held in Brook in 1990.

The men who worked to reclaim and seed Brook Green in 1974. From left: Bert Morris, Bill Cook, Peter Jackman and George Humber.

*Be vigilant and look after your village green!*

In 1921 General Jack Seely gave the strip of land opposite the Seely Hall to the village to be used as a green. The gift was never written down however and when the Seely Estate was sold in 1958, the land was claimed by Brook Farm. By 1962 the villagers were becoming concerned about the state of the land, which had been fenced off and was being used for breeding pigs. Mr Bert Morris, Parish Councillor, raised the matter and Brighstone Parish Council put in a claim on behalf of the public. On the death of farmer Joliffe Kingswell, the farm sale included the land of the village green. Letters passed between solicitors and the Parish Council, until finally, in February 1972, the executors no longer contested the ownership of the land and the green was returned to the public. Thanks to Mrs Win Hollis who had championed the cause, the original 1920s posts and chains, which had been stored in a barn, were also withdrawn from the sale. In 1974/5 the green was levelled and re-seeded and the posts and chains painted and re-installed.

The green was restored by Bert Morris and Peter Jackman assisted by Bill Cook and George Humber. The financial cost was borne by the Parish Council and the labour was given free as was the gift of the trees. The green was officially opened on 6th September 1975 by Mrs Brenda Ross, wife of Island M.P. Stephen Ross. She said: *Be vigilant and look after your village green! In these sad days of erosion of the countryside due to road widening and, in some cases, bad planning, it is a joy to find some land which is actually being restored to the public. When the land was fenced off it would have been the end of the story but for the tenacity of one man, Mr Bert Morris, who led the fight to get it back.*

The Men of Wight Morris Men perform at the opening ceremony in 1975.

# Brook Women's Institute

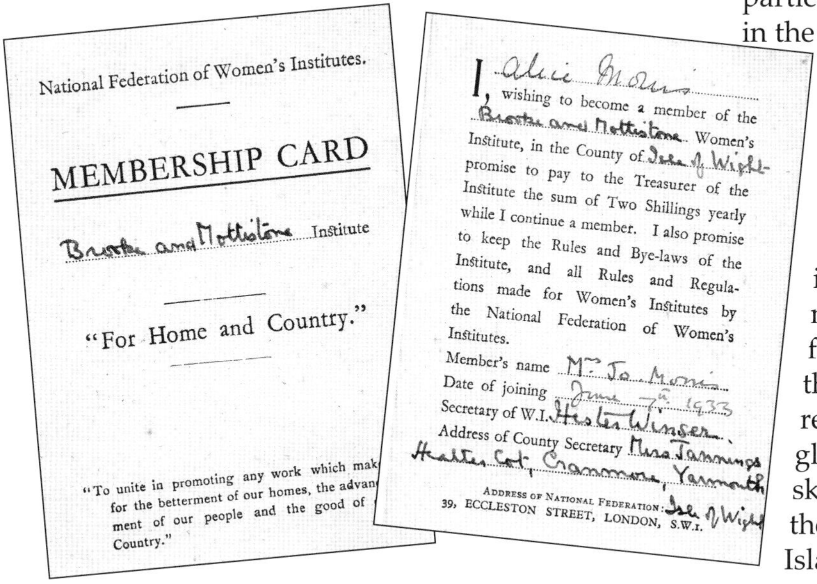

National Federation of Women's Institutes.

MEMBERSHIP CARD

Brooke and Mottistone Institute

"For Home and Country."

"To unite in promoting any work which mak[es] for the betterment of our homes, the advan[ce]ment of our people and the good of [our] Country."

I, Alice Morris, wishing to become a member of the Brooke and Mottistone Women's Institute, in the County of Isle of Wight promise to pay to the Treasurer of the Institute the sum of Two Shillings yearly while I continue a member. I also promise to keep the Rules and Bye-laws of the Institute, and all Rules and Regulations made for Women's Institutes by the National Federation of Women's Institutes.

Member's name Mrs Jo. Morris

Date of joining June 7th 1933

Secretary of W.I. Hester Winser

Address of County Secretary Miss Jennings Heather Cot, Cranmore, Yarmouth, Isle of Wight

ADDRESS OF NATIONAL FEDERATION: 39, ECCLESTON STREET, LONDON, S.W.1.

In June 1933, fifty years after the Reading Room was built, Brook Women's Institute (WI) was formed and went from strength to strength, meeting at the Seely Hall for 25 years. Thirty-two ladies from Brook and the surrounding district joined and Miss Emily Seely, daughter of Gen. Jack Seely, became its first President. The Rector's wife became secretary and the local schoolmistress looked after the finances. When the Second World War was declared, WI members were asked to keep 'everything going'. They preserved food, canned fruit, collected rose hips and herbs, knitted for the service men and collected clothes for people in bombed areas. Tea parties and games were given for local children in the Rectory garden.

After the war, the membership increased and Brook carried on as a very busy WI. Throughout its life WI members played an active part in the life of the community. Reading through the records shows how resourceful and gifted they were in entertaining themselves and others at meetings. The ladies learned many skills from the talks and demonstrations given at their meetings and extra classes. There are records of painting, dressmaking, basketry, glove-making and a recorder group. Their skills in needlecraft and cookery enabled them to take part in exhibitions across the Island. Members enjoyed talks on many subjects ranging from 'Design for Living' to 'Smuggling'. Money was raised for many causes, which included providing a piano and curtains for the Seely Hall. They sewed bedspreads for

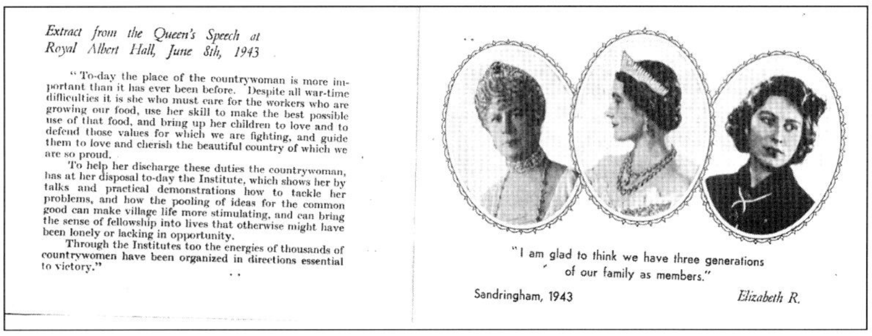

*Extract from the Queen's Speech at Royal Albert Hall, June 8th, 1943*

"To-day the place of the countrywoman is more important than it has ever been before. Despite all war-time difficulties it is she who must care for the workers who are growing our food, use her skill to make the best possible use of that food, and bring up her children to love and to defend those values for which we are fighting, and guide them to love and cherish the beautiful country of which we are so proud.

To help her discharge these duties the countrywoman, has at her disposal to-day the Institute, which shows her by talks and practical demonstrations how to tackle her problems, and how the pooling of ideas for the common good can make village life more stimulating, and can bring the sense of fellowship into lives that otherwise might have been lonely or lacking in opportunity.

Through the Institutes too the energies of thousands of countrywomen have been organized in directions essential to victory."

"I am glad to think we have three generations of our family as members."

Sandringham, 1943 *Elizabeth R.*

Brook Women's Institute in the 1980s.
Back row from left: xxx, Dora Hookey, Miss Smith, Jean Peck, Mrs Summerfield, Mrs Smith (Mottistone Farm), xxx, xxx, Joan Newbery-Smith, Miss Johnson (with spade), Rene Allen, Margaret Stone, Mrs Phillips, Mrs Sheath. Front row: xxx, Gladys Morris, xxx,xxx, xxx, Lesley Cave.

people in the home for the blind and flowers were picked and sent to London hospitals. Visits were made to the residents of Pitt Place (now Brighstone Grange), a local home for the elderly. At the same time the Institute was not insular. Members were in contact with the Country Women's Association in Australia and New Zealand and supported local, county and world issues. They discussed and voted against anything they felt was detrimental to the good of the World. Two members served on the County Federation Executive, and several on County sub-committees. By the 1960s Brook and Mottistone WI also embraced the village of Brighstone and one of the enduring reminders of those days is the fascinating Village Scrapbook made by members in 1958. The Scrapbook is handwritten and beautifully illustrated, it includes the history of the area and members' memories of the old days. Sadly the Brook W.I. was suspended in October 1989.

## Brook Ladies Choir

Despite Mrs Smith saying 'we were terrible when we first started,' another successful activity that the Seely Hall and the W.I. made possible, was the Ladies' Choir. The Choir was formed in 1953 under the leadership of Mrs Smith and developed into what a newspaper called 'one of the finest ladies' choirs in the Island, if not the finest.' They brought much honour and glory to Brook, frequently winning awards at the Isle of Wight Music Festival (they never failed to bring home at least one cup) and giving concerts all over the Island. The choir hit the headlines (left) when a surprise change to the competition rules meant they could no longer enter for a particular cup. The new rules stipulated a minimum of twenty voices which was more than they could muster (having regularly won this same cup with thirteen voices).

# Top choir drops a bombshell

NOT ENTERING MUSIC FESTIVAL

A SURPRISE switch in the rules of the Isle of Wight Music Festival has brought a shock decision from Brooke W.I. choir — one of the leading choirs in the Island.

Front row from left: Mrs Smith (conductor), Mrs Tickner, Mrs Polington, Mrs Morris, Mrs Stone, Miss Way, Miss Attrill, Mrs Reynolds. Middle row: Mrs Buckett, Mrs Thompson, Mrs Cooper, Mrs Newbery, Mrs Dedamous, Mrs Barnes, Mrs Isaacs, Mrs Cotton, Miss Russell, Mrs Sheath, Mrs Warnby. Back row: Mrs Summerfield, Mrs Saunders, Mrs Page.

# Hanover Stores and tea rooms

Hanover stores and tea rooms when it first opened in 1933. Note the hand-painted sign and all important roller to keep the lawn smooth.

A lynchpin of Brook life for 36 years was the village shop and tea rooms at Hanover House.

In the spring of 1933 H & M Morris was formed. It was the start of a successful family business. Brother and sister Herbert (known as Bert) and Margaret (known as Madge) were the children of Mr and Mrs Joe Morris. They were a long-established Brook family and rented Hanover House from the Seely family. Margaret married Walter Stone and Bert married Gladys Winser and the four of them ran the business until their retirement in1969.

M. Emmett 1950 2

Church Cottage, Mottistone

H. & M. MORRIS,

GROCERS & PROVISION MERCHANTS,

HANOVER STORES, BROOKE, I.W.

Phone: Brighstone 281

## The shop

With £25 borrowed from their mother Alice, Bert and Margaret bought a small amount of stock and opened the shop. The shop was a small building at the side of the house off Coastguard Lane. Its sloping roof and low doorway caught many a customer a crack on the head. Margaret was shopkeeper and served behind the counter. Their first customer was their next door neighbour, Mrs Daisy Newbery of Meadow Cottage, who purchased 2lb of loose sugar. Rita Whitewood remembered the first day the shop opened: *Being still at school we were keen to be the first customers, my friend and I had a few coppers and we purchased some sweets, sherbet fountains I think. From then on we always purchased our weekly shopping there. I think it amounted to about £2 for all our weekly shopping.* After that first day the shop kept Brook supplied with the essentials from 1933 to 1969. Behind the counter were fully-stocked shelves of sweets and chocolate. More glass jars of loose sweets stood next to brass weighing scales. Below the sweets was a cigarette and tobacco cupboard. Most of the stock was 'loose' and was weighed

*It always amazed me that Mrs Stone didn't fall into the huge deep freeze as she was so short, she almost disappeared into it when in search of something at the bottom...*
Ann Male (Hailey)

The Newbery sisters wait outside Hanover Stores, Myrtle standing and Rosemary in the pram.

in strong blue paper bags which were then neatly folded and tied with string. The shop was well-supported by the villagers and gradually Bert and Madge were able to build up their stock. Their father, Joe, grew fresh vegetables for them to sell and their range of services extended to include paraffin and later bread from Orchard Bros. at Freshwater Bay. Villagers supplemented their home grown fruit and vegetables by doing their weekly shopping at Hanover and saved themselves a fortnightly trip to Newport. Cosy with six people at the counter, the shop had very little space. A big clock ticked away. Floor to ceiling shelves held the stock, with the non-perishables on the top under the eaves. A marble slab was used for cutting the cheese, bacon and ham and later a chest freezer arrived. A whopping great tray of Carters' seeds was permanently behind the low doorway. In summer, a little window was opened beneath the fig tree onto the lawn and ice creams were sold from here. Often a bird found its way in through this window. Open from 8am until 6pm, the shop closed for an hour at lunchtime and on Thursday afternoon and Sunday. It was not unheard of for villagers to call at the back door when they had forgotten something, although this was not encouraged. Ken Barnes remembers: *One thing that will always stick in my mind, was Mrs Stone's kindness. I needed a cycle battery one Sunday morning as I worked in Freshwater and needed a light for Monday morning. When I asked Mrs Stone if I could buy one, she explained the situation, that the Sunday trading laws were very strict, but she still let me have a battery...* At holiday times villagers were a bit put out when they couldn't get into the shop because there were so many holiday-makers. Walter Stone, Margaret's husband, delivered groceries as far as Brighstone on a Thursday. On Tuesdays, (Newport market day), Hanover often hung out the flag to get Shotters, the carrier, to call. It was a red flag with a yellow diagonal cross and was poked out of Bert and Gladys' bedroom window. The carrier would buy whatever they needed in Newport and bring it back in the evening. Hanover later offered a library service at 2d per week per book. Titles included *The Upfold Farm Mystery* by A. Fielding, *Belinda Tries Again* by Richard Starr and *The Way of a Fool* by Lilian Clifford.... Gripping stuff.

*They also sold a nice line in pottery with 'Brook' printed on. The young campers loved to take a piece home for their mums.*

In the late 1950s when the Hulverstone Post Office closed Margaret also opened as a post office. A 3ft square area was allocated for this beside the counter with a wire mesh surround for security. The shop contributed enormously to the village until it closed in 1969, by which time many villagers had cars and could shop in Freshwater and Newport at cheaper prices.

*Happy*
*memories of a sunny garden,*
*awaiting Mrs Morris bearing heaving trays*
*of succulent scones, sweet strawberry jam and*
*piled cream. Around us the fellow tourists*
*chatter and wave their hands to disperse*
*the threatening wasps.*
Rosy Burke (Denaro)

## The tea rooms

After the shop was established, Hanover also opened as a tea room. Bert seeded the lawn ready for making a tea garden. When Gladys Winser came from Devon to visit her aunt she helped out with the cooking. Eventually marrying Bert, Gladys was the lynchpin in the kitchen. The tea room changed little over the years, with its bow window and polished horse brasses hanging from the dark beams. Two bells were used for service; one, a ship's bell from a wreck, is now in Brighstone Museum. There were nine highly polished tables inside and twelve more outside when the weather was good.

HANOVER HOUSE.
BROOKE.
ISLE OF WIGHT.
**For Teas & Refreshments**
PARTIES CATERED FOR.
BED AND BREAKFAST.
*M. & H. MORRIS, Proprietors.*

In the winter there was always a welcoming fire. It was very cosy when full and everyone seemed to chat to everyone else. It provided a good meeting place for people. The tea rooms were open all year round and a sausage and mash supper was made regularly for the Vectis Cyclists for 1/6 (one shilling and sixpence). During the Second World War, soldiers stationed in Brook would have breakfast and other meals at Hanover, (see *The War Years*) and the Land Army girls occasionally came for a treat of beans on toast instead of their usual sandwiches. All this meant a lot of hard work in a very small space. Everyone had a job and Gladys, who got up at 5.30 each morning to make all the scones and cakes, is remembered well for carrying huge, heavy trays and cheerfully serving the customers. Molly Humber was the only outside helper and was invaluable. On busy Sundays in the summer people queued at the gate. Janet and Susan, (Margaret and Walter Stone's daughters), remember the washing up as a nightmare which often lasted from 4pm to 7 or 8pm. By the 1960s a cream tea cost three shillings with strawberries available in season, as were fresh prawns from Brook Bay. Clotted cream was delivered from the Creameries in Newport and the daily milk was fetched fresh from Downton Farm across the road in two, six and eight pint cans. In 1969, the last year of business for the family, the tea gardens were well known all over the Island and served 10,000 cream teas and salad meals.

Vectis Road Cyclists were regular customers, and here pose after stopping off for tea at Hanover in 1935. In 1937 teas cost 1/= (one shilling) and from then until after the War they consisted of bread, butter and jam - as much as you liked - and a homemade plain cake.

The small summer house in the garden (below) was thatched by Bert using straw casings from wine bottles that he got from the Sun Inn at Hulverstone.

A real Brook gathering in the garden of Hanover House to celebrate the golden wedding of Joe and Alice Morris in 1953

*My childhood memories of Hanover are of Uncle Walter and Uncle Bert in their smart suits and chauffeurs caps driving their impressive taxis. Of Margaret scurrying here, there and everywhere and Gladys for her amazing food and her Devonshire sayings like, 'there's none so queer as folks.'*

Edward Whitewood

1 Hilda Barnes
2 Barry Oatley
3 Mrs Oatley
4 Robert Cassell
5 Charlie Smith
6 Joan Shepheard
7 Lance Barnes
8 Erica Newbery
9 Daisy Newbery
10 Mrs Sheath
11 Dorothy Atkins
12 Walter Stone
13 Joan Morris
14 Gladys Morris
15 Bert Morris
16 Mrs Tickner
17 Walter Newbery
18 Daisy Newbery
19 Mabel Newbery
20 Muriel Cassell
21 Gerty Webb
22 Mr Bucket
23 Muff Young
24 Mrs Bucket
25 Mr Young
26 Ann Sharpe
27 Nan Sharpe
28 Mr Leal
29 Ella Hookey
30 Babs Jackman
31 Mrs Jackman
32 Mr Jackman
33 Mrs Heal
34 Mabel Newbery
35 Louisa Newbery
36 Gerty Pitman
37 Mrs Leal
38 Sophie Phillips
39 Mrs Barnes
40 George Phillips
41 Bessie Winser
42 Edie Morris
43 Fred Morris
44 Bill Morris
45 Joe Morris
46 Alice Morris
47 Mr Barnes
48 Janice Morris
49 Janet Stone
50 Susan Stone
51 Margaret Stone

In his 1903 diary (below), the vicar of Brook, Rev. R L Morris, records the marriage of Alice and Joe Morris (no relation) alongside the productivity of his bees and a visit to Brook by a young Winston Churchill.

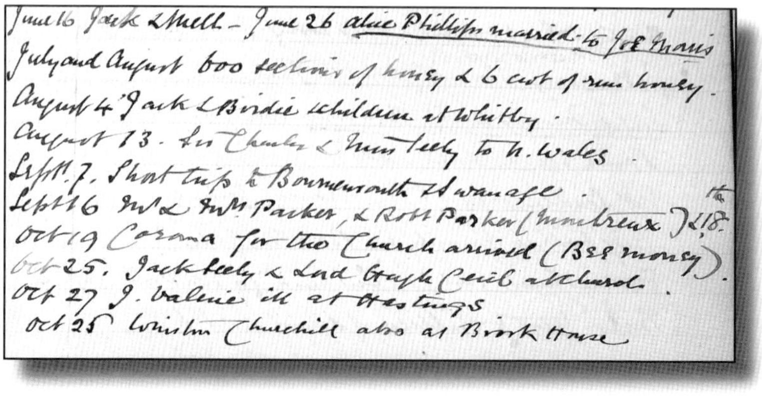

June 16 Jack & Nell – June 26 Alice Phillips married to Joe Morris
July and August 600 sections of honey & 6 cwt of run honey.
August 4 Jack & Birdie children at Whitby.
August 13. Sir Charles & Mrs Seely to N. Wales.
Sept 7. Short trip to Bournemouth & Swanage.
Sept 16 Mr & Mrs Parker, & Robt Parker (Montreux) £18.
Oct 19 Corona for the Church arrived (Bee money).
Oct 25. Jack Seely & Lord Hugh Cecil at Church.
Oct 27 J. Valerie ill at Hastings
Oct 25 Winston Churchill also at Brook House

CYCLE : MOTOR CYCLE : CAR : & : GENERAL ENGINEERS

**H. & M. MORRIS,**

HANOVER GARAGE

**BROOKE, ISLE OF WIGHT.**

EST 1933. TEL: BRIGHSTONE 281.

SPECIALIST IN HIGH CLASS LIMOUSINE HIRE CARS

## The taxi service and garage

Walter Stone, a friend of Bert's, joined the family 'firm' when he married Margaret. These two men were fitters and turners by trade. They could turn their hands to any job, and they did, repairing cars, lawn mowers, bicycles, irons, kettles. You name it, they had a go at it, usually with success. There were many jobs around the village too; stone walls to repair, even house building and plumbing work. As Hanover House was such an old house there were always plenty of repairs to be done at home too ....

Bert with the Humber 'YY'

but it wasn't always top priority. In the 1930s Bert bought a car, a Morris Cowley, registration number PO 3535, and started a taxi service. This proved popular and he was commissioned to take local people on outings and to visit relations in other parts of the Island. Dressed up with white ribbons it also served as a wedding car.

The fleet grew and as well as the 'PO,' (the car was named after its registration number), there was soon a Humber, known as 'YY' and later a Wolsely, 'FJJ',which was bought with the £600 made from the salvage of raw rubber bales washed up from a wreck on Brook Bay. The cars had glass wind-down screens between the driver and passengers and the Humber had a sort of telephone arrangement to enable the passengers to communicate with the driver. 'YY' also had extra fold down seats in the back so it could seat 5 people. Walter Stone and Bert Morris wore navy blue suits and chauffeur's caps when driving. Some notable local people used the taxi service included Lord Sherwood and J B Priestley. As well as housing four to six cars, accumulator batteries bubbled away in the garage. There were all kinds of car spares, pulleys, chains, tools and numerous boxes of 'this and that,' as well as stocks of bicycle tyres hanging from the walls and other bike accessories. A vulcaniser stood nearby for mending punctures and there was a large pit for car repairs. Big green sliding doors made the place secure.

*I had a model steam engine for Christmas one year, it ran by heating the boiler with a spirit lamp. Being rather careless I let the boiler run dry and the solder around the base melted and leaked. I took it to Mr Stone who soldered it back for me, it was then as good as new.*

Ken Barnes

Bert Morris and Walter Stone at work with a saw at Hanover.

Both couples took an active part in village life, Bert and Walter did car repairs, plumbing and general maintenance. They were members of the Cliff Rescue Service; Bert was churchwarden for many years and Margaret played the organ and was in the Brook Ladies' Choir. However busy she was, Gladys always attended church and provided delicious food for all the village occasions. In September 1969 the *IOW County Press* reported:

Retirement presentation to Mrs Margaret Stone and Mrs Gladys Morris by Mr Lance Barnes (Old Myrtle Cottage), with the Rev. Robert Bowyer in the background.

**PRESENTATION AT BROOK**

A presentation on their retirement from Hanover Stores and Tea Garden was made to Mrs W J Stone and Mrs H F Morris by the people of the village on Sunday evening. The ceremony was held in the garden of the Rectory at Mottistone and the large gathering was entertained to tea by Mrs R Bowyer. The presentation was made by Mr Lance Barnes, an old friend of the family and one of the few remaining residents of Brook who was born in the village, He gave each a card with the names of all subscribers on it. Welcoming the guests, the Rector said that it was doubtful whether Mrs Stone and Mrs Morris had really sat down during those long years of their service to the village and so the choice of a garden seat was especially appropriate. He remembered hearing of the famous little shop when he was in the Midlands before he had even seen Brook and he recalled an occasion when he had been unable to buy some article he wanted at another village store in Knightsbridge, called Harrods, but had obtained them on his return at Hanover Stores. In thanking Mrs Stone and Mrs Morris for their life's work the Rector welcomed the new owners of the stores and tea gardens, Mr and Mrs Hedley.

Courtesy of *Isle of Wight County Press.*

From left to right: Rev. Robert Bowyer, Mrs French,Geoff Mariner, Terry Mears, Susan Mears (Stone), Bert Morris, Gladys Morris, Walter Stone, Lily Stone, Margaret Stone (Morris), xxx, Ethel Smith, xxx, xxx, Hannah Hutchinson, xxx, xxx, xxx, Lance Barnes, Stanley Eade, Mr Bob French, Stanley Dowden.

# A king, a queen, a writer, a politician, a film star and... a horse

Clockwise: Queen Mary, J B Priestley, Winston Churchill, General Jack Seely, Warrior, Jane Birkin, John Seely, General Guiseppe Garibaldi, Henry VII.

Either for pleasure or as a refuge from the public eye, a number of monarchs, politicians and well-known writers and performers have regularly visited or lived in this part of the Isle of Wight. King Henry VII famously feasted at Brook Manor in 1499. Charles Seely lost favour with Queen Victoria when he hosted the Italian liberator General Garibaldi in Brook in 1864. In the early 1900s Queen Mary took refuge from Cowes Week by visiting the Seelys at Brook and Mottistone. Although the locals who worked there were very discreet, we are told that Edward, Prince of Wales, later Duke of Windsor, partied up at Brook Hill between the wars. Lloyd George, Lord Hugh Cecil and Winston Churchill all visited Jack Seely and family when they lived at Brooke House and Lord Boothby regularly joined shooting parties arranged by Hugh Seely, Lord Sherwood. Winston Churchill and Jack Seely became lifelong friends and the Rector's diary notes that Winston regularly visited Brook in the early 1900s. A chine (where the Military Road now has traffic lights), became known as 'Winston's Chine' after he and Jack Seely dug it out trying to improve drainage and halt coastal erosion. Alfred, Lord Tennyson would walk from Freshwater Bay across the downs above Brook in his large black hat and cloak. Like Tennyson, when J B Priestley came to Brook Hill after the Second World War he was the equivalent of a superstar today and glad of the beauty and seclusion of Brook. Farm workers have told us that if they met Priestley out walking they were advised not to talk to him in case they disturbed his flow of thought. The list of Priestley's visitors at Brook Hill included Compton Mackenzie, A J P Taylor and Sir Julian Huxley. John Betjeman referred to the 'sheer delight' of Mottistone during one of his visits to his friends Rev. Robert and Elizabeth Bowyer. Judy Campbell, the actress known as Noel Coward's muse, and who sang 'A Nightingale Sang in Berkeley Square', loved the family house in Hulverstone. Jane Birkin, her daughter, is remembered as the tomboy who rushed down Brook Shute on her bike and worked for pocket money in the market garden of Brook House. John Seely, second Lord Mottistone, became a successful architect and with his partner Paul Paget became Surveyor to St Paul's Cathedral. While not a human being, we cannot leave out General Jack Seely's horse, Warrior, nor A. J. Munnings, the artist, who drew Warrior in the trenches and battlefields of northern France and later in the peaceful fields of Brook and Mottistone. In the next few pages we focus on just a few of those mentioned here.

# J B Priestley at Brook Hill House

The novelist described the local landscape as the scenery of our dreams, and captures the view from his study window as if in a painting, framed and frozen in time:

*Down below are downlands and heath, green slopes and gorse in bloom…Lower and nearer, a glimpse of a tiny church and the ruin of a large manor house. Further off, but dominating the scene, is the long chalk cliff that ends in the Needles. And full in the middle panes of my window is that flashing mirror, that blue diamond or that infinite haze, that window for the mind, which is the sea. And delight shall soar into ecstasy when a great shaft of late afternoon sunlight reaches the upper downland, bright against a sea of pewter, and my rheumy eyes seem to stare at the fields of Paradise.*

Delight (1949)

View over to Tennyson Down and on to Swanage from Brook Hill

We are told that when Priestley lived at Brook Hill the working day would start with a huge breakfast, with hot dishes of kidneys and kippers on the sideboard at a stated hour, after which Priestley would disappear into his study until lunchtime,

to re-emerge for fierce tennis on a private court, tea on the terrace, cocktails, and a late, lavish dinner. At night, the great man would challenge his guests that they could look

*The house was high on the hill facing south-west, Jack used to sit by the window growling 'I hate wind.'*

at the lights of Bournemouth and 'thank God you're not there.' In 1953 he was in his late 50s and most of his important writing was behind him; Literary projects completed at Brook Hill included nine plays, including Dragon's Mouth (1952). Here he wrote the rumbustious

*Concerts were held in the large central hall, with some guests sitting up the stairs, and would stretch over several evenings.*

satire Festival at Farbridge (1951), set in a claustrophobic local community preparing for the Festival of Britain. It targets pomposity and village rivalries. Tom Priestley recalls how:

*We didn't often walk down to the village, JBP did not drive and so we were quite isolated. He was community-minded in spirit and had local friends. We 'stubbed our toes' on class in the Island. My father, not being 'County' meant he was not much liked. We were friendly with the Mew family, he was the Master of Foxhounds and Alfred Noyes was another IOW friend.*

*On Sundays, Priestley would march his guests to The Albion and give them a 'Dog's Nose', an odd mixture of gin and draught ale.*

It was while they were living at Brook Hill that the Priestleys' marriage broke down. Both JBP and his wife remarried, with Jack marrying Jacquetta Hawkes in 1953. Jacquetta was a distinguished archaeologist and had been awarded the OBE in 1952. Her first major discovery was a Neanderthal skeleton in Palestine and she was archaeological adviser to the 1951 Festival of Britain. Her widely acclaimed book *A Land* combined her archaeological knowledge with her poetic imagination. In the Isle of Wight she excavated the Neolithic longbarrow at the Longstone with Jack Jones, then County Archaeologist, assisted by her son Nicolas Hawkes and Mr Frank Hayles, the gardener at Brook Hill. Jacqetta believed in making use of all forms of mass media to popularize archaeology, and in the late 1940s produced an innovative film about pre-history, with an Iron Age site reconstructed at Pinewood Studios. During the 1950s she frequently appeared on the popular BBC television programme *Animal, Vegetable, Mineral.* Jacquetta also wrote poetry and plays, collaborating with JBP on several pieces. In 1957 Jacquetta and JB Priestley and a number of friends, including Canon John and Diana Collins, founded the Campaign for Nuclear Disarmament and she was often to be seen leading the famous Aldermaston marches. In 1958 she organised a major public meeting in Sandown Pavilion to promote the campaign on the Isle of Wight, which coincided with the local, successful campaign against a proposed nuclear power station at Newtown. Despite his famed grumpiness, Priestley was known as 'Jolly Jack' to his close friends: *When Jack Priestley was there, those were gay days. We celebrated New Year's Eve by a special party. Jack had a special bottle of drink concealed under his chair. We had a string quartet*

*We 'stubbed our toes' on class in the Island. My father, not being 'County' meant he was not much liked.*

*At night, the great man would challenge his guests that they could look at the lights of Bournemouth and 'thank God you're not there.'*

JBP and Jacquettta Hawkes in what Johanna Jones describes as a typical Sunday morning scene.

*If Salzburg and Edinburgh could have festivals, why not Brooke Hill, Isle of Wight?*
*J B Priestley, Picture Post, 1950*

Sir Arthus Bliss and J B Priestley 'settle down after a talkative walk to the shaping of the libretto of a new opera.' *The Picture Post*, September 1950.

*playing high grade stuff.* Jack and Jacquetta Priestley entertained many guests at Brook Hill, including such well-known figures from the arts and sciences as Leon Goossens, Iris Murdoch, Julian Huxley, Mortimer Wheeler, Compton Mackenzie, Dilys Powell, Michael Denison and Dulcie Gray, Marghanita Laski, and John and Diana Collins. Parties included poet Louis MacNiece, historian A J P Taylor (who lived in Yarmouth), Gerald Abraham, Professor of Music at Liverpool, Jack and Johanna Jones, when he was Curator at Carisbrooke Castle, Dr Richard and Mary Sandiford and the Rev. Robert Bowyer, Vicar of Brook and Mottistone and his wife Elisabeth. Nicolas Hawkes, Jacquetta's son described a New Year's Eve party in 1953 in his diary: *a great event for this teenager! Guests: The Abrahams, Revd and Mrs Bowyer (vicar of Mottistone) the Hutchinsons plus Jugoslav student, the Sandifords, the Taylors, and important new friends Jack & Johanna Jones, of Carisbrooke Castle Museum plus 4 of us. Miss Pudduck prepared a magnificent supper, which was eaten standing. Games brilliantly organized by JBP: 1. Miming Game (like Washing the Elephant) in 2 teams; 2. The acting Titles Game in 4 teams of 4 each; 3. Fortune-telling, in which each person dropped a spoonful of molten lead into cold water, the resulting, often fantastic, shape was used by JBP to tell the person's fortune. Much merriment! Finally Bishop, or mulled port, was served to see the New Year in. There was NO Auld Lang Syne, GSTQ, kissing etc. They preferred it that way.*
Professor Abraham, alongside J B Priestley, famously organised concerts of chamber music at Brook Hill House, inviting such brilliant ensembles as the Dartington Quartet and soloists Leon Goossens and Reginald Kell. In his diary Nicolas Hawkes describes the music concerts: *The large central hall at Brook Hill was ideal, with excellent acoustics and the guests sitting on the wide staircase and on the gallery above. Audiences were about 150 and it was always a capacity house with the long approach drive choked with slow moving vehicles. 11-13 Sept 1953 The New London Quartet with Erich Gruenberg, Lionel Bentley (violins), Keith Cummings (Viola), Douglas Cameron (cello). Leon Goossens, the world famous oboeist and Eric Harrison (Piano) also played. In January 1954 Harrison and Goossens returned for a single concert and in September 1957 The Robert Masters Piano Quartet played; RM (1st violin), Nannie Jamieson (viola) and Muriel Taylor (cello).*
Jack Jones recalls how: *Priestley would introduce the players and programme, after which he would disappear into the large drawing room where he would enjoy the music from the depths of an armchair, and the aroma of cigar smoke would be discernible.* When the Priestleys left Brook Hill in 1959, it was not without regrets: *If we were so happy up there at Brooke Hill House why did we sell, pack up and leave the Island? It was all very well for us living there, but our family and friends had to keep getting to and from the Island. This was not very easy in winter with its sudden blinding fogs cutting us off from the mainland… So we took pity on our family and friends and moved somewhere more accessible. But I am not sure we were right.*

Jack Priestley outside Brook Hill with the Ford motor car that, when they left the Island, Jacqetta thoughtfully left to Jack Jones to replace the electric bicycle he used to visit archaeological sites on the Island.

We are grateful to Dr Brian Hinton who provided much of the material on JB Priestley in Brook.

# Jane Birkin

Jane Birkin is known by many as the young actress in the 1960s who became the partner of French songwriter Serge Gainsbourg, the mother of actress Charlotte and who is now a singer in her own right. Perhaps few people know that, as a child, she spent her school holidays in Brook and Hulverstone. After renting Little Brook for the summer, her parents bought Bank Cottage and the Post Office in Hulverstone when the Seely Estate was sold in 1957. Brook in those days was an open and less developed place: *Being a 12-year-old on a bike on the Isle of Wight with my brother and sister and Ma and Pa is for me the epitome of happiness. We didn't stay on the chic side of the Island, but near Brook beach, where there's black sand. We would ramble and have adventures together – it was wonderful. We used to get up at six in the morning and get on our bikes and we just went to discover things. There were wrecks from the last war, and there was a porcupine washed up which we tied onto our bikes with a few mines that we'd found on the beach.* Jane Cotton remembers the Birkins in the 1950s when her father was foreman of the Seely Estate: *The Birkin family first came to stay at Little Brook for the school holidays in 1955. Lt Commander Birkin was a tall, thin man and he was a painter. He had been awarded the Légion d'Honneur for his role in the war. Mrs Birkin was a celebrated actress whose stage name was Judy Campbell. She was very striking-looking, tall and slim with very dark hair and a deep husky voice. I have happy memories of several holidays spent with their children,*

Jane at Brook in 1960.

*We used to get up at six in the morning and get on our bikes and we just went to discover things.*

*Andrew, Jane and Linda. Despite our differences in education and background, we got on really well and played around the Brook Estate, in the garden of Little Brook and on the beach.* Jane's life changed dramatically a few years later when aged 19, she was briefly married to John Barry, already well-known as the composer of the James Bond film music. A year later in 1966, she appeared in the cult film *Blow-Up*. In 1968 she went to Paris where she met Serge Gainsbourg and later released the song, *Je t'aime… moi non plus*, which caused a furore, leading it to be banned by the BBC and condemned by the Vatican. Back in Brook in 2010 to make documentary about her life, Jane and her brother Andrew found the 'treasure' they had hidden 50 years ago - a hoard of threepenny pieces under a small waterfall.

Kate Barry, Jane Birkin with baby Charlotte and Serge Gainsbourg in Hulverstone in 1971.

# Seely and Paget

John Seely, the second Lord Mottistone, was a talented architect who, together with his partner, Paul Paget, formed the firm of Seely and Paget in 1926. One of their first commissions involved designing the opulent former Eltham Palace for Stephen and Virginia Courtauld and their pet ring-tailed lemur. They restored many damaged church buildings after World War Two and restored parts of Windsor Castle in the 1960s. They also became surveyor to St Paul's Cathedral, where the candles on the choir stalls are called 'Mottistone candles.' The Shack in the grounds of Mottistone Manor was used by the architects as a retreat and country office. Built in the 1930s, it is an example of Modern Movement design. Local examples of John Seely's work include Mottistone Manor, Little Brook and Shalfleet Church Hall. It is he who is to be thanked for gifting much of Mottistone to the National Trust and ensuring that the countryside, coast and downland did not become overdeveloped in the 1960s.

Lord Mottistone presenting the prize for 'best beast' to Mr Willie Wykeham (of Jack's Hill and Chilton Farm) and Primrose, at the Agricultural Show.

# General Guiseppe Garibaldi (1807-1882)

Garibaldi arrives at Brooke House in April 1864. *Illustrated London News*

When he died at his home in Caprera, aged 75, Garibaldi had worked as a sea captain, fought for freedom causes in Brazil and Uruguay and seen the realisation of his greatest ambition, the unification of Italy. Garibaldi visited England in 1864, to thank the British people who had given him support during his campaign of 1860. Charles Seely (1803 - 1887), a Liberal MP who supported the unification of Italy, invited the great liberator Garibaldi to stay at Brooke House when it was thought (quite rightly) that he would be mobbed by adoring crowds in London. Garibaldi landed at Southampton on Sunday 3 April 1864, and in reply to the mayor said: *Without the help of the English nation it would have been impossible to complete the deeds we did in southern Italy.* Charles Seely incurred Queen Victoria's severe displeasure, some say because the crowds for Garibaldi were much larger than

*Queen Victoria became very perturbed at the excitement of the populace in acclaiming this revolutionary general.*

those for herself. As Mary Seely writes to him after his visit: *The Inspector* (of police) *told Charles that the progresses of her Majesty had never been nearly so enthusiastic.* Garibaldi spent time at Brooke House, the home of Charles Seely, before travelling to London where he was greeted by an estimated half a million people. The crowds were so immense it took him six hours to travel three miles through the streets. Garibaldi later returned to Brook for a few days before he returned to Italy. Garibaldi arrived at Cowes on Monday, 4 April 1864 and a crowd estimated at 2,000 welcomed him to streets decorated with flags and banners. The shipbuilders J.S. White gave their workers the afternoon off and the band of the Isle of Wight Rifles played *See the Conquering Hero Comes*. The Isle of Wight Observer reported: *Cowes claims the honour of being the first spot in the Isle of Wight trod by the greatest man who ever set foot on our soil.* The crowds escorted Garibaldi all of the 15 miles to Brooke House. While there, Garibaldi planted

*They recited poetry to each other, Garibaldi repeating Italian verses of which Tennyson apparently understood not a word.*

an oak tree in the garden which the Seely family called the 'Tree of Liberty' and which survived until the hurricane of 1987. Locals tell another story about the Garibaldi oak dying and another being planted by head gardener, Mr Tribbick, in its place. While at Brook, Garibaldi visited Farringford, the home of the poet Alfred Tennyson. Emily Tennyson records hearing: *the sounds of welcome as Garibaldi passed thro' the village to Farringford. People on foot and on horseback and in carriages had waited at our gate for two hours for him.* Tennyson took Garibaldi to his study and advised him not to discuss politics in England. They recited poetry to each other, Garibaldi repeating Italian verses of which Tennyson apparently understood not a word. While at Farringford Garibaldi was accosted by a woman

Garibaldi on cliffs in England (an engraving made in 1864).

Garibaldi is cheered by crowds at Newport Guildhall in April 1864. *Illustrated London News*

*The streets were decorated with flags and streamers and a banner with 'Viva Garibaldi' spanned Newport High Street.*

on her knees. It was Julia Margaret Cameron who held her black, chemical-stained hands up to him, asking him to sit for a photograph. He is said to have thought she was a well-dressed beggar and she to have said: *this is not dirt but art!* On Thursday 7 April when Garibaldi's carriages passed through Newport, the streets were decorated with flags and streamers and a banner with 'Viva Garibaldi' spanned the High Street. To the cheers of thousands he was greeted by the mayor, Mr. W.B. Mew at the Guildhall and took his place on a purpose-built platform to express his gratitude for the warm welcome. On 11 April Garibaldi left Brooke House and travelled to London where he was greeted by crowds estimated at half a million people. He stayed at Charles Seely's London residence, 26 Princes Gate. The whole country shut down for three days. On the 20th he was awarded the Freedom of the City of London and also met with the Liberal Prime Minister Lord Palmerston and the Prince of Wales, the future Edward VII. The impact Garibaldi had on the populace continued to worry Queen Victoria. She instructed Palmerston to write to Charles Seely urging Garibaldi to leave the country. In *Adventure* (1930), Jack Seely writes:

> ...when Garibaldi arrived in London he was given the Freedom of the City, and that on his journey to the City and back he was acclaimed by crowds more vast than any that has assembled in living memory. The Austrians were much offended, and Queen Victoria became very perturbed at the excitement of the populace in acclaiming this revolutionary general. She urged that Garibaldi should be induced to return to Italy, and correspondence ensued between the Prime Minister of the day and my grandfather.

After London, Garibaldi returned to Brook for a few days and then left for home aboard the Duke of Sutherland's private yacht. Letters from both Mary and Charles Seely to Garibaldi and his replies in Italian show the strength of their mutual affection. Garibaldi was a charismatic and attractive figure and, as his portraits show, was seen as a romantic, revolutionary leader. While people at this time were given to expressing themselves (especially in letters) in an expan-

*Everyday my wife and I talk about you and we long to have you back again all to ourselves in our quiet little village of Brooke.*

sive way, the letters indicate a strong affection. A lock of Garibaldi's hair survives as a keepsake on a piece of card and the inscription reads: *I cut this lock of hair from off General Garibaldi's head in the Library at Brooke House, Isle of Wight, on the sixth of April 1864. Mary Seely.* After Garibaldi has left Brook, *Mary writes: When, alas! you had left me yesterday, and my heart was heavy with grief, I went to your little bed full of emotion and sorrow that your dear and revered head would not rest there again.* Writing from his home on the island of Caprera near Sardinia in June 1864, Garibaldi refers to her as *my precious friend*, adding: *I am given to melancholy, but become cheerful when I think of you.* He says: *When I think of your face, which I carry engraved on my heart, I forget my gloom and am happy.* Charles Seely writes to him in July 1864 and as well as giving him political news says: *You will never know the intense interest you excited in this country and I may add the personal love - I wonder when I shall see you again - Everyday my wife and I talk about you and we long to have you back again all to ourselves in our quiet little village of Brooke.* In one letter of October 1864 Garibaldi discusses the political situation in Italy and then the progress of the turnip seeds he was given to plant in Caprera. He writes in English: *The Brookes' turnips are growing magnificent! And I visit them every morning, translating myself deliciously in the beautiful and dear birthplace of it.* When Louis and Julia Denaro bought the Coach House of Brooke House in the Estate auction of 1958, they discovered a vast oil painting of Garibaldi propped up, damp and dusty in a greenhouse. The massive frame was repaired by master carpenter, Walter Newbery, in Carpenters' Lane, Brook. In 2009 the painting was professionally restored by the Isle of Wight Heritage Service and is now on permanent display at the Newport Guildhall where Garibaldi once waved to the crowds.

*The Brookes' turnips are growing magnificent! And I visit them every morning, translating myself deliciously in the beautiful and dear birthplace of it.*

Oil painting of Giuseppe Garibaldi at Brooke House in 1864, painted by Attilio Baccani. The Italian and British flags are carved at the top and the words *Liberta* and *Indepenza* painted on each side. The portrait is now on permanent display at Newport Guildhall.

# Queen Mary

Not as fond of sailing as George V, Queen Mary visited her friends, General Jack and Evelyn Seely at both Brooke House and later Mottistone Manor, during Cowes Week. She planted trees in the grounds and there is a memorable description of her having been stung by a bee while taking tea in the garden of Brooke House. Daisy Newbery worked in the gardens of Brooke House for thirty years and remembered: *Once, when I was working, General Seely brought Queen Mary around and introduced me to her. The Queen was very kind and asked how my shoulder was (it had been giving some trouble).* The first bunches of the famous and abundant black Hamburg and Muscat of Alexandria grapes planted by Mr Tribbick and looked after by Daisy in the Brooke House vinery were sent annually to Buckingham Palace.

*Queen Mary was once stung by a bee while taking tea in the garden at Brooke House.*

Jack Seely introduces Warrior to Queen Mary on an informal visit at Mottistone Manor in 1934. It was probably during Cowes Week as he is in sailing clothes. Prince George is apparently behind the Queen.

THIS HORSE WILL NOT RUN TODAY

Lord Mottistone celebrated his seventieth birthday yesterday by riding near his home in the Isle of Wight on Warrior, thirty-year-old horse which went through the war without a scratch. Twenty years ago Warrior carried his master, then General Jack Seely, fifty miles on a night ride to a threatened part of France.

# Warrior

*My faithful friend, who never failed and never feared.*

Bred at Yafford in 1908, Warrior was taught to be fearless in battle by walking into the roughest waves at Brook Bay by Jack Seely. He had many narrow escapes but survived the 1914 - 1918 war in which 484,000 horses were killed. In September 1914, for example, he had to gallop 10 miles across country to escape encirclement by the advancing enemy. In 1915 a shell cut the horse beside Warrior clean in half and a few days later another shell destroyed his stable, seconds after he had left it. In 1917, only frantic digging extricated him from mud in Passchendaele, and only three days before on March 30, 1917, a direct hit on the ruined villa in which he was housed left him trapped beneath a shattered beam. He took part in one of the last great cavalry charges at Moreuil Wood on 30 March 1918. After his injury in 1918, Warrior recovered sufficiently to join the victory parade in Hyde Park and in 1921 came back to win the Isle of Wight Point to Point. After 20 years of peaceful retirement in Brook and Mottistone, Warrior lived until 1941 when it was felt that the extra corn rations needed to keep the 33-year-old gelding could not be justified in wartime.

There are still a number of local people today who have memories of seeing or sitting on Warrior when they were young. He was one of the most famous warhorses ever known. As Jack Seely described it: *as I rode along, whether it was in rest billets, in reserve, approaching the line, or in the midst of battle, men would say, not 'Here comes the General,' but 'Here's old Warrior.'*

Detail from a painting by A J Munnings in France in WW1, "the unfortunate Munnings kept breaking into the mud beneath until I had him mounted on some duck boards..." *My Horse Warrior.*

The field called Sidling Paul on Brook Shute, where Warrior spent his young days. Jasper Morris, who looked after Warrior during these years, explained to me: "What I likes about Sidling Paul is that she has water at each end so the colts be encouraged to walk first one way and then the other on the steep sides. That makes their legs strong, and their hearts big."
*My Horse Warrior.* Drawing by A.J. Munnings

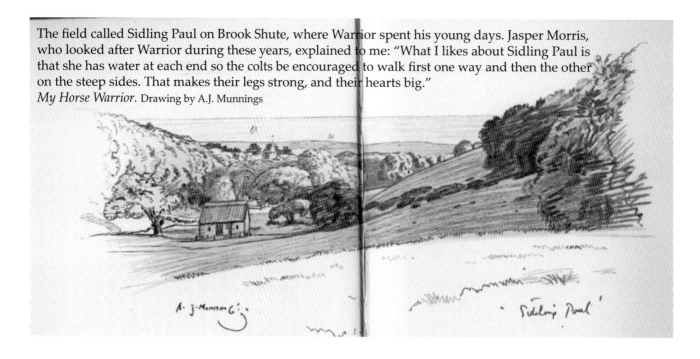

# Bibliography


*Adventure*, J E B Seely, 1930
*An Eventful Life,* Robert Cassell, 1997, ed. Dina Broughton
*Back of the Wight*, G F Mew, 1934, IOW County Press
*Brighstone, Brook and Mottistone W.I. Scrapbook.*
*Brooke Lifeboat*, Robert Cassell, ed. Dina Broughton
*Coastguard! An Official History of HM Coastguard,* William Webb, HMSO, 1976, ISBN 0 11 510675 8
*Forever England,* J E B Seely, 1932
*Galloper Jack*, Brough Scott, 2004, 0330491687
*Hanover House*, Susan Mears, 1999
*In Living Memory, IOW Federation of* Women's Institutes, 1994, Countryside Books, 1853062898
*Launch!*, J E B Seely, 1932
*My Horse Warrior,* J E B Seely, 1934
*Paths of Happiness,* J E B Seely,1938
*Put Out the Flag,* Derek Sprake, 1993, Cross Publishing, 1873295 00 6
*Shipwrecks of the Isle of Wight,* J C Medland, 1986, West Island Printers, 0951149806
*The Isle of Wight An illustrated History,* Jack and Johanna Jones, 1987, Dovecote Press, 0946159440
*The Isle of Wight at War*, Adrian Searle, Dovecote Press, 2000
*The West Wight Remembered*, Eric Toogood, 1984, West Island Printers
*The West Wight Remembered*, Eric Toogood, 1989, West Island Printers

# Acknowledgements

Our thanks are more than due to all of the following people,
in particular: Bert Morris, Julia Denaro and Rita Whitewood.

**Research:** Chris Bull, George Jupe, Christine Harmer, Pauline Tyrell. **Memories:** Pat Tyrrell, Avice Mariner (French), Erica Browitt (Newbery), Myrtle Lewis (Newbery), Alison Long, Rosemary Whitehead (Newbery), David Hollis (Snr), George Thompson, Robert Cassell, Rita Whitewood, Tony & Mary Pettitt (Taylor), Robin Shepheard (Newbery), Renella Phillips (Humber), Evelyn O'Neill, Joyce Downer, Ann Male (Hailey). **Transcription and proof-reading:** Gillian Belben, Anne Simmonds, Georghia Ellinas, Avice Mariner, Iris Tracey, Belinda Walters, Brough Scott, Rosy Burke, Terry Mears. **Photography:** Mike Osborne, Andrew Sim, Susan Mears, Lawrence Greswell, Louis Denaro. **Heritage photographs and artefacts:** The collections of Bert Morris, Brighstone Museum, Blackgang Chine, Calbourne Mill, Jane Phillips, David, Lord Mottistone, Anne Ham (Hookey), Sheila Warne (Hookey), Eric and Nancy Sheath (Newbery), Paul Cutmore, Paul Manley, Peter Phillips, Hilary Higgins. **Photographic reproduction:** Barry Smith.

Contributors to particular chapters include:

**Churches and Chapel:** Chris Bull, Avice Mariner (French), Erica Browitt (Newbery), Kate Slack (Morris), Ann Male (Hailey), Dick Robinson and the Appleton family. **Early History:** Alison Long, Ruth Waller. **Farms and farming:** Jane Phillips, Ralph Cook, George Thompson, Pat Tyrell, David Baker, David Stephens, Pauline Tyrell, Robert Cassell, Tod and Jackie Carder, Hilda Barton (Jackman), John Jackman, Robin Minchin, Patrick and Susannah Seely **Fishing:** Pat Tyrell, Simon Homes, Chris Braund. **Lifeboats and wrecks:** John Medland, Geoff Cotton, Rob Snow, Dot Lobb, Marjorie Clark, Chris Bull. **Smuggling and coastguards:** Fred Mew, Joe Hulse, Bob Cassell. **High Days and Holidays:** Barbara Heal (Hookey), Peter Phillips (Newbery), Paul Manley (Newbery). **Self-sufficiency and lucrative pastimes**: Rita Whitewood, Carol Worrall (Woolbright), Robin Shepheard, Joyce Downer, Audrey Rann (Barnes), Evelyn O'Neil, Patrick Court. **Village trades and occupations:** Robin Shepheard, David Hollis, Michele Kaiser. **School:** Ken Barnes, Audrey Rann (Barnes), Ron Emmett. **Wartime:** Myrtle Lewis (Newbery), Ron Emmett. **The Seely family and Brooke House:** David Seely, Lord Mottistone, Brough Scott, Mark Fletcher, Caroline Clarke, Patrick Seely. **Seely Hall and Women's Institute:** Valerie Downer (Cook), Renella Phillips (Humber), Win Hollis. **Hanover Stores and tea rooms:** Ken Barnes, Edward Whitewood. **A king, a queen, etc:** IOW Heritage Service, John Medland for Garibaldi; Brian Hinton, Tom Priestley, Nicolas Hawkes, Rachel Whitehead, Margaret Jackson for J B Priestley; Andrew Birkin for Jane Birkin; David, Lord Mottistone for Queen Mary and Seely and Paget. **Historical context:** Crispin Keith, Chris Bull.
**Newspaper reports and photographs:** are courtesy of the *Isle of Wight County Press*.

*Brook - A Village History* Get Together in May 2009. From left at back: Pat Tyrrell, Barbara Thompson (Sivier), George Thompson, Pauline Emmett, Anne Ham (Hookey), Richard Minchin, Robin Minchin, Janet Ash (Stone), Avice Mariner (French), Myrtle Lewis (Newbery), Doris Baker (Emmett), Joan Irons (Emmett), Mary Pettitt (Taylor), Tony Pettitt, Jim Abbott, Janice Hackshaw (Simpson), Brough Scott, Renella Phillips (Humber), Nancy Sheath (Newbery), Jean Storie, Audrey Rann (Barnes), Libby Farquhar (Wykeham). Front from left: Jane Cotton, Susan Mears (Stone), Cecil Baker, Marjorie Clark (New), Carol Worrall (Woolbright).

A get-together at the Seely Hall in 2009 for people who were born, worked and lived in Brook, Mottistone, Hulverstone or Chessell between the 1920s and the 1960s.

1. Joan Irons (Emmett), Joyce Downer, Doris Baker (Emmett); 2. Libby Farquhar (Wykeham); 3. Marjorie Clark (New) and Carol Worrall (Woolbright); 4. Roger Attrill; 5. Renella Phillips (Humber); 6. Robin and Richard Minchin; 7. Anne Ham (Hookey), Pat and Pauline Tyrell; 8. Cecil Baker, Ron and Marlene Emmett; 9. Jim Abott, Myrtle Lewis (Newbery); 10. Janice Hackshaw (Simpson); 11. Susan Mears (Stone), Audrey Rann (Barnes); 12. Tony and Mary Pettitt (Taylor); 13. Erica Browitt (Newbery); 14. Jane Cotton, Brough Scott; 15. Avice Mariner (French), Brough Scott, Janet Ash (Stone); 16. Eric and Nancy Sheath (Newbery); 17. George and Barbara Thompson (Sivier), Anne Ham (Hookey).